الداء والدواء

Purification of the Heart and Soul
(Illness & Cure)

By

Imam Ibn Qayyim Al-Jawziyyah

Translated by
Abdul Ali Hamid

Revised by
Dr. Zubair Chaudhry

TABLE OF CONTENTS

Purification of the Heart and Soul

By Ibn Qayyim Al-Jawzi
In the name of Allah, the Most Beneficent, the Most Merciful.
His help we ask for.

Foreword

This is a book which was composed by the most learned scholar of his time, Ibn Qayyim al-Jawziyyah in reply to a question put to him. The question was about someone who was inflicted by love: Is there any cure for him? It seems that the author wrote extemporaneously, which shows his vast knowledge and ability to write on any subject at any time. As a matter of fact his writings cover almost every area of Islamic subject from Tafsir, Hadith, Seerah, fiqh, belief, morality and Arabic literature and so on.

When he speaks about any subject he demonstrates profound knowledge of it. However, I noted that his knowledge of two areas is vey excellent, deep and impressive: they are Satan and love. He speaks about the Devil and his tricks in alluring and deceiving mankind as though he has gone through his mind and acquired all information about them. He wrote a book about the subject, إغاثة اللهفان في مصايد الشيطان Which I translated in English and was published under the title of "Supporting the distressed against the tricks of Satan". It has useful and interested sections. He dealt with this topic in many of his other books as well. As of the subject of love he exhibits his understanding of human psychology, and inner feelings of the lovers. This book shows it clearly. His other books also go deep in discussing the human nature and weaknesses in the matter of love.

This book deals with morals and characters, education, training and purification of the souls. He spoke about invocation, its importance, its secrets and the manners of supplication as well as other matters related to it. Invocation is closely connected with Divine decree; it affects the decision of Allah, the Exalted. He forwarded many evidences from the Qur'an and the Sunnah to prove it. He also dealt with the various types of punishment designed by Allah Almighty for those who lost their way: some connected with heart others with body and others to affect the sinner in this world and the worst ones are those which Almighty has prepared in the Hereafter for the one who does not heed the commands of Allah, The Glorious.

He also discussed shirk, association of partners with Allah, the Most High, and stated that it had various categories and could happen in worship, speech, deeds as well as in intentions. He mentioned the shirk of the Christians and the shirk of those who take intercessors and mediators from among the creation to gain the favour of Allah. He talked in detail about the major sins and their evil consequences. He discussed in detail the punishments meted out by Allah for those who disobey Him. He cited 54 punishments and spoke about each one of them. This section is really an eye opener to those who do not heed the warning given by Allah Almighty. He dealt with injustice, murder, adultery and other serious offences. He discussed the evil of sodomy, which seems to be common in the society at his time. How a person is dragged to commit a sin is also detailed. Here he speaks from experience and says that the first thing which a person in confronted is thought, which Satan puts in his mind and persuades him to follow his instruction. The next stage is talking when the man speaks about his intention and the final step is to proceed to commit it. He described the procedures followed by the Devil and tells us how the cursed one advises his disciples to incite the mankind toward the evils. He tells them to attack first of all the soul and the heart; once the heart is won then everything will be easier. He tells them to approach the man from the side of his eyes, ears, tongue, mouth, hand and feet. How to control and get hold of them is described by the Devil.

He talked extensively about love and said that love was the basis of every good or evil deed. The good deed emanates from a person the love of Allah; an act of worship is meaningless unless it is done with the love of Allah. When the love of Allah is mixed with the love of others it is shirk which will never be forgiven as Allah has announced. The author spoke about the stages of love and its name in every stage. As a matter of fact he wrote a beautiful book about love and lovers called in Arabic روضة المحبين ونزهة المشتاقين which means "the meadow of the lovers and amusement of the longing". He cited in it 51 words denoting the stages of love. When he speaks about love he does not miss to quote lines of poetry which makes his discussion more interesting.

Love is something which every person experiences in his life. He mentioned number of outstanding scholars who fell in love and spoke about it in their poems. If it is an avoidable matter, then Allah has provided spouses for the people; they should express their love to them instead of going to illegal areas.

At the end he prayed that Allah make us among those who make the love of Allah dominate the love of his desires, and devoted to seeking His pleasure.

The book in its original form in Arabic was printed many times. The first edition came out in Egypt in 1282 AH, followed by other editions in many Arab countries. New editions are still coming. It shows the popularity of the book among the readers.

Now it is the first attempt to present it in English language. Since it was written in answer to a question, as said earlier, it was not divided into chapters. I am grateful to Dr. Zubair Chaudhry who fixed chapters for the topics. Dr. Chaudhry has been very helpful to me in my works of translation. He takes the trouble of correcting the text from grammatical errors and polishing the language and putting it in a readable form. He also prepared the Table of Contents and Index. Usually books on religious topics do not have index, which I find very useful for the readers. Luckily I have Dr. Chaudhry who is happy to do it for me. My thanks to him for all that he has done and assured support for future as well. May Allah reward him for his effort in the best way.

A short biography of the Author

He is Abu Abdullah Muhammad ibn Abu Bakr ibn Ayyub ibn Sa'd al-Zara'i al-Dimashqi well known as Ibn Qayyim al- Jawziyyah. (691-751AH/ 1292- 1350 CE) He got this nickname Ibn Qayyim al-Jawziyyah from his father who was the caretaker of the school called al-Jawziyyah in Damascus.

He attended the famous schools of his time and acquired knowledge of all the subjects taught in them. Later he joined the circle of Shaykh al-Islam Ibn Taymiyyah, and become the most devoted disciple of him, and 33remained with him until the death of his mentor. When Ibn Taymiyyah was put in prison, he joined him there as well, and remained until he passed away. He is described by his colleagues and biographers as a man of good character, cooperative and helpful to others. He followed what he taught in his books about being nice and gentle.

Like his teacher he suffered great deal of atrocities from the authorities. He left a number of books and touched almost on all the topics related to religion of Islam, plus some books on Arabic literature. Many of his books are printed but there are still some which remain in manuscript form. The editor of one of his books counted them to be 57. Definitely they are more than that. His books are very popular among the readers. He wrote on every subject known in his time. His style is fascinating and beautiful. He was a good poet and has composed a *qasidah* (long poem) called *al-Nooniyyah,* to outline the belief of the people of the Sunnah and Jama'ah, which is read and commented upon. In his books he quotes lines of other poets which make his style more attractive.

He followed the path of his teacher in his belief and defended it in many of his books. He criticized those who denied the Attributes of Allah or tried to give them a wrong interpretation.

May Allah, the Most Forgiving, the Most Merciful shower His mercy upon him and give him the best reward for his work in spreading the correct knowledge among the masses.

Glossary

Tawhid: It is to declare and believe that there in no one comparable to Allah. It has three sections;

i.   To take Allah Almighty as the sole object of worship. Nothing else should be worshipped beside Him, and no one else should be approached for help or assistance.

ii. To believe that Allah alone is the Creator of everything. He has no helper in this matter. He alone is the Creator, Provider and Sustainer.

iii. Allah has given some excellent Names for Himself, which should not be used for others. His Names are His qualities of maintaining the world and all that is in it.

Shirk: It is opposite of Tawhid and designates believing that Allah has partners in His domain. Worshipping any other object or turning to anything, man, Jinn, angel, tree, stone or anything else is part of shirk.

Jahmiyyah: It is a group that denies any Attribute to Allah

Al-Mu'attilah: These are people who deny any work by Allah in this world.

Al-Mu'tazilah: A very intelligent and rationalist group which accepted the Attributes in principle but gave them a rational interpretation.

Purification of the Heart and Soul

By Ibn Qayyim Al-Jawziyyah

CHAPTER 1   - INTRODUCTION

Shaykh, Imam, the most learned, outstanding scholar and distinguished writer Shams al-Din Abu Abdullah Muhammad ibn Shaykh Taqiy al-Din Abu Bakr, well-known as Ibn Qayyim al-Jawziyyah,- May Allah grant him plenty of His bounty - was asked the following question:

"What do the eminent, knowledgeable the *leaders of the religion – may Allah be pleased with them all - say about a man who was afflicted by a tribulation and is aware that if it remains with him for long it will destroy his life in the world and the Hereafter? He tried to get rid of it by all means but instead it increased in its intensity and fierceness; what is the way to remove it? And how can he get rid of it? May Allah show mercy to the one who helps a man in trouble? Allah is in the support of the slave as long as he is in the help of his brother[1]. Advise us expecting the reward from Allah. May He show mercy to you!"*

Shaykh responded in writing with the following reply:

"All Praise belongs to Allah.
It is reported in Sahih of Al-Bukhari on the authority of the Abu Hurayrah, may Allah be pleased with him, that the Prophet, Allah's blessing and peace be upon him, said:

"Allah did not send a disease but sent a cure for it   [2]."

It is also reported in Sahih of Muslim on the authority of Jabir ibn Abdullah that the Messenger of Allah, Allah's blessing and peace be upon him, said

"For every disease there is a medication; if the suitable medication is applied, it will cure with the permission of Allah."   It recorded in the Musnad of Imam Ahmad on the authority of Usamah ibn Sharik that the Prophet, Allah's blessing and peace be upon him, said:

---

[1] A Hadith reported by Muslim (2699)
[2] Bukhari (5354, 5678)

"Allah did not send a disease but sent a cure for it as well. Some knew it and others did not."[3]

In another report he said:

"Allah did not create a disease but created a cure or medicine for it except one disease."

The Companions asked: 'Which one is that, O Messenger of Allah?'
He replied: "The senility."[4]
Tirmidhi declared this report as authentic.

The above Hadith includes all the diseases of the heart, the soul and the body, and their medication. The Prophet, Allah's blessing and peace be upon him, declared ignorance to be a disease and made its cure asking the learned.
Jabir ibn Abdullah reported:

'We went out on a journey and one of us was hit by the stone which fractured his head. He had wet dream and asked his colleague whether he was permitted to make *tayammum* (dry ablution). They told him that they do not find for him permission when he had water. He took bath and then died. When we came to the Prophet, Allah's blessing and peace be upon him, and told him about it, he said:

"They killed him. May Allah kill them! Why did they not ask when they did not know? The remedy of incapable is asking. It was enough for him to use mud and tie a piece of cloth on his wound and wipe by his wet hand on it, and wash the rest of his body."[5]

The Prophet declared ignorance as disease and its cure to ask.

Allah, the Glorious, has declared the Qur'an as cure. He said:

"If We had made it a foreign Qur'an, they would have said, 'Why its verse were not made clear (in our language)? Is it a foreign speech to an Arab?' Say, 'For those who have faith it is guidance and healing." (41:44)

---

[3] Musnad (1: 443, 4: 278)
[4] Tirmidhi (2038), Abu Dawud (3855) Ibn Majah (3436)
[5] Abu Dawud (336)

"We send down of the Qur'an that which is healing and mercy to those who believe." (17:82)

The whole Qur'an is healing as it is said in the first verse. It is healing for the hearts from the disease of ignorance, doubt and uncertainty. Allah, the Glorious and Most High, did not send down from the heaven a healing more comprehensive, more useful, more excellent and more successful in removing the disease than the Qur'an.

It has been proved by the following report of Abu Sa'id:
'A party of the Companions of the Prophet, Allah's blessing and peace be upon him, went on a journey. They came across an Arab tribe and asked them to provide them with hospitality, but they refused. Later the chief of the tribe was stung by a scorpion and they tried all sort of treatment but nothing worked. Some of them said, 'If you go to these people who have camped nearby, they may have something!' They went to them and said, 'Our chief has been stung by a scorpion and we tried to treat him by all medicines but nothing worked. Have you got anything which can cure?' One of the Companions said: 'Yes, By Allah, I know some spiritual formula, but we asked you to help us by giving the provision of guests but you refused. I will not use my spell till you fix a compensation for me.' They agreed on band of sheep. He went and started to blow on the chief and reading the Opening chapter: "All praise belongs to Allah, the Lord of the universe". The man was cured as though he was freed from the shackles. He started walking without having any pain. The tribe paid their agreed compensation in full. Some of them suggested dividing it between them. The person who had used the spell said 'We will not do anything until we go to the Prophet, Allah's blessing and peace be upon him, and tell him what happened, and see what he says.'
When they came to the Messenger of Allah, blessing and peace of Allah be upon him, and told him the story, he said: "How did you know that it was a spiritual formula? You did the right thing. Divide the compensation and include me and give me a share." [6]

The opening chapter is the easiest and simplest healing. If a person uses it for treatment, he will see its amazing impact in healing. I stayed in Makkah for a period suffering from diseases without having a doctor or medicine. I started treating myself with this chapter and noticed amazing impact. I described it to those who complained any pain, and many of them were cured quickly.

---

[6] Bukhari (2276) See also Abu Dawud (149)

However, there is a point to be taken in account. It is that these invocations, the Qur'anic verses and prayers which are recited for the purpose of treatment and healing are in themselves useful and healing, but they require the readiness of the subject and the resolution and zeal of the person who does it. If cure is not achieved, it is due to the weakness of the effectiveness of the doer or unpreparedness of the affected subject or due to a strong impediment which blocks the working of the treatment. It happens in the case of diseases and physical treatment. They do not work because the natural disposition does not accept that treatment. Or it could be for another strong impediment which bars the effect of the medicine. When the nature accepts the medicine fully, the body's reaction will be in accordance with it. In the same way when the heart receives the invocation and supplication with full acceptance and the person administering it has an effective soul and powerful resolution, his incantation will work in removing the illness.

It is the same with supplication which is a very effective means of repelling the undesired matter and achieving the desired one. But sometimes it fails to work because of a defect in it for being an unjust supplication which Allah does not like. The failure could be due to the weakness of the heart and lack of focusing and concentration at the time of supplication. In this case it is like a loose bow from which the arrow shoots very slowly. The reason of ineffectiveness of the supplication may be for other reasons like consuming forbidden materials, doing injustice, coverage of the heart by sins or domination of heedlessness, lust and distraction. It is supported by the report of Abu Hurayrah who said that the Prophet, Allah's blessing and peace be upon him, said:

"Invoke Allah while you are sure of His answering, and remember that Allah does not answer a prayer from a heedless and inattentive heart."[7]

Supplication is an effective treatment which removes the illness, but the heedlessness of the heart spoils its power. Similarly consuming forbidden materials weakens the power of supplication and renders it useless. Abu Hurayrah reported that the Messenger of Allah, blessing and peace of Allah be upon him, said:

"People, indeed Allah is pure and does not accept but pure, and Allah has ordered the believers what He ordered His messengers saying:

---

[7] Hakim (1: 493) see also Tirmidhi (3479)

"O Messengers, eat good food and do righteous deed. Indeed, I know what you do." (23:51)

Then the prophet recited: **"Those who believe, eat from the good thing which We have provided for you." (2:172)**

Then he mentioned a man who makes long journey, his hair dishevelled and covered in dust, and he raises his hands to he sky and says: 'O Lord, O Lord!' His food is unlawful, his drink is unlawful, his dress is unlawful and he has been fed with unlawful materials. How then his supplication be answered?"[8]

It is reported that the Children of Israel were afflicted by tribulation, and they went out for invocation. Allah inspired to their prophet to tell them: 'You go out to the plain with impure bodies and raise hands by which you have shed bloods, and have filled your houses with unlawful materials. Now you come when My wrath upon you has increased. You are going to be farther from Me.'[9]

---

[8] Muslim (zakat: 3419))
[9] Al-zuhd of Ahmad (1:176)

CHAPTER 2 - FUNDAMENTALS OF SUPPLICATION

2.1 Supplication is the weapon of the believer

Supplication is the most effective treatment. It is repellent of mishap, combats and pushes it away. It bars its happening and makes it light if it comes. It is the weapon of the believer.
Ali ibn Abi Talib reported that the Messenger of Allah, blessing and peace of Allah be upon him, said:

"Supplication is the weapon of the believer, the pillar of the religion and the light of the heavens and the earth." [10]

It has the following three positions with the mishap:
1. It could be stronger than the affliction and thus can drive it away.
2. It may be weaker than the affliction and so the affliction gets control, and the believer suffers. Yet it can make it lighter even if it is weak.
3. Both are equal in strength and engaged in battle, each trying to have the control.

'A'ishah reported that Allah's Messenger, blessing and peace of Allah be upon him, said:

"Precaution cannot help against the Divine decree, but supplication helps from what has happened and that which has not occurred. The mishap comes down and meets supplication and both wrestle among them till the Day of Judgement." [11]

Ibn 'Umar narrated that the Prophet, Allah's blessing and peace be upon him, said:

"Supplication is useful against what has happened and what has not occurred. The servants of Allah stick with supplication." [12]

Thawban reported that the Prophet, Allah's blessing and peace be upon him, said:

---

[10] Hakim (1: 492)
[11] Hakim (1: 492) See also Ahmad (5: 234)
4 Hakim (1: 493) See also Tabarani in Awsat (4615), al-Bazzar (3: 29) See majma' al-Zawa'id (10: 146
1. Hakim (1: 493), Tirmidhi (3548)

"Nothing can repel the fate except supplication, nothing adds to the age but good deed. A man is deprived of provision because of a sin he committed."[13]

2.2   Persistence in calling on Allah

One of the most effective treatments is to persist in calling upon Allah. Abu Hurayrah reported that the Messenger of Allah, blessing and peace of Allah be upon him, said:

"Whoever does not ask Allah He becomes angry with him."[14]

Anas related that the Prophet, Allah's blessing and peace be upon him, said:

"Do not fail in making supplication; no one can perish with supplication."[15]

'A'ishah reported the messenger of Allah, blessing and peace of Allah be upon him, saying:

"Indeed Allah loves those who persist in calling upon Him."[16]

Qatadah reported from Murriq having said:

'I did not find an example for the believer except a man in the sea on a piece of wood, and he calls upon his Lord: 'O Lord! O Lord! He hopes that Allah may rescue him.'[17]

2.3   Matters that impede the invocation

One of the matters that hinder the effect of invocation is to be in haste and consider the answering delayed. When a person shows hurry he feels frustrated and abandons invocation. He behaves like a person who puts seed or plants a tree in the ground and takes care of it by watering it, but

---

[13] Hakim (1: 493), Ibn Majah (4022), Ahmad (5: 277) Ibn Hibban (1090)
[14] Tirmidhi (3370), Ibn Majah (3827), Ahmad (2: 422), Hakim (1: 491)
[15] Hakim (1: 4930 It is a weak report
[16] Tabarani in al-Dua' (20)
[17] Al-Zhuhd of Ahmad (2:273), al-Hilyah of Abu Nu'aym (2: 235)

when he feels that the plant is not growing fast, he abandons it and leaves it.

Abu Hurayrah reported that the Messenger of Allah, blessing and peace of Allah be upon him, said:

"The supplication of one of you is granted as long as he does not show haste. He starts saying that 'I supplicated but it was not granted.'" [18]

In another report the Prophet, Allah's blessing and peace be upon him, said:

"A person's supplication is answered if he does not ask for committing sin or cutting the bonds of relation, as long as he is not in hurry."
He was asked: 'What means to be in hurry, Messenger of Allah?'
He replied:
"He says: 'I supplicated, I supplicated, but I feel that my supplication is not granted.' At that point he loses the hope and abandons supplication." [19]

Anas reported that the messenger of Allah, blessing and peace of Allah be upon him, said:

"A believer remains in good as long as he does not show haste."

They asked: 'How does he show haste, Messenger of Allah?'He replied:
"He says, 'I supplicated my Lord, but He did not answer my supplication." [20]

2.4   Matters that increase the chances of the acceptance of invocation

When supplication is made with the full attention of the heart and concentration on the subject and it happens in one of the six period of answering, it is surely granted. The six periods are:

1. The last third part of the night,
2. When call for prayer (*adhan*) is made,

---

[18] Bukhari (6340), Muslim (Dhikr: 2735) Ahmad (2: 396, 478)
[19] Muslim (dhikr: 2735)
[20] Ahmad (3: 193, 210)

3. Between *adhan* and the *iqamah*,
4. After the obligatory prayers,
5. When the Imam ascends the pulpit on Friday till the prayer is finished,
6. The last moment after *'asr* prayer,

When supplication is made in these periods with humility in the heart, submissiveness before the Lord, showing humbleness and servility, and the servant faces the Qiblah and is pure. He is also required to raise his hands and start with the praise and glorification of Allah followed by sending blessing to Muhammad, Allah's Messenger and His servant. He should start by turning to Allah in repentance and asking Him forgiveness then start his supplication showing persistence in asking, and begging with hope and fear and trying to approach Allah with His Names and Attributes and declare His oneness, and forward charity before supplicating, this supplication is rarely rejected. Especially when he asks Allah with those words which the Prophet, peace be upon him, has said that they are likely to be granted or they contain the greater Name of Allah.

Below are some of those words which the Prophet, Allah's blessing and peace be upon him. Has recommended:

Buraydah reported that the Messenger of Allah, blessing and peace of Allah be upon him, heard a man saying:
'O Allah, I am asking You while I witness that You alone are Allah, there is no being worth worshipping except You. You are One, Eternal, Who begot no one nor was begotten. No one is comparable to Him.' He said:

"This man has asked Allah with the Great Name by which when He is asked, He gives and when He is invoked, He grants."

In another version the Prophet said:

"You asked Allah with His Great Name."[21]

Anas reported that he was sitting with the Messenger of Allah, blessing and peace of Allah be upon him, and a man was performing prayer. He then supplicated saying:

---

[21] Ahmad (5: 349, 360; 3: 120), Abu Dawud (1493), Tirmidhi (3475), Ibn Majah (3857), Ibn Hibban (891)

'O Allah, I ask You, praise belongs to You. There is no god except You, the Benefactor, the Originator of the heavens and the earth! O Owner of majesty and honour, O Ever Living, O Sustainer of existence!'
The Prophet, Allah's blessing and peace be upon him, said:

"This man has asked Allah with His Great Name by which when He is invoked he grants and when asked He gives."[22]
Asma' bint Yazid related that the Prophet, Allah's blessing and peace be upon him, said:

Allah's Great Name is in these two verses:

'Your god one God, there is no being worthy of worship except Him. He is the Most Merciful, the Most Beneficent' (2:163)

And the opening of the chapter of the family of 'Imran:

'Alif Lam Mim. Allah, there is no god but Him, the Ever Living, the Sustainer of the existence.' (3:1-2) [23]

Abu Hurayrah, Anas ibn Malik and Rabi'ah ibn 'Amir reported that the Prophet, Allah's blessing and peace be upon him, said:

"Stick with 'O the Owner of majesty and honour'." [24]
The meaning is to keep repeating and persistently saying it.

Abu Hurayrah reported that when any matter disturbed the Prophet, Allah's blessing and peace be upon him, he raised his head to the sky, and when he exerted in supplication he said:

'O Ever Living, O Sustainer.'[25]

Anas reported that when the Messenger was disturbed by anything he said:

"O Ever Living, O Sustainer, I seek help in Your mercy."[26]

---

[22] Nisa'i (3: 52), Abu Dawud (1495), Tirmidhi (3544), Ibn Majah (3858), Ibn Hibban (893) Ahmad (3: 158, 245, 265)

[23] Tirmidhi (3544), Abu Dawud (1496), Ibn Majah (3588), Ahmad (6: 461)

[24] The report of Abu Hurayrah is in Hakim (1: 499), that of Anas is in tirmidhi (3525) and the report of Rabi'ah is in Ahmad (4:177), Hakim (1:498)

[25] Tirmidhi (3432) \it is a weak report

[26] Tirmidhi (3532)

Abu Umamah reported from the Prophet, Allah's blessing and peace be upon him, that he said:

"The Great Name of Allah is in three chapters of the Qur'an: the cow (Chapter 2), Family of 'Imran (Chapter 3) and Taha (Chapter 20)."

Al-Qasim (one of the reporters) said that I searched for it and found 'the Ever Living, the Sustainer'[27]

Sa'd ibn Λbi Waqqas reported that the Prophet, Allah's blessing and peace be upon him, said:

"The invocation of the man of the whale (i.e. Jonah) when he invoked from inside the belly of the whale was 'there is no god but You, glory be to You, I was of the wrong doers.' (21:87) No Muslim invokes with it in any matter but Allah will answer him."[28]

Sa'd also reported that he heard the Prophet, Allah's blessing and peace be upon him, saying:

"Shall I not tell you the Great Name of Allah? When a person afflicted with worrying matter, and invokes with it Allah will remove his worry. It is the invocation of Jonah."

Sa'd also reported that the Prophet, Allah's blessing and peace be upon him, said:

"Shall I not tell you the Great Name of Allah? It is the invocation of Jonah."

A man asked: 'Was it especially for Jonah, O Messenger of Allah?'
He replied:

Do you not hear Allah's statement:

'We responded to him and saved him from the distress? Thus We save the believers.' (21: 88)

---

[27] Hakim (1; 505)
[28] Tirmidhi (3500), Hakim (1:505; 2:382) Ahmad (1462)Hakim (1:505, 506) It is a weak tradition

So any Muslim invokes forty times with it in his illness and dies in that illness, he will be given the reward of a martyr, and if he recovers, he will recover being forgiven."[29]

Ibn Abbas reported that the Messenger of Allah, blessing and peace of Allah be upon him, used to say at the moment of distress:

"There is no god but Allah, the Great, the Clement. There is no god but Allah, the Lord of the Great Throne. There is no god but Allah, the Lord of the seven heavens, the Lord of the earth the Lord of the Noble Throne."[30]

Ali ibn Abi Talib said:
'The Messenger of Allah, blessing and peace of Allah be upon him, taught me to say when I was distressed:

"There is no god but Allah, the Clement, the Generous. Glory be to Allah! Blessed is Allah the Lord of the Great Throne. Praise belongs to Allah, the Lord of the universe." [31]

Abdullah ibn Mas'ud reported that Allah's Messenger, Allah's blessing and peace be upon him, said:

"No one is affected by grief or distress and says:
'O Allah, I am Your slave, the son of Your slave, the son of Your maid, my forehead is in Your hand, Your decree is effective with me, Your judgment about me is just; I ask You, O Allah, with every name You have You named Yourself with it, or taught it to any of Your creation, or revealed it in Your Book or kept it secret with You, to make the Great Qur'an the spring of my heart, the light of my breast, removal of my grief and dispeller of my distress,'
but Allah will take away his grief and distress, and replace them with happiness."

It was said: 'Should we not learn it O Messenger of Allah?'
He replied:

"Yes, indeed. It is desirable for anyone who listens to it to learn it."[32]

---

[30] Bukhari (6346), Muslim (2730)
[31] Ahmad (701), Hakim (1: 508)
[32] Ahmad (1: 391, 452), Hakim (1: 509), Ibn Hibban ((772) Abu Ya'la (5297)

Ibn Mas'ud said:

'No prophet was afflicted with distress but sought help of Allah with glorification.'

Anas ibn Malik reported that a man from the Helpers of the Companions of the Prophet, Allah's blessing and peace be upon him, called Abu Mi'laq was a trader who used to trade with his merchandise and other people's merchandise. He used to travel to remote regions. He was a pious and godly man. Once he went on his trip and was confronted with an armed and masked thief. He told him to put down what he had because he was going to kill him. He said to him: 'What do you have with my blood? Your concern is money so take it.'

He said: 'Money is for me but I am after your blood.'

He said: Well, if you refuse, then let me perform four rak'ahs of prayer.'

He said: 'Pray as you wish.'

The trader performed ablution and performed four rak'ah prayer and prayed in the last prostration: 'O the Most Loving, Glorious Owner of the Throne, Who does whatever He wants, I am asking by Your power which cannot be overcome, and Your sovereignty which cannot be tempered and Your light which has illuminated the pillars of Your Throne, to save me from the evil of this robber. O Helper, help me! O helper, help me! He said it three times.'

All of a sudden a horseman appeared holding a spear between the ears of his horse. When the robber noticed him came towards him and the horseman hit him with the spear and killed him. He then went to the trader and told him to stand up. He asked him: 'Who are you, may my father and mother be ransom for you! Allah saved me by you today.'

He said: 'I am an angel from the fourth sky. When you called first time, I heard a rattle in the gates of the sky. Then you called the second time, I heard noise among the people of the sky. When you called the third time, it was said to me, it is the prayer of a distressed man. Then I asked Allah to give me power to kill him.'

Anas said:

'Whoever performs ablution, make four rak'ah prayer and invokes with this supplication, he will be helped whether he is distressed or not. [33]

---

[33] Ibn Abi al-Dunya: Mujabu al-da'awat (23)

2.5   The Secret of the invocation

We often find that some people invoked Allah with particular supplication and it was answered. It may be the result of the need of the person and his full devotion to Almighty. It may as well be the result of some good deeds which Allah accepted and made the answer of his supplication a sort of appreciation of his good deed. Or it may have been made at the time in which the supplication is granted, and so on, and his supplication was granted. Some people may think that the secret was in the words of that supplication and he takes them in isolation from those conditions which accompanied that person. It is like a person who used a useful medicine in its proper time and in the way it was prescribed and got cured. So, someone thought that the mere use of that medicine was enough in treatment. He is mistaken. It is a situation in which many people make mistake.

Another case is that the prayer of a distressed person near a grave is granted and an ignorant person thinks that it was due to that grave. He did not know that the secret is the need of the person and his sincere refuge to Allah, the Most High. If it happens in a house from the houses of Allah, it will be better and more desirable to Allah.

The prayers and seeking refuge are like weapons. The weapon works by its user's skill not only by its sharpness. When the weapon is perfect without any defect and the hand using it is strong, and there is no impediment, it will work on the enemy. But when any of these elements is missing the desired result will not be achieved. If the prayer itself is inadequate or the person's heart and tongue were not joined together or there was any other barrier, the effect of the invocation will not be seen.

2.6   A Popular Query

Here is a popular question:
If what is being asked has been decreed, it will definitely take place whether someone asks for it or not. On the other hand if it has not been decreed, it will not happen whether it is being asked or not.

Some people considered the question valid and abandoned supplication saying that there was no use in it. These people apart from their excessive ignorance and misguidance are inconsistent. The exclusive application of their view will invalidate all the causes. One of them may be asked: If satiation and satisfaction are decreed for you, they will happen whether you eat or not, but if they are not decreed then they will not happen whether you eat and drink or not. In the same way if a child is decreed for you, it will definitely be born whether you had intercourse with your wife or not, and if it was not decreed then there is no need to have a wife. There are many such examples.

Can any reasonable person or human being say it? Even an animal is created to apply the causes on which its life and sustenance depend. Animals are more intelligent and understanding than these people who are like cattle rather further astray.

Some of them tried to be smart and said that invocation is mere showing the submission for which Allah will give reward to the one who gets involved in it; it has no effect in any way in the desired matter. There is no difference in the view of this clever man between supplication and holding the tongue and heart away from it in producing the result.

Another group smarter than this one said that supplication was mere indication which Allah has designated for the fulfilment of the need. When Allah helps a man to supplicate, it is a sign that his need has been fulfilled. It is like a black cold cloud in the winter which is a sign of rain. They said that was the rule of good deeds with reward and the disbelief and sinful acts with punishment; they are only indications of reward and punishment and not causes for them. To them the breaking which results in smashing, burning which results in destroying and to stifle that leads to death are not the causes and there is no connection between them and their outcome. It is only normal relation and not the cause and effect. In this way they have gone against the senses, reason, religion and instinct and the rest of the reasonable people. Rather they made the intelligent people laugh at them.

The correct matter is that there is a third category apart from what the questioner has said and that is, what happens is attached with causes one of them being the supplication. Nothing is decided without a cause, but everything is attached with some causes. When the cause is found the decreed matter takes place. If the cause is not found, the decreed matter will not take place. This is how the satiation and satisfaction are decreed with eating and drinking, the child with intercourse, growing of the plant with seed and getting the soul out of the animal by slaughtering. In the same way entrance into Paradise is conditioned with good deeds and going to Hell with evils deeds. This category is the right one and the questioner missed it.

Now supplication is the most effective cause. Since the result is acquired by supplication, it is wrong to say that there is no use in supplication. It is absurd to say that there is no use in eating, drinking and doing anything. No cause is more effective and competent than supplication. The Companions of the Prophet, Allah's blessing and peace be upon him, were the most knowledgeable of the community about Allah and His Messenger and more understanding of His religion. They, therefore, resorted to this cause, applied its conditions and maintained its etiquettes.

'Umar ibn al-Khattab used this method for seeking help against his enemy. He considered it the greatest of his soldier. He used to say to his people: 'You are not helped by big number; your help comes from the heavens.'

He also said: 'I do not worry about granting of the supplication, I am concerned with the supplication. When you are inspired to make supplication, the answering will come with it.'

A poet took this message and put it is his saying:

'If you had not intended to grant what I hope and seek from the generosity of your hands, you would have not made me used to asking you.'

Whoever is inspired to supplicate has a desire to be granted. Allah, the Glorious, said:

"Call upon Me, I will respond to you." (40:60)

He also said:

"When My servants ask you concerning Me, I am near, I respond to the invocation of the supplicant when he calls upon Me." (2:186)

Abu Hurayrah reported that the Messenger of Allah, blessing and peace of Allah be upon him, said:

"Whoever does not ask Allah, He gets angry with him." [34]

It shows that Allah's pleasure lies in begging and obeying Him. When Allah is pleased every good will be achieved, and when He is angry it will result in all kinds of affliction and mishap.

---

[34] Tirmidhi (3373), Ibn Majah (3827)

Imam Ahmad cited a statement from Allah saying:

'I am Allah. There is no god but Me. When I am pleased I bless, and there is no end for My blessing; and when I get angry I curse, and My curse reaches to seventh generation.'[35]

The tradition, the reason, the instinct and the experiences of the people of different races, religions and sects agree that getting closer to the Lord of the universe, seeking His pleasure and showing kindness to His creation is one of the greatest sources of good, and their opposites are the mean cause of evil. Allah's favour was not procured and His resentment was not repelled by anything like His obedience and getting close to Him and being kind to His creation.

Allah, the Blessed and Glorious, has made acquiring the welfare and success in the world and the Hereafter, and the affliction of evil and mishap in the world and the Hereafter, the result of deeds as the cause and effect and condition and result. Almighty has described it in His Book in many places more than thousand times.

Sometimes He makes the incident as the result of the Divine Decree and religious order in proper way, as in the following verses:

"When they persisted in doing what they had been forbidden to do, We said to them, 'Be apes, despised." (7:166)

"Cut off the hands of thieves whether man or woman, as punishment for what they have done, a deterrent from Allah." (5:38)

"The Muslim men and the Muslim women, the believing men and the believing women, the obedient men and the obedient women, the truthful men and the truthful women, the patient men and the patient women, the humble men and the humble women, the charitable men and the charitable women, the men who guard their private parts and the women who do so, and the men who remember Allah often and the women who do so - for them Allah has prepared forgiveness and a great reward." (33:35)

There are many other statements like these.

Sometimes Almighty puts it in the form of condition and effect as in the following verses:

---

[35] Al-Zuhd (52)

"If you remain mindful of Allah, He will give you a criterion and wipe out your bad deeds and forgive you." (8:29)

"If they repent, keep up the prayer, and pay the prescribed alms, then they are your brothers in faith." (9:11)

"If they had stayed on the right way, We would have given them abundant water to drink." (72:16)

And other verses.

Sometime He cites with letter *'Laam'* (ل) which is used for justification as in the following verses:

"This is a blessed Book which We revealed to you (Muhammad), so that they might reflect upon its verses and that those with understanding take heed." (38:29)

"We made you (believers) a just community, so that you bear witness (to truth) over others and so that the Messenger may be witness over you." (2:143)

Sometimes *Kay* (كي) is used to show the cause like the following verse:

"So that it dose not become a matter of distribution among those who are rich." (59:7)

Another time the preposition *'ba'* (ب) is used to indicate the reason as in the following verses:

"This is for what your hands have sent forth." (3:182)

"He will tell you what you used to do." (5:105)

"Thus We make some of the wrongdoers allies of others for what they used to earn." (6:129)

"That is because they disbelieved the verses of Allah." (3:112)

Sometimes لأجلمفعول is brought either openly or being omitted. The examples are as follows:

"If two men are not available, then a man and two women from those whom you accept as witnesses – so that if one of them errs, then the other can remind her." (2:282)

"Lest you should say on the Day of Resurrection, indeed we were of this unaware." (7:172)

"Lest you say, 'the Scripture was only sent down to two groups before us and we were unaware of their study." (6:156)

Allah, the Exalted, sometimes uses the letter 'fa' (ف) to indicate the reason as in the following verses:

"They called him a liar and hamstrung her (i.e. she camel). So their Lord destroyed them for their crime and levelled them." (91:14)

"They disobeyed the messenger of their Lord, so He seized them with an ever tightening grip." (69:10)

"They called them both liars, and so were of the destroyed people." (23:48)

And similar verses.

Sometimes the agent 'lamma' (لـما) is used to indicate the effect as in the following verse:

"When they provoked Us, We punished them and drowned them all." (43:55)

Sometime the word 'inna' (انّ) is used as in the following examples:

"They used to hasten to good deeds and supplicate Us in hope and fear." (21:90)

"They were a people of evil, so We drowned them all." (21:77)

In other places the agent 'lau la' (لَوْلا) is used to show the connection of what is before it with what come after as in the following:

"If he had not been one of those who glorify Allah, he would have stayed in its (i.e. the Whale's) belly until the Day when all are raised up." (37:143-144)

Sometimes the word *'lau'* (لُو) is used which indicates the condition as in the following:

"If they had done as they were told, it would have been far better for them." (4:66)

In short, the Qur'an from the beginning to the end indicates clearly that the recompense is based on good or bad deeds, and the cosmic system and religious rules and regulations are all attached with the principle of cause and effect. In reality all the rules of the word and the Hereafter and their benefits or harms are connected with causes and deeds.

Anyone who understands this matter and gives it a proper thought will benefit greatly, but the one who relies on decree out of ignorance, incapability and laxity, his trust is in incapability and vice versa.

The real intelligent is the one who tries to repel the decree by the decree and removes a decree by another decree. This is the only way for a human to survive. The hunger, thirst, cold and all other sources of fear and troubles are all by the decree, and all the people are struggling to combat this decree by another decree.

Whoever has received support from Allah, and Almighty has inspired him good sense, he will struggle to repel the decree of punishment of the Hereafter by the decree of repentance, faith and good deeds in the world. It is like the decree of troubles and their repelling in the world. The Lord of both abodes is One, His wisdom is one and there is no contradiction among them.

It is one of the noble issues for those who understand its value and takes due care of them. Allah's help is sought.

However, there remain two issues for him, which will be helpful in achieving the happiness and success:

The first is to know the details of the causes of good and bad. He should develop understanding of what he observes in the world and what he has experienced as well as what he heard of the news of the nations both at present and of the past. The most effective source in this respect is to contemplate on the Qur'an. It will open his mind and provide him with the help. The Book shows explicitly the causes of good and bad in detail. Then he has to turn to the Sunnah, which is supplementary to the Qur'an and the second revelation. Anyone who turns his attention to them both, they will be sufficient for him. They will show him the good and evil and their causes as if you can see them openly.

After that if you look in the stories of the nations and Allah's dealing with the people who obeyed or disobeyed Him, you will notice that they faced exactly what you have learnt from the Qur'an and the Sunnah. You will realize the truth of what Allah has said and promised. You will also learn by looking in the verses dealing with the universe that the Qur'an is truth, the Messenger is truth and that Allah definitely will fulfil His promise. History is a detailed account of what Allah Almighty and His Messenger have informed us. It is the exposition of the causes of good and evil.

The second matter is that he should be careful not to be deceived by the causes. It is very important. The servant knows certainly that disobedience and negligence are the harmful causes for him in his world and the Hereafter, but his soul deceives him sometimes by relying on the forgiveness and pardon of Allah and by turning in repentance later sometimes. He is also deceived by asking for forgiveness by tongue and by doing desired acts. He takes refuge in knowledge and sometimes in decree. Another source of deception is argument by comparison and sometimes by claim of following the great people.

2.7 Misconception concerning supplication

Many people think that if they do what they do and say 'I seek forgiveness of Allah' the impact of the sins will disappear and it will be wiped out. A man associated to *fiqh* said to me: 'I do what I do then say, 'Glory be to Allah and praise be to Him' hundred times, all my misdeed is erased.'

He argued by what is reported from the Prophet, Allah's blessing and peace be upon him, that

"Whoever says in a day, 'glory be to Allah and praise be to Him' hundred times, his sins will be erased even if they are like the froth of the sea." [36]

Another man from Makkah said to me that one of us makes a mistake, then takes bath and goes around the Ka'bah seven rounds, his mistake is wiped out.

Another person said to me: 'It is reported through authentic chain from the Prophet, Allah's blessing and peace be upon him, that he said:

---

[36] Bukhari (6405), Muslim (2691)

"A man commits a sin then says, 'My Lord, I have committed a sin, so forgive me', Allah forgives him. Then after a while he commits another sin and says, 'My Lord, I have committed a sin, for give me.' Allah forgives his sin. He commits another sin again and says, 'My Lord, I have committed a sin, forgive me.' Allah says: 'My servant knows that he has a Lord who forgives sins and takes account of them. I have forgiven My servant, let him do what he wishes." [37]

He said: I do not have doubt that there is a Lord for me Who forgives the sins and takes account of them.'

These people stick to the texts related with hope and rely on them and hold it by both hands. When they are reprimanded on committing sins and indulging in them, they cite to you all that they remember about the extent of the mercy and forgiveness of Allah, and the texts of hope.

There are strange and amazing statements by the ignorant people from this category. Some of them said:
'Commit as many sins as you can because you are going to face a Generous Lord.'
Another said:
'Keeping away from sins is ignoring the extent of the pardon of Allah.'
Another said:
'Abandoning sins is audacity against the forgiveness of Allah, and contempt of it.'
Abu Muhammad ibn Hazm said:
'I saw some of these people saying in their supplication: 'O Allah, I seek refuge in You from infallibility.'

Among these deceived people are those who takes refuge in the issue of compulsion and believes that a man has no choice in his deed; he is compelled to commit sins.
There are others who are deceived by the issue of delay. They follow the principle that belief is only attestation of faith and deeds are not part of it. The faith of the most vicious person is like the faith of Gabriel and Mika'il.
Some others are cheated by the love of the poor and righteous people. They visit their grave regularly and beg them, seek their intercession and help to Allah, and ask Him by their rank to Him and their honour to Him.

---

[37] Bukhari (7507), Muslim (2758)

Some are deluded by their forefathers and ancestors thinking that they have position and rank with Allah and they will surely free them from their faults. They compare it with the situation of the kings of the world who grant their close friends power to get the faults of their sons and relatives forsaken. If any of them happens to commit a horrible mistake, they will be saved by their father, grandfather because of their rank and position with Allah, the Great.

Some other are misled by the thought that Allah has no need to punish them as the punishment is not going to increase in His kingdom and His mercy will not decrease His kingdom at all. One of them says, 'I am in need of His mercy and He is the most Self-sufficient. If a poor and needy who is desperate to drink water approaches the house of someone who has a flowing stream, he will not stop him from it. So, Allah is more Benevolent and Kind; forgiving does not decrease His power and punishment does not increase it.

There are people who are deluded by wrong perception of the texts of the Qur'an and the Sunnah and depend on it. Some of them for instance relied on the saying of Allah Almighty:

"Your Lord will grant you so much that you will be satisfied." (93:5)

They say that he (i.e. the Messenger) will not be pleased that anyone of his community be left in the Fire.

It is the most disgraceful ignorance and the clearest lie on the Prophet, Allah's blessing and peace be upon him, as he will be pleased with what his Lord is pleased. Allah is pleased with tormenting the unjust, sinful, faithless and persistently involved in committing grave sins. Great is the Messenger of Allah, Allah's blessing and peace be upon him, and free (from assumption of the ignorant) by not agreeing with what His Lord, the Most Exalted, agrees.

Some others take resort to His saying:

"Indeed, Allah forgives all the sins." (39:53)

This approach as well is the extreme ignorance. This verse includes association of partners with Allah, which is the root and basis of all sins. There is no dispute among the scholars that this verse is about those who make repentance. Allah Almighty will forgive the sin of every person who repents no matter how grave his sin is. If the verse were to be taken in the case of those who did not repent, all the texts of warning will be rendered null and void, and reports of bringing the people who believe in the oneness of Allah out of the Fire by the intercession will lose their significance.

These people are victims of the lack of knowledge and understanding. In this verse Allah, the Exalted, spoke in general terms and it was understood that He meant those people who repented. On the other hand in chapter of women (ch. 4) He specified and restricted and said:

"Allah will not forgive association of partners with Him, and will forgive anything less than that for whoever He will." (4:48)

So, Allah has clearly declared that He will not forgive association of partners with Him and He may forgive less than that. If the statement concerned with the people who repented, He would have not differentiated between association and other sins.

Some other ignorant people argued on the basis of the following verse:

"You human, what has lured you away from your Generous Lord?" (82:6)

They say it was His generosity that lured them! Some of them said that He taught the deceived his argument. This is a serious ignorance. It is Satan who deceived these people regarding their Lord, and they were deluded by the soul which is commanding evil and makes them follow their lust.

Almighty used the word '*Karim*' 'generous' to show that He is the Master, Tough, Great and obeyed. One should not be deceived by Him and abandon His rights. This deceived person put the word in its inappropriate meaning and was unnecessarily deceived.

Another group was misled by Almighty's sayings:

"In which none but the most wicked will burn, who denied the truth and turned away." (92:15-16)

"The Fire has been prepared for the disbelievers." (2: 24)

This misguided person did not know that saying of Allah:

"So, I warned you about raging Fire." (92:14)

Above verse is concerning a special fire from the various stages of Hell. If all Hell was meant, He would have said, 'no one will enter it.' He rather said **"None but the wicked will burn in it"**. Not burning does not mean that he will not enter it. Burning is more specific than entrance and negation of specific does not mean negation of the general. If this deceived person had considered the verse after this one, he would have known that he was not to enter it.

He argued by the Divine statement **"It has been prepared for the disbelievers"** and did not pay attention to His saying about Paradise **"It was prepared for the righteous people." (3:133)** Preparation of the Fire for the disbelievers does not mean that the vicious and unjust will not enter it. In the same way preparation of Paradise for the righteous people does not bar the people who have an atom's weight of faith in their heart and never did any righteous deed from being admitted into it.

Some other people are deceived by relying on the fast of 'Ashura' (the tenth Muharram) or the fast of day of 'Arafah. Some of them claimed that fast of the 10th Muharram wipes out the sins of the whole year and the fast of the day of Arafah remains for the increase in reward. This misguided man did not realize that the fast of Ramadan and five daily prayers are greater and more valuable than the fast of Arafah and 'Ashura. Fast on these two days will wipe out the sins committed between them as long as the grave sins are avoided. Ramadan to the next Ramadan and Friday to the next Friday cannot wipe out the minor sins unless the grave ones are avoided. When those good deeds are performed and major sins are avoided only then the minor sins will be erased.

How the supererogatory fast of one day can obliterate every major sin which a person committed with persistence and did not think of repenting? It is impossible. However, it is not impossible for the fast of the tenth of Muharram and the fast of the day of 'Arafah to wipe out the general sins of the whole year. This will be based of the texts of promise surrounded by conditions and impediments. One of the barriers is to persist on committing the major sins. If a person does not persist on committing the major sins, the fast together with his avoidance of major sins will be able to obliterate his sins. In the same way when Ramadan and five daily prayers are combined together with the abundance of grave sins are able to obliterate the minor sins. Allah, the Glorious, said:

"If you avoid the grave sins you have been forbidden, We shall wipe out your minor misdeeds." (4:31)

We learn from this verse that making a matter cause of obliteration of sins does not bar it from joining with cause of the obliteration. The obliteration of sins with both causes will be more perfect and comprehensive than with only one cause. When the causes of the obliteration are stronger their power will be stronger and more perfect and comprehensive.

Another group rely on the Divine Hadith in which Allah, the Exalted, said:

"I am at the good opinion of My servant about Me, so let him think about Me as he wills" [38]

No doubt the good opinion will work with good deeds. A devoted person who does good deeds has good opinion about his Lord to be rewarded for his good work. He is certain that his Lord will not break His promise and will respond to his repentance. On the other hand a man who is persistently involved in grave sins, injustice and violations of the commands, his bad deeds will prevent him from having good opinion about his Lord. This is witnessed in the observation. A slave who runs away and does not obey his master does not have good opinion about his master. The estrangement of bad behaviour cannot come together with good opinion. A person who is involved in evil deeds feels strange in accordance with his evil deeds, and the best person to have good opinion about his Lord is the one who is more committed to His obedience.

Al-Hasan Basri said:
'The believer has good opinion about his Lord so he is involved in good deeds, and the wicked person has evil thought about his Lord so he continues doing evil deeds.'[39]

How can a person who is running away from his Lord have good opinion about his Lord? He is moving in activities that cause His anger and displeasure and thus makes himself the target of His affliction. He took the command and rights of his Lord lightly and neglected them. He did not take His prohibitions seriously and continued in committing them. How can a person have good opinion about his Lord who has undertaken upon himself opposing His command? He takes His allies as enemies and His enemies as allies, rejects His perfect Attributes and holds bad opinion about what He and His Messenger described Him. He considered those

---

[38] Ahmad (3: 491), Ibn Hibban (633), Tabarani in Kabir (22: 211) and awsat (1205)
[39] Ahmad in al-Zhud (348)

descriptions, out of ignorance, as misguidance and disbelief. How can a person have good opinion about the One Whom he thinks that He does not speak, does not command or forbid, is not pleased or gets angry?

Allah said concerning those who had doubt about His listening to the secret talks:

"That was your assumption which you assumed about your Lord, which led to your ruin, and you became among losers." (41:23)

These people assumed that Allah does not know many things they do, and it was a bad assumption concerning their Lord, which brought ruin to them. This is the case of all those who deny the perfect Attributes and the Majestic Characteristics of Allah, the Most High, and describe Him with what is not appropriate for Him. If these people think that this act will take them to Paradise, it is mere deception, self delusion and seduction of Satan; it is not good opinion about the Lord.

Pay attention to this issue and consider the extreme need of it. How the following two things can come together in the heart of a person: his belief that he is going to meet with Allah, and He listens his talk and watches his position, knows his open and secret, nothing is hidden from Him; he will have to stand one day before Him and be asked about all that he has done; and his attitude of consistently doing deeds which cause His anger, is violating His commands and abandons His rights? Nevertheless, he has good opinion about his Lord, which is the delusion of the souls and wishful thinking.

Abu Umamah Sahl ibn Hunayf said:

'I and 'Urwah ibn al-Zubayr went to see 'A'ishah and she said: 'If you had seen the Messenger of Allah, blessing and peace of Allah be upon him, in his illness! I had six or seven Dinars, he ordered me to distribute them. I was kept busy by his pain till Allah granted him relief. He asked me about them and said:

"What did you do with six Dinars? Did you distribute them?"

I replied: 'No, by Allah. Your condition kept me busy. He asked them to be brought to him, put in his hand and said:

"What will be the assumption of the Prophet of Allah, if he meets with him and these are with him?"

In another wording:

"What will be assumption of Muhammad if he meets with Allah and these are with him?"[40]

How unfortunate will be the assumption of the people of major sins and unjust people with Allah when they meet Him and their unjust deeds are with Him? Will it avail them if they say, 'We had good opinion about You and thought that You are not going to punish a tyrant or vicious man?' If it is going to work then let a person do whatever he wishes and commit all those things which Allah has forbidden and have good opinion about Allah that the Fire will not touch him. Glory is to Allah! How far can the deception take a man? Abraham peace be upon him said to his people:

"How can you choose false gods other than Allah? So what is your opinion about the Lord of all the worlds?" (37:86-87)

That is what do you think He will do to you when you meet Him when you have worshipped objects other than Him?

If a person pays due attention to this issue, he will realize that good opinion about Allah is nothing but good deeds. A person is engaged in good deeds because he has good opinion about Allah that He will reward him and accept his good deeds. It was his good opinion about his Lord that prompted him to do good deeds. When a person's opinion about his Lord is good, his deeds will be good, otherwise only good opinion while running after the desires is incapacity. It is reported by Shaddad ibn Awas that the Prophet, Allah's blessing and peace be upon him, said:

"Astute person is the one who subjugates his soul, and works for what is after death; and the incapable is the one who follows his desires and wishes good from Allah."[41]

In general, the good opinion comes with belief in the sources of redemption; it is not available with the belief in the sources of destruction, if it is said that yes it was possible. The cause of the good opinion is the comprehensiveness of the forgiveness, mercy, pardon and the kindness of Allah Almighty, and the fact that His mercy overwhelms His anger, and the punishment is not going to befit Him nor the pardon will harm Him.

---

[40] Ahmad (6: 104), Ibn Hibban (686)
[41] Tirmidhi (2459), Ibn Majah (4260), Ahmad (3: 124), Tabarani (7143) Hakim (1: 57)

The answer will be that the matter is like that. Allah is above all and He is the most Majestic, Kind, Generous and Merciful, but He puts these things in their proper places. Almighty is described to have attributes of wisdom, might, retribution, stern punishment, punishing those who deserve it. If the basis of the good opinion were only His Names and Attributes, the wicked and pious, the believer and disbeliever, His ally and enemy- all will be included. But His Names and Attributes are not going to avail a criminal who incurred the wrath of Allah and were subject of His curse. Such a person has gone too far in infringing the forbidden matters and intruding the sanctity of His orders. The good opinion will work with those who repent, regret and desist, and replace their evil with good and resume his remaining life in doing good deeds and obeying Allah. Such a person's good opinion will work while the first category's opinion is mere deception. Allah's help is sought for.

You should not consider this discussion too long because every one needs it badly. People have to know the difference between having good opinion about Allah and being deceived with Him. Allah, the Exalted, said:

"Those who believed, migrated, and strove for Allah's cause, it is they who can look forward to Allah's mercy." (2:218)

Almighty specified the people who have hope and not the corrupt and wicked ones. He, the Most High, said

"For those who migrated after they were persecuted, then strove and remained steadfast, your Lord is Most Forgiving, Most Merciful." (16:110)

Here Allah, the Glorious, said that He is forgiving and merciful for those who went through these trials.
A learned person puts the hope in its proper place, and a deceived ignorant one places it in a wrong position.

2.8   Forgiveness and command of Allah

Many ignorant people rely on the mercy of Allah and His forgiveness and kindness and neglected His order and prohibition. They forgot that He was severe in retribution and His punishment was not to be turned away from criminal people. The one who relied on pardon with persistence of committing sins is like obdurate.

Ma'ruf said:

'Your hope for the mercy of the One Whom you do not obey is stupidity and frustration.'

Some learned scholars said:

'The One who ordered cutting off your hand in the world for stealing three dirham do not feel safe from His punishment in the Hereafter being like that.'

It was said to Hasan:

'We see you weeping frequently?'

He said: 'I fear that He may throw me in the Fire and will not care.'

He said:

'Some people were distracted by the hopes of forgiveness until the departed from the world without repenting. One of them would say:

'I have good opinion about my Lord. He is a liar. If he had good opinion, he would have done righteous deeds.'

A man asked Hasan: 'Abu Sa'id, what can we do with those people who when they speak, they frighten us to the extent of making our hearts driven out?

He replied:

'By Allah, it is better for you to sit with people who frighten you until you reach safety than to sit with people who pass feeling of safety in your hearts till you are caught by dangers.'

Usamah ibn Zayd reported:

'I heard the Messenger of Allah, blessing and peace of Allah be upon him, say:

"A man will be brought on the Day of Resurrection and thrown into the Fire. His intestines will come out and he will go round them like the donkey goes round its mill stone. The people of Hell will go to him and say: 'So and so, what happened to you? Did you not order us for good and forbid evil? He will say: 'I used to order you good and did not do it, and prohibited the evil but I did it."[42]

Abu Rafi' reported:

'The Messenger of Allah, blessing and peace of Allah be upon him, passed by Baqi' and said: **"Uff to you, uff[43] to you!"**

I thought he means me. He said:

---

[42] Bukhari (3267), Nuslim (Zuhd: 2989)
[43] An expression of disgust.

"No, it is the grave of so and so. I send him as collector to the family of so and so, and he stole a sheet which has been turned in the coat of fire for him."[44]

Anas ibn Malik narrated that the Prophet, Allah's blessing and peace be upon him, said:

"I passed on the night I was taken to the heavens by a people their lips were cut by the scissors of the fire. I asked: Who are they?. They told me: They are the speakers of your community among the people of the world. They ordered people to do good and forgot themselves. Don't they understand?"[45]

Anas also related that the Messenger of Allah, blessing and peace of Allah be upon him, said:

"When I was taken up to the heavens I passed by some people who had nails of copper and they were scratching with them their faces and chests. I asked: 'who are they, Gabriel?' He said: 'they are the ones who used to eat the flesh of the people and involved in slandering them."[46]

Anas related that the Prophet, Allah's blessing and peace be upon him, used to say frequently:

"O Turner of the hearts, keep my heart firm on Your religion."

We said: 'Messenger of Allah, we have believed in you and that which you brought, are you afraid about us?'
He said:

"Yes, the hearts are between two fingers of Allah, He turns them as He wills."[47]

Anas also reported that the Messenger of Allah, blessing and peace of Allah be upon him, said to Gabriel:

"Why I never see Mika'il smiling?"

---

[44] Ahmad (6: 392), Nisa'i (2: 115)
[45] Ahmad (3: 120, 239)
[46] Ahmad (3: 224), Abu Dawud (3878)
[47] Ahmad (3: 112), Tirmidhi (2226) Hakim (1; 526)

He replied: 'He never smiled since the Fire was created.'[48]

Anas related that the Messenger of Allah, blessing and peace of Allah be upon him, said:

"The most affluent person of the world will be brought and be dipped once in the Fire and then asked: 'Did you experience any good at all? Did you enjoy any comfort at all?' He will say: 'never, my Lord!' The most wretched person of the world will be brought and give the taste of Paradise and then asked: 'Son of Adam, did you experience any hardship at all? Did you endure any trouble?' He will reply: 'No, my Lord, I never saw any distress, I never experience any hardship at all."[49]

Al-Bara' ibn 'Azib reported:
'We went out with the Prophet, Allah's blessing and peace be upon him, in the funeral of a man from the Helpers. We reached the grave and it was not yet ready. The Messenger of Allah, blessing and peace of Allah be upon him, sat and we sat down around him silently as though there are birds on our heads. The Prophet had a straw and scratched up the ground with it. He raised his head and said:

"Seek refuge in Allah from the torment of the grave."

He said it two or three times. Then he said:

"When a believing person reaches near the end of his worldly life and close to the Hereafter, angels from the heavens come down to him with bright faces as though they are sun. They will be holding shrouds from Paradise and perfume from Paradise. They sit there as far as the eye can see. Then the angel of death comes and sits near his head and says: 'O reassured soul, come out. Come out to the forgiveness and pleasure of Allah. It will flow as the drop flows from the mouth of the water skin. He takes it, and when he takes it, the other angels do not leave it for a twinkling of an eye but they take it and put it in that shroud and perfume. It diffuses the fragrance of the best of musk found on the face of earth. They go up with it and do not pass by any group of the angels of the heaven but they ask: 'Who is that pleasant soul?' They say: so and so, they mention him with the best name he was called with in the world. They carry it to the lowest

---

[48] Ahmad (3: 224)
[49] Muslim (Sifat al-Qiyamah: 2807)), Ahmad (3: 203(

sky and ask for it to be opened. It will be opened and in every sky it will be escorted by the closest angels to the next one till they reach the seventh sky. Allah will say: 'Write the book of My servant in 'Illiyyin, and return him to the earth. I created them from it, and in it I will return them and from it I bring them out again.''

The Messenger went on:

"His soul will be returned to the earth. Two angels will come to him and make him sit and ask him: 'Who is your Lord?' He will answer: 'My Lord is Allah.' 'What is your religion? They will ask. He will reply: 'My religion is Islam.' They will ask him: 'Who is this man who was sent to you?' He will answer: 'He is Muhammad, the Messenger of Allah.' They will ask: 'How did you know?' He will reply: 'I read the Book of Allah, and believed in it and attested it.' Then a caller will call from the sky: 'My servant has spoken truth, so spread for him from Paradise and give him dress from Paradise and open a gate for him from Paradise.'

It will be done and its fragrance and pleasant smell will come to him. His grave will be extended as far as an eye can see.

Then a man with handsome face, beautiful dress and pleasant fragrance will come to him and say: 'Get good tiding of what will make you happy. This is the day you were being promised.' He will say: 'Who are you? Your face is the one which brings good.' He will say: 'I am your good deeds.' He will say: 'My Lord, establish the Hour. My Lord, establish the Hour so that I can return to my family and property.'

The Prophet, Allah's blessing and peace be upon him, went on:

"When a disbelieving person comes to the end of his life in the world and heads toward the Hereafter, angels with black faces come down from the sky to him carrying coarse sheet. They sit as far as the eye can see. Then the angel of death comes and sits near his head and says: 'O evil soul, come out to the wrath and anger of Allah.' It spreads in his body and the angel pulls it out as the skewer is pulled out from wet wool. He takes it and then the other angels do not leave it in his hand but put it in that rough material. It diffuses the most evil smell of a decomposed body found on the face of the earth. They carry it up and do not pass by any group of the angels but they say; 'what is this evil soul?' They answer: 'This is the soul of so and so.' They call him with the ugliest name he was called with in the world. They ask the door of the sky to be opened but it is not opened.''

Here the Prophet, Allah's blessing and peace be upon him, read:

"The gates of the heaven will not be opened for them, nor will they enter Paradise until a thick rope enters into the eye of a needle." (7:40)

Allah will say: 'Write his book in 'Sijjin' in the lowest part of the earth.' So, his soul is dropped. Then the Messenger, Allah's blessing and peace be upon him, recited:

"Anyone who assigns partner with Allah is like someone who has been hurled down from the skies and snatched up by the birds or flung to a distant place by the wind." (22:31)

"His soul is returned to his body and two angels come to him and seat him and ask: 'Who is your Lord?' He will say: 'Ha, ha I do not know.' They will ask him: 'what is your religion?' He will say: 'Ha, ha I do not know.' They will ask: 'who is this man who was sent to you?' He will say: 'Ha, ha I do not know.'
A caller then will call from the sky: 'My servant has told lie, spread for him from the fire and give him dress of fire and open a gate for him from the Fire.' When it is done its heat and hot wind will reach him, his grave will be tightened on him till his ribs will entangle. Then a man with ugly face ugly dress and evil-smelling will appear and say: 'Receive the news which you will not like. This is the day you were promised.' He will say: 'Who are you? Your face is the one which brings evil news.' He will say: 'I am your evil deed.' He will say: 'My Lord, do not bring the Hour.'
Then a blind, dumb and deaf will be sent to him with an iron rod, if a mountain is hit by it, it will become dust. He will hit the man with it and he will be smashed to dust. Then Allah will return him as he was, and he will be hit another time. He will scream loudly which will be heard by every creation except the human and the jinn. Then a gate from the Fire will be opened and bed of fire will be spread for him."[50]

Al-Bara' also reported:
'While we were with the Messenger of Allah, blessing and peace of Allah be upon him, he noticed a group of people, and asked:

"For what these people have gathered?"

He was told that they were digging a grave. So the Messenger, Allah's blessing and peace be upon him, was terrified and rushed to the grave and

---

[50] Ahmad (4: 287, 288, 295), Abu Dawud (4754), Hakim (1: 37-40)

knelt on his knees. I sat in front of him to see what he is going to do. He cried till he made the ground wet by his tears and faced us and said:

"My brothers, for a day like this make preparation."[51]

Buraydah reported:
'One day the Messenger of Allah, blessing and peace of Allah be upon him, came out to us and called three times:

"O people! Do you know the likeness of me and you?"

They replied: 'Allah and His Messenger know best.'
He said:

"My likeness and yours is like a people who were scared of an enemy coming to them. They sent a man to find out. He saw the enemy and came to warn them. He feared to be apprehended before reaching his people, so he made gesture by his cloth saying: 'People, you are going to be attacked, people, you are going to be attacked.' He called three times."[52]

Jabir related that the Messenger of Allah, blessing and peace of Allah be upon him, said:

"Every intoxicant is forbidden. Allah has vowed that anyone who drinks the intoxicant, He will make him drink 'tinat al-khabal'."

He was asked what *tinat al-khabal* was? He replied:
"It is the sweat of the people of Hell or the pus of the people of Hell."[53]

Abu Dharr reported that the Messenger of Allah, blessing and peace of Allah be upon him, said:

"I see what you do not, and I hear what you do not. The heavens moan and they have right to moan. There is no place size of four fingers but in it is an angel in prostration. If you happen to know what I know, you would laugh little and cry much, and would not

---

[51] Ahmad (4: 294), Ibn Majah (4195)
[52] Ahmad (5: 348)
[53] Muslim (drink: 2002) Ahmad (3: 361)

enjoy your wives in beds, and go out to plain seeking help from Allah."

Abu Dharr said: 'I wish I would be a tree to be cut.'[54]

Hudhayfah reported:
'We were with the Messenger of Allah, blessing and peace of Allah be upon him, in a funeral. When we arrived to the grave, the Prophet sat on its corner and looked in it again and again, then said:

"The believer is squeezed in it so forcefully that his testicles will be separated, and it will be filled with fire for a disbeliever."[55]

Jabir reported:
'We went with the Messenger, Allah's blessing and peace be upon him, in the funeral of Sa'd ibn Mu'adh. When the Messenger, Allah's blessing and peace be upon him, performed the prayer on him and he was placed in his grave and it was levelled, he glorified for long and we joined him, then he exalted Allah and we did with him for long. He was asked for the reason of glorification and exaltation and he said:

"The grave of this righteous man was tightened over him till Allah relaxed it."[56]

Abu Sa'id reported that the Messenger of Allah, blessing and peace of Allah be upon him, said:

"When the funeral is ready and the people lift it on their shoulders, if it is righteous, it says: 'Take me ahead, take me ahead.' If it was not righteous, it says: 'Owe to it, where are they taking it!' Its voice is heard by everything except for the humans. If a man hears it, he will fall unconscious."[57]

Abu Umamah reported that the Messenger of Allah, blessing and peace of Allah be upon him, said:

"The sun will be brought close to one mile on the Day of Resurrection and its heat will be increased so much that the heads will be boiling

---

[54] Ahmad (5; 173), Tirmidhi (2312) Ibn Majah (4190), Hakim (2: 510)
[55] Ahmad (5: 405)
[56] Ahmad (3: 360, 377), Tabarani in Kabir (5346)
[57] Bukhari (1251)

like the cooking pots. People will sweat according to their sins, for some the sweat will reach to their ankles; others will have it up to their legs, some to their middle and some will be bridled with the sweat."[58]

Ibn Abbas narrated the Prophet, Allah's blessing and peace be upon him, as saying:

"How can I be comfortable when the angel of the horn has put it in his mouth and lowered his forehead to listen when he will be ordered to blow it?"

His Companions said: 'What should we say?' He replied:

"Say: 'Allah is sufficient for us and He is the best helper. In Allah we put our trust."[59]

Ibn 'Umar reported from the Prophet, Allah's blessing and peace be upon him, that he said:

"Who considers himself big in his mind or struts about in his walk, he will meet Allah while He will be angry with him."[60]

Ibn 'Umar also reported that the Messenger of Allah, blessing and peace of Allah be upon him, said:

"People who make pictures will be punished on the Day of Resurrection; it will be said to them: 'Put life in what you made."[61]

Also from Ibn 'Umar that the Prophet, Allah's blessing and peace be upon him, said:

"When one of you passes away his seat is presented to him in the morning and the evening. If he is one of the people of Paradise, he will be shown his place in Paradise, and if he is from the people of the Fire, his place in the Fire will be shown to him. It will be said to him; 'this is your seat until Allah raises you."[62]

---

[58] Ahmad (5: 254)
[59] Ahmad (1: 326), Hakim (4: 559)
[60] Ahmad (2: 118), Hakim (1: 60)
[61] Bukhari (5705) Muslim (2108)
[62] Bukhari (1371), Muslim (jannah: 2866)

Again Ibn 'Umar reported that the Messenger of Allah, blessing and peace of Allah be upon him, said:

"When the people of Paradise are taken to Paradise and the people of Hell to Hell, death will be brought and stopped between Paradise and Hell then slaughtered. A caller afterward will call: 'people of Paradise, it is eternity and no death; people of the Fire, it is eternity and no death.' The people of Paradise will be happier than before and the people of Hell will increase in their distress."[63]

Ibn 'Umar said that the Prophet, Allah's blessing and peace be upon him said:

"Anyone who bought a piece of cloth with ten dirham in which one dirham was unlawful Allah will not accept his prayer as long as the cloth was on him."

Ibn 'Umar put his two fingers in his ears and said:
'They become deaf if I did not hear the Prophet, Allah's blessing and peace be upon him, say it![64]

Abdullah ibn 'Amr reported that the Prophet, Allah's blessing and peace be upon him, said:

"Whoever abandons prayer because of intoxication once it will be as though he had the world and what is in it and then it was taken away from him. If someone neglects prayer four times because of heedlessness, Allah has right of making him drink the mud of al-khabal."

They said: 'What is the mud of al-khabal, Messenger of Allah?' He replied:

"The pus of the people of Hell."[65]

Ibn 'Umar reported that the Prophet, Allah's blessing and peace be upon him, said:

---

[63] Bukhari (6548), Muslim (2850)
[64] Ahmad (2: 98)
[65] Ahmad (2: 178), Hakim (4: 146)

"When a person drinks wine once, Allah does not accept any prayer from him for forty days. If he repents, Allah will accept his repentance. If he goes back and drinks again, Allah will not accept his prayer for forty days. If he turns to Allah in repentance, Allah will turn to him."

'I do not know whether the Prophet said in the third or fourth time:

"If he goes back to drink, Allah will surely make him drink from the mire of al-khabal on the Day of Resurrection."[66]

Abu Musa reported that the Messenger of Allah, blessing and peace of Allah be upon him, said:

"Whoever dies and he was addicted to wine Allah will make him drink from the stream of al-Ghutah.

He was asked what the stream of al-Ghutah was and he replied:

"A stream which flows from the vagina of the prostitutes; the smell of it irritates the people of the Fire."[67]

Abu Musa also reported that the Prophet, Allah's blessing and peace be upon him, said:

"The people will have three presentations on the Day of Judgement two of them will be argument and excuses, at the third one the records of the people will be spread, some holding them in their right hands and some in their left hands."[68]

Ibn Mas'ud narrated that the Messenger of Allah, blessing and peace of Allah be upon him, said:

"Be aware of the despised small sins; if they multiply on a person will destroy him."

The Prophet, peace and blessing of Allah be upon him, gave an example saying:

---

[66] Ahmad (2: 35), Tirmidhi (1863)
[67] Ahmad (4: 399), Ibn Hibban (5346), Hakim (4: 146)
[68] Ahmad (4: 414), Tirmidhi (2425), Ibn majah (4277)

"It is like some people who halted in a desert, and the protégé of the group came and the people started collecting fire wood, a man bringing one piece and the other another piece until they collected enough and lit fire and cooked what they wanted."[69]

Abu Hurayrah reported that the Messenger of Allah, blessing and peace of Allah be upon him, said:

"The bridge will be set on Hell and I will be the first person to cross it. The supplication of the messengers at that time will be: 'O Allah save us.' There will be hooks like the thorn of Sa'dan, which will grab the people according to their deeds. Some will collapse because of his deeds; some will be ground then will escape. When Allah completes the judgement between the servants and wishes to bring out from the Fire those whom He wills from among those who witnessed that there is no god but Allah, He will order the angels to take out some. They will recognize by the marks of prostration and bring them out while they have been burnt. Then water called 'the water of life' will be poured on them and they will grow as the grain springs out on the riverbank after the flood."[70]

Abu Hurayrah reported that the Messenger of Allah, blessing and peace of Allah be upon him, said:

"The first people to be judged on the Day of Resurrection will be three:
The first will be a man who was martyred. He will be brought and Allah will remind him of His bounties, he will acknowledge them. Then he will be asked: 'What did you do with them?' He will reply: 'I fought for You till I was killed.' Allah will say: 'You are a liar. You fought so that people say, 'he is very brave,' and it was said.' He will be dragged on his face and thrown to the Fire.
The second person will be a learned man who acquired knowledge and taught and read the Qur'an. He will be brought and Allah will remind him of His favours to him. He will acknowledge them. Then He will ask him: 'What did you do with them?' I acquired knowledge for the sake of You, taught it to others and read the Qur'an.' He will reply. Allah will say: 'You are telling a lie. You learnt so that it is said that he was a learned man. It was said, and you read the Qur'an so that people say he is a good reader, and it was said.' Then He will

---

[69] Ahmad (1: 402)
[70] Bukhari (6573) Muslim (182)

order him to be dragged on his face and thrown into Hell. The third will be a man whom Allah gave plenty of wealth, he had all sorts of materials. He will be brought and Allah will remind him of His bounties, which he will acknowledge. Then He will ask: 'What did you do with them?' He will say: 'I did not leave any place You liked to be spent in but I spent in it for your sake.' Allah will say: 'You are telling lie. You did it so that it is said that he was a generous man. It was said.' He will be dragged on his face and thrown in Hell."

In another version:

"They will be the first three men from the creation of Allah by whom the Fire will be kindled on the Day of Judgement."[71]

I heard Shaykh al-Islam Ibn Taymiyyah saying:
'As the best people are the prophets, the worst ones are those who imitate them and claim that they are among them while they are not. Then next best people are the learned, the martyrs, the sincere truthful ones, and the worst people are those who pretend to be among them while they are not.

Abu Hurayrah reported that the Prophet, Allah's blessing and peace be upon him, said:

"Anyone who committed an act of injustice against his brother concerning money or honour should go to him and get it settled before he is caught and has no Dinar or dirham. If he has good deeds, his good deeds will be taken and passed to his victim; if he has no good deeds, his victim's evil deeds will be taken and transferred to him, and he will end up in the Fire."[72]

Abu Hurayrah also reported that the Prophet, Allah's blessing and peace be upon him, said:

"Whoever takes one span of hand of land unjustly will be made to sink in the ground on the Day of Judgement to the seventh level of the earth."[73]

Abu Hurayrah reported that the Messenger of Allah, blessing and peace of Allah be upon him, said;

---

[71] Muslim (imarah: 1905)
[72] Bukhari (2449), Ahmad (2: 506)
[73] Bukhri (2454)

"This fire which the sons of Adam light is only one of the seventy parts of the fire of Hell."

The Companions said: 'By Allah, this fire was sufficient.'

The Prophet said:

"It was made superior to it by sixty nine degree, each having similar heat."[74]

Mu'adh reported:
'The Messenger of Allah, blessing and peace of Allah be upon him gave me the following instructions:

"Do not associate partners with Allah, even if you are killed or burnt; do not disobey your parents even if they ask you to abandon your family and property; do not neglect the prescribed prayer deliberately because anyone who neglects a prescribed prayer deliberately Allah's protection will be removed from him; do not drink wine because it is the main source of every evil; Keep away from engaging in evil deeds because getting involved in sin causes wrath of Allah."[75]

The Traditions in this respect are many more than we have cited. It is, therefore, not appropriate for a person who means well for himself to ignore them and leave himself loose and hang on the rope of hope and good opinion.

Abu al-Wafa' ibn 'Aqil said:
'Be careful with the Prophet, Allah's blessing and peace be upon him, he cut off the hand in stealing three dirham,[76] executed the punishment of drinking wine for drinking equivalent of the needle of wine,[77] told us that a woman went to the Fire because of neglecting a cat[78] and the cloak became fire on the one who dishonestly took it though he was killed as martyr.[79]

---

[74] Bukhari (2665), Muslim (2843)
[75] Ahmad (5: 238)
[76] Bukhari (6401, 6411)
[77] There is no report about it. The Prophet said: "Every intoxicant is forbidden."
[78] Muslim (2242)
[79] Muslim (115)

Tariq ibn Shihab reported the Prophet, Allah's blessing and peace be upon him, saying:

"A man entered Paradise because of a fly, and another person went to Hell because of a fly."

The Companions asked, 'how was it, Messenger of Allah?'
He replied:

"Two persons passed by a people who had an idol. No one passed by them but he had to offer something to it. When these two men came there, they said to one of them: 'Offer something.' He said; 'I had nothing with me.' They said to him: 'Offer even a fly.' He did and they left him go. This is how he entered the Fire. They asked the other man to offer something. He said: 'I am not going to offer anything for anyone except for Allah Almighty.' They killed him and he was admitted into Paradise. One word which a person speaks makes him fall because of it in the Fire farther than the distance between the east and the west."[80]

Some of the deceived people may be misguided when they see that Allah has bestowed His bounty on him, and thinks that He will not change it. He thinks that He gave him that because He loved him and He would give him better than that in the Hereafter. This is the utter deception.

'Uqbah ibn 'Amir reported that the Prophet, Allah's blessing and peace be upon him, said:

"When you see that Allah gives a person what he loves of the world despite his disobedience, then be sure that Allah is testing the person as he is allured to his own destruction. The he recited:

"When they forgot that warning they had received, We opened the gates to everything for them. Then, as they revelled in what they had been given, We struck them suddenly and they were dumbfounded." (6:44)[81]

Some early scholars said:

---

[80] Ahmad in Zuhd (15) Abu Nu'aym (1: 303) reported it from Yariq from Slaman l-Faris 's statement.
[81] Ahmad (4: 145)

'When you notice that Allah continuously giving you His bounty while you commit disobedience of Him, be careful. These bounties are a trial from Allah and could act as a trap or proof against oneself'.

Allah said:

"If it were not that people might have become one community (of disbelievers), We would have given everyone who disbelieves in the Lord of Mercy house with roofs of silver, sweeping staircases to ascend, massive gates for their houses, couches to sit on, and golden ornaments. All of these are mere enjoyments of this life; you Lord reserves the next life for those who take heed of Him." (43:33-35)

Allah, the Glorious, has refuted this kind of thought by saying:

"When the Lord of human beings tries him through honour and blessings, he says, 'My Lord has honoured me,' but when He tries him through the restriction of His provision, he says, 'My Lord has humiliated me.' No, indeed! "You treat not the orphans with kindness and generosity" (89:15-17)

It makes clear that no every man who has been provided immensely by Allah and given all kind of sources of enjoyment is honoured by Him, neither all those people whose provision is restricted are humiliated by Him. Rather it a trial, one is tried by the favour and grace and the other by affliction.

The Prophet, Allah's blessing and peace be upon him, said:

"Allah gives the worldly materials to those whom He loves as well as those whom He does not love. But He gives faith exclusively to those whom He loves."[82]

Some early scholar said:
'There are many who are allured by the favours of Allah without knowing, and there are others who are deceived by the covering of Allah and they do not know. There are people who are beguiled by the praise of the people without knowing.'

---

[82] Ahmad (1: 387), Hakim (1: 34)

2.9 The world is the biggest source of deception

The most deceived person is one who is deceived by the world and its available materials, and gives it precedence over the Hereafter and prefers it over the life to come. Some of them say: 'The world is cash in hand and the Hereafter is credit, and cash is better than credit.'
Some others say: 'A tiny available is better than a promised pearl.'
Another said: 'The pleasures of the world are sure and the pleasures of the Hereafter are doubtful; I am not going to leave the certain for the doubtful.'
This is the greatest deception and delusion of satan. The dumb animals are more intelligent than these people. When an animal fears the danger of something, it does not approach it even if it is beaten for it; but one of these people goes ahead for what is destructive and he is divided between agreeing and denying. If these kinds of people believe in Allah and His Messenger and meeting Him and retribution, they will be the greatest in the regret because they ventured on it with knowledge. If they do not believe in Allah and His Messenger, then they may get lost!

Their statement that cash is better than credit will be correct if the cash and the credit were equal, then definitely the cash is better; if they are different and the credit is more and better then it is better. Here the whole world from the beginning to the end is like one breath of the Hereafter.
Al-Musawrid ibn Shaddad reported that the Messenger, Allah's blessing and peace be upon him, said:

"The world compared with the Hereafter is as one of you puts his finger in the sea; let him see how much water it gets!"[83]

Preference of this cash over that credit is the gross self-deception and greatest ignorance. If this is what the whole world values compared with the Hereafter, then what will be the value of the age of the human compared with the Hereafter? Which one is then more appropriate for an intelligent person. Preference of the little in this short period and being deprived of the permanent good of the Hereafter or abandoning small valueless material which will vanish soon for what which is precious, significant and has no limit and no end?

As for the claim of others that 'I am not going to leave a certain thing for the doubtful one', he will be told that either you have doubt about the

---

[83] Ahmad (4: 229), Tirmidhi (2322) see also Muslim (2858)

promise of Allah, and His threat and the truth of His messengers, or you are certain about them. If you believe in them, then you have not abandoned but a little material which will vanish soon for a sure matter which is beyond doubt and has no end. If you have doubt, then check the signs of the Lord Almighty which indicate His existence, His power, will, oneness and the truth of His messengers about what they have informed. Think independently and look deeply into the signs of Allah until it becomes clear to you that what the messengers of Allah have brought is the truth without any doubt, and that the Creator of this universe and the Lord of the heavens and the earth is free and above, what people attribute to Him falsely.

Any person who ascribes qualities other than what Allah has permitted, he has abused Him, denied and rejected His Lordship and Kingdom. Any man with stable disposition and sound understanding will consider it absurd and impossible that the true King be incapable or ignorant, and unable to know anything, or lack hearing, seeing, speaking or commanding or forbidding. He will find it inconceivable that the Creator is unable to reward and punish, give honour to whoever He wishes and humiliate whoever He wishes. It is also unthinkable that He does not send His messenger to the corners of His kingdom and leave His subjects alone without taking care of them.

False attribution will belittle the power of ordinary king and considered unsuitable for him, then how could it be attributed to the True and Supreme King?

When a man looks at his condition from the beginning when he was a drop of sperm to the stage of his perfection and maturity, he will realise that the one who has carried him from embryological phase to development and maturity, will not leave him alone or abandon him without commanding and forbidding and without telling his rights and obligations and rewarding and punishing him.
If a man pays full attention to his affairs, he will find out that all that he sees and what he does not see are a proof of oneness, prophecy and the life to come. He will come to believe that the Qur'an is His words.
We have explained the evidence of all that in our book 'The oaths of the Qur'an' at His statement:

"I swear by what you see and by what you cannot see: this (i.e. the Qur'an) is the word (spoken by) an honourable messenger." (69:38-40)

Also I clarified some parts of it in the explanation of His saying:

"(There are signs) in yourselves, do you not see?" (51:21)

I clarified that the man himself is an evidence for the existence of his Creator, His Unity, the truth of His messengers and the affirmation of His perfect Attributes. It is clear that the one who in unmindful is deceived on both assumptions: the assumption of his affirmation & conviction and that of his denial & being in doubt.

If it is said: 'How can a sure attestation without doubt in the life to come and Paradise and Hell be in alignment with negligence in acts? Is it in the human nature to know that he is going to be confronted by some kings to be punished severely or be fully honoured yet he be unmindful and neglectful and not to remember his standing in front the king and not preparing himself and be ready for that?'

It will be said in answer that by Allah it is a correct query about most of the creation and the combination of these two conditions is the most amazing matter. This negligence of the duties is result of the various causes:
One of them is lack of knowledge and failing in certainty. If a man thinks that knowledge does not differ, his thought is false and vain. Abraham, the friend of Allah, asked his Lord to show how to bring dead of dead back to life openly while he knew the power of Allah. His act was in order to increase in certainty and see the unseen in the form of perceivable reality.
Ahmad reported that the Prophet, Allah's blessing and peace be upon him, said:

"The one who brings the news is not like the one who witnesses."[84]

When the following disasters join together, then the faith of a person is in danger. These are the lack of knowledge combined with not remembering and its absence from the heart because of its engagement in what is opposite of it, in addition to the corruption of the nature, domination of the desire, overwhelming of lust, delusion of the soul, deception of Satan, finding the promise too late, long hope, slumber of heedlessness, love of the present, opportunity of interpretation and love of the familiar customs

---

[84] See Musnad (1842), See also Tabarani in Kabir (12451) and awsat (284), Ibn Hibban (6213), Hakim (2: 321)

– then only the One Who holds the heavens and the earth from vanishing can save the faith.

For this reason the people differ in faith and deeds until a man reaches the point of the least of an atom's weight of faith. The basis of all these reasons is lack of insight and patience. This is why Allah, the Glorious, praised the people of patience and certainty and made them the leaders of the religion. He said:

"We raised leaders among them guiding according to Our command when they became steadfast and believed firmly in Our verses." (32:24)

2.10 Difference between the good opinion and deception

Now the difference between good opinion and deception has become clear. If the good opinion prompts to work, induces to it and leads to it, then it is right. Reversely, if it leads to inactivity and engaging in evil deeds, then it is deception. Good opinion mean hope, so if a person's hope leads to obedience and keeps him away from the evil deeds, it is a right hope. On the other hand, if his hope is based on inactivity and sluggishness, then it is deception and the person holding it is deceived.

It could be explained by the following example. A man has a land and he expects that it will produce yields for his benefit, but he neglects it and does not sow seeds in it nor does he till it and still has the good opinion that he will get from its produce without tilling, sowing seeds, irrigating and taking care of it, the people will consider him the most stupid person.

In the same way if a person's opinion is good and his hope is high that he will have a child without intercourse or will become the most learned of his time without seeking knowledge and putting big effort in it, he will be regarded as foolish. The same applies to a person who has good opinion and strong hope for achieving the highest ranks and enduring pleasure without carrying out the acts of obedience and fulfilling the duties and avoiding the prohibitions, he is living in dream. Only Allah can give help. Allah, the Most High, said:

"Those who have believed and those who have emigrated and strove in the cause of Allah, they expect the mercy of Allah." (2:218)

Look how Almighty fixed their expectation with fulfilling these acts of obedience? The deceived people assume that those who neglect the dues of Allah, abandon His commands, commit injustice to His servants and cross the boundaries set by Him are the ones who expect the mercy of Allah.

The secret of the issue is that hope and good opinion will be useful if accompanied with causes required by the wisdom of Allah and His religion, decree and reward and honour. The slave carries them out and has good opinion about his Lord, and hopes that He will not desert him, but will help him to continue doing deeds which are beneficial for him, and to turn him away from the matters which are opposed to them and destroy their effects.

2.11 The requirements of hope

It is useful to know that anyone who hopes to acquire something has to do three things:
- to love that thing,
- to be afraid of losing it,
- to work hard as much as he can to acquire it,

Expectation that does not have these elements is only wishful thinking. Expectation is one thing and wishful thinking is another. Every hopeful person is scared, and when a person walking on the path is scared, he will be quick in his walk with the fear of losing it.

Abu Hurayrah reported that the Messenger of Allah, blessing and peace of Allah be upon him, said:

"The one who is scared sets out at night and the one who sets out in night reaches the destination. Beware Allah's commodity is expensive, beware Allah's commodity is expensive."[85]

Allah, the Exalted, has made hope for the people of the righteous deeds; similarly He has put fear for the people of righteous deeds. This indicates that useful hope and fear are those which are joined with the good deeds. Allah, the Glorious, said:

"Those who stand in awe of their Lord, who believe in His messages, who do not ascribe partners to Him, who always give what they give with hearts that tremble at the thought that they

---

[85] Tirmidhi (2452), Hakim (4: 307)

must return to Him, are the ones who race toward good thing, and they will be the first to get them. (23:57-61)

'A'ishah reported:
'I asked the Messenger of Allah, blessing and peace of Allah be upon him, about this verse and said: 'Is this about the people who drink wine, commit adultery and steal?' The Prophet, blessing and peace of Allah be upon him, said:

"No! O daughter of Siddiq. They are those who fast, perform prayer, give out charity and are scared that these deeds may not be accepted from them. They are the ones who hasten toward the good deeds."[86]

This narration was reported by Abu Hurayrah as well.
Allah, The Supreme, described the lucky people with doing good deeds while they have fear, and He described the unfortunate ones with torment while they feel safe. Anyone who looks in the conditions of the Companions will discover that they were engaged in righteous work with extreme fear. We have combined between carelessness or rather negligence and safety. Look at the Siddiq (i.e. Abu Bakr) who said:
'I wish I were a hair in the side of a believer.'[87]
It is said about him that he used to hold his tongue and say: 'This is the one which caused me destruction.'[88]
He used to cry frequently and say: 'Cry, if you cannot cry, pretend to cry.'[89]
When he stood for the prayer he was as though he was a piece of wood.
He was served with a bird for meal; he turned it upside down and said:
'No game was hunted, and no tree was cut but because of neglecting the glorification of Allah.'[90]
When the time of his death approached he aid to 'A'ishah:
'My little daughter, I received this cloak, milk cow and this slave from the property of the Muslims, immediately pass them on to the son of al-Khattab.'[91]
He said: 'By Allah, I wish I were this tree to be cut off and consumed.'
Qatadah said: I learned that Abu Bakr said: 'I wish I were green vegetable to be eaten by the cattle.'[92]

---

[86] Tirmidhi (3175), Ibn Majah (4198), Hakim (2:393), Ahmad (6:159, 205)
[87] Ahmad in al-Zuhd (2:13)
[88] Malik in Mu'atta (2:988), Ibn al-Mubarak (369)
[89] Ahmad in Al-zuhd (2:13)
[90] Ibid (2: 15)
[91] Ibid (2: 16)
[92] Ibid (2: 17)

'Umar read Surat al-Tur (Chapter 52) when he reached the verse, **"The torment of your Lord is coming." (52:7)**, he cried intensely to the extent that he fell ill and people visited him.

He said to his son at the time of his death:
'Owe to you! Put my cheek on the ground. That may make Him to show mercy to me.' Then he said: 'Woe unto to my mother! if I was not forgiven. He said it three times, and then passed away.
He used to pass by a verse in his recitation in the night and become scared, and would remain in the house for days being visited. The people thought he was ill.[93]
Ibn Abbas said to him:

'Allah founded cities by you and made you conquer areas and He bestowed further victories and bounties.' He said: 'I wished to be rescued without reward or punishment.'[94]

And look at 'Uthman ibn 'Affan. When he stood at a grave, he started crying till his beard got wet.[95]
He said: 'If I were between Paradise and Hell and I did not know which one I will be taken in, I would prefer to be ash before knowing where I will end up.'[96]

Here is Ali ibn Talib and his crying and fear. He was greatly fearful of long hope and following the desires. He said:
'The long hope makes one forget the Hereafter, and the following the desire turns him away from the truth. Beware the world has turned its back and the Hereafter is approaching. Each one of them has its offsprings. Try to be the sons of the Hereafter and not the sons of the world. Today are works and no accounting and tomorrow will be accounting and no work.'[97]

Abu al-Darda' used to say:
'The worst thing, I am scared to happen to me on the Day of Judgement is that it will be said to me: 'Abu al-Darda', you had knowledge, then did you act according to what you knew?'
He also said:

---

[93] Ibid (2:29)
[94] Ibid (2: 34)
[95] Tirmidhi (2424), Ibn Majah (4267) Abu Nu'aym in al-Hilyah (1: 61)
[96] Ahmad 92: 42), Abu Nu'aym (1: 60)
[97] Ahmad (2; 48) Abu Nu'aym (1: 76)

'If you were to know what you are going to face after death, you would not eat food with appetite, nor drink water, nor enter a house for relaxing. You would rather go out to open ground beating your chests and crying over yourself. I wish I were a tree which is cut down then is eaten by cattle.'

Abdullah ibn Abbas's lower eye was like worn out shoelace because of the tears.
Abu Dharr used to say:
'I wish I were a tree to be cut down, and I wish I would have not been created'.
He was offered support for maintenance and he said:
'We have a goat which we milk and donkeys we move on them and a free slave who serves us, and a spare cloak. I am fearful of accounting about these things.'

Tamim al-Dari read one night the Surat al-Jathiyah (Chapter 45). When he came to the verse:

"Do those who commit evil think that We will deal with them in the same way as those who believe and do righteous deeds?" (45:21)

He continued repeating it till morning.

Abu 'Ubaydah ibn al-Jarrah said:
'I wish I were a sheep which my family slaughtered and ate my meat and sipped my soup.'

There is an extensive section of quotes of the righteous people, which can be followed.

Imam Bukhari set a chapter in his Sahih,
"The fear of the believer from getting his deeds destroyed while he does not realise"

Ibrahim al-Taymi said:
'Never did I compare my talk with my deeds, but I was scared of being a liar.'

Ibn Abi Mulaykah said:
'I met thirty Companions of the Prophet, Allah's blessing and peace be upon him, every one of them was fearful of hypocrisy. None of them said that his faith was like the faith of Gabriel and Michael.'

Hasan said:

'No one fears Him except a believer, and no one feels safe from Him but a hypocrite.'

'Umar ibn al-Khattab used to ask Hudhayfah: 'I implore you by Allah, did the Messenger of Allah, blessing and peace of Allah be upon him, mention my name to you i. e. among the hypocrites? He replied: 'No, but after you I will not vindicate anyone else.'

I heard our Shaykh, i.e. Ibn Taymiyyah saying: 'He did not mean that he would not clear anyone beside 'Umar from hypocrisy; rather he meant that he was not going to open the door and answer everyone who asked him whether the Messenger of Allah, blessing and peace of Allah be upon him, named him.

I say: it is like the saying of the Prophet, Allah's blessing and peace be upon him, to the person who asked him to pray to Allah to put him among those seventy thousand who will enter Paradise with accounting: "Ukkashah went ahead of you."[98]

The Prophet did not intend to say that Ukkashah is only to deserve this honour out of all the Companions, but he prayed for him, another person would have requested and the door would be opened for more requests. It was possible that someone who did not deserve it would also have requested it, so it was better to stop. Allah knows better.

2.12 The harm of the sins and evil deeds

Let us go back to our discussion of the treatment of the disease which if persists will spoil the world and the Hereafter of a believer. It is worth noting that the sins and evil deeds are harmful without any doubt. Their harm to the hearts is like the harm of poison in the bodies with varying degrees of damage. Is there any evil in the world or the Hereafter but its cause is sin and evil deed?

What expelled the parents (Adam and Eve) from Paradise, the abode of delight, pleasure and joy to the abode of pain, grief and afflictions?

What caused the banishment of Iblis from the domain of the heavens? He was expelled and cursed and his external and internal forms were disfigured; his face was distorted and turned into ugliest and most repulsive one, and his inner self was changed to the most abominable and

---

[98] Bukhari (6175), Muslim (216)

disgusting form. His closeness was turned into remoteness; the mercy he enjoyed was replaced by curse and his beauty was turned to ugliness. He was taken from Paradise to blazing fire. His faith was substituted with disbelief and the friendship of the Praiseworthy and Benefactor with the greatest enmity and hostility. He used to sing the glorification, exultation and unity of Allah, which was replaced with the words of disbelief, association of partners to Him, engagement in lie, accusation and abhorrent talks. Instead of the dress of belief he donned the garment of disbelief, defiance and disobedience. The result was that he became utterly despicable, and dropped immensely in His estimation. Allah's anger descended upon him and he lost his status. Allah despised him tremendously and caused his ruin. He became pimp for every defiant and criminal. He agreed to be pimp after enjoying the worship and supremacy. O Allah, we seek refuge in You from disobeying Your commands and violating Your prohibitions.

What was the cause of all the people of the earth to be drowned till the water went above the summit of the mountains? What made the storm being released against people of 'Ad which brought them down dead on the face of the earth as though they were hollow palm-trunk? Their towns, fields, plants and cattle were destroyed and they became a lesson for the nations until the Day of Resurrection.
Why was the blast sent on the people of Thamud which tore their hearts inside their chests and destroyed them all?
What was the cause of lifting the towns of the people of Lot to height till the angels heard the barking of their dogs and then turning them over them and making them upside down? They were all destroyed and the rain of stone of hard clay followed. On them the types of punishment were combined which was not inflicted on any other nation. Their brothers are going to suffer similar torment. Allah's punishment is not far from the wrongdoers.
What caused the clouds like shadow to be sent over the people of Shu'ayb and when they reached above their heads, they rained on them blazing fire?
Why Pharaoh and his people were drowned in the sea, then their souls were moved to Hell? The bodies were drowned and the souls were cast in the Fire for burning.
What was the cause of Corah (Qaroon) to be sunk in the ground together with his house, wealth and family?
Why the communities after Noah were destroyed by various punitive measures and completely annihilated?
Why the people of the man mention in surah Yasin, were destroyed by the blast which made all of them perish?

What was the cause of sending people of great force upon the children of Israel, who ravaged their homes, killed the men, enslaved the women and children and plundered their properties? Many powerful groups were sent again until they ransacked all that they found and utterly annihilated whatever within their power.

Why various punitive measures were applied to them, by killing, taking them prisoners, ruining their towns, subjecting them to the atrocities of the kings and transforming them to apes and pigs? The last thing was the swearing of the Lord, the Glorious and Blessed that:

"He will impose on them till the Day of Judgement people who will subject them to terrible suffering." (7:167)

Jubayr ibn Nufayr reported:
'When Cyprus was conquered and divided among the warriors, people started crying. I found Abu al-Darda' sitting alone and crying. I said to him: 'Abu al-Darda', what makes you cry on this day when Allah has given power to Islam and its followers? He replied: 'Woe to you Jubayr! How mean people are to Allah when they neglect His orders! They are powerful and victorious, have authority, but neglected the orders of Allah so they ended up to what you see.'[99]

A man reported that the Prophet, Allah's blessing and peace be upon him, said:

"People will not perish unless they fail to find excuses for themselves."[100]

Umm Salmah reported that she heard the Messenger, Allah's blessing and peace be upon him, saying:

"When the evil deeds become common in my Community, Allah will bring all-embracing punishment upon them."

Umm salmah said:
'Will there be no righteous people among them?'
He replied:
"Yes, there will be."
'Then what will happen to them? She asked.

---

[99] Ahmad in Zuhd (1: 86)
[100] Ahmad (4; 260), Abu Dawud (4347)

He said:

"They will suffer from what the people suffer, then they will return to the forgiveness and pleasure of Allah."[101]

Hasan reported that the Prophet, Allah's blessing and peace be upon him, said:

"This Community will remain under the protection and shelter as long as its religious leaders do not conform to its rulers, and the righteous people condone its evil ones, and their good people are not humiliated by the bad ones; When they do it Allah will withdraw His help from them and establish their tyrants as ruler over them who will subject them to terrible torment, then He will inflict poverty and indigence on them."[102]

Thawban reported that Allah's Messenger, Allah's blessing and peace be upon him, said.

"A man is deprived of the provision because of the sins he commits."[103]

Thawban also reported that the Prophet, Allah's blessing and peace be upon him, said:

"It is almost that the nations will rally on you from every corner as the eaters rally around the plates."

We said: 'Messenger of Allah, it will happen because we will be few in number?'
"He said:

"You will be plenty at that time, but you will be like the scum of the flood. Allah will take away fear of you from the hearts of your enemies and cast *wahn* in your heart."

They asked: 'What is *wahn*?'

He replied:

---

[101] Ahmad (6: 304)
[102] Al-Darimi (282)
[103] Ahmad (5: 277), Ibn Majah (4022), Hakim (1: 493)

"It is the love of the world and dislike of death."[104]

Anas reported that the Prophet, Allah's blessing and peace be upon him, said:

"When I was taken to the heaven I passed by a people who had nails of copper and scratched their faces and their chests. I said: 'Who are they, Gabriel?' He replied: 'They are the ones who used to eat the flesh of people and disparage them."[105]

Abu Hurayrah reported that the Messenger of Allah, blessing and peace of Allah be upon him, said:

"At the end of the time there will appear men who will swindle the world with religion. They will wear soft skin of sheep to deceive the people, their tongues will be sweeter than sugar and their hearts will be the hearts of the wolves. Allah, the Mighty and Sublime says: 'Is it Me who they try to delude or is it against Me whom they conspire? By Me, I swear to send upon these people a trial that will leave the intelligent person utterly confused."[106]

Ali said:
'There will come a time when only name of Islam will remain, and only the script of the Qur'an will be seen. The mosques will be full in those days but will be empty from guidance. Their learned religious men will be the worst people under the shade of the sky. From them the problem will start and to them it will return.'[107]

Abdullah ibn Mas'ud said:
'When adultery and usury spread in a town, Allah allows its destruction.'[108]

Hasan reported that the Prophet, Allah's blessing and peace be upon him, said:

"When the people disclose knowledge and miss acts, express love by tongues and hide hatred in hearts and cut off the bonds of blood, then

---

[104] Ahmad (5: 278), Abu Dawud (4297), Tabarani in Kabir (1452)
[105] Ahmad (3:120), Abu Dawud (4878)
[106] Tirmidhi (2404)
[107] Al-Bayhaqi in Sh'ab al-iman (1763)
[108] Abu Ya'la (4981), Tabarani in Kabir (10329)

Allah will reject them and make their ears deaf and blind their eyes."[109]

Abdullah ibn 'Umar said:
'I was one of ten people of the Emigrants with the Messenger of Allah, blessing and peace of Allah be upon him, and he faced us and said:

"Assembly of the Emigrants, there are five matters I seek Allah's refuge from getting you: no immorality appeared in a people and they made it public but they will be afflicted with plagues and diseases which were not found with their ancestors; no people cheated in measurement and weight but were afflicted with drought, lack of food and oppression of the ruler; no people stopped paying zakat of their wealth but would be deprived of the rain from the sky, if there were no cattle, they would not have rain at all; no community broke the pledge but Allah would give power over them to their enemy who would take some of their wealth; no religious leaders of a community neglect following what Allah, the Most High has revealed in His Book but Allah will create hostility among them."[110]

Abdullah ibn Mas'ud reported that the Messenger of Allah, blessing and peace of Allah be upon him, said:

"When a man from the community before you committed a sin, the warner went to him and reprimanded him. The following morning he went to him and sat with him and participated in eating and drinking with him as though he had not seen him committing a sin. When Allah, the Exalted, saw this He created enmity between their hearts for one another, then He cursed them on the tongues of David and Jesus, the son of Mary, because they disobeyed and persistently overstepped the limits. By the One in whose hand is Muhammad's soul, you will order what is good and forbid what is evil, and hold the hand of the silly and force him to follow the truth or Allah will create enmity in your hearts for one another then curse you as He cursed them."[111]

Ibrahim ibn 'Amr al-San'ani said:
'Allah revealed to Yusha' ibn Nun: 'I am going to destroy forty thousand people of their good ones and sixty thousand of evil ones.'

---

[109] Tabarani (6: 323), Abu Nu'yam in al-Hilyah (3: 109) from the report of Slman
[110] Ibn Majah (4019) Hakim (4: 540)
[111] Ahmad (1: 291), Tirmidhi (3047), Abu Dawud (4336), Ibn Majah (4006) Tabarani in Kabir (10262)

Yusha' said: 'My Lord, the evils are alright, but what is the fault of the good ones?'
He replied: 'They did no care for My anger, they joined them in eating and drinking.'[112]

Abu Hizzan said:
'Allah sent two angels to a town ordering them to destroy them with those who are there.' They went and found a man praying in a mosque. They said: 'Lord, Your servant so and so is praying.' Allah the Almighty said: 'Destroy the town including him because his face never frowned for Me in disapproval.'[113]

Mis'ar said:
'An angel was ordered to destroy a town; he said: 'My Lord, there is a devoted righteous man in it.' Allah said to him: 'Start with him, because his face never changed in disgust against them for My sake.

Wahab ibn Munabbih said:
'When David committed the sin, he prayed to Allah: 'My Lord, forgive me.' Allah said: 'I forgave you and put its shame on the children of Israel.'
David said: 'My Lord, how is it? You are the Just Arbiter, do not wrong anyone, how it is that I commit a sin and You put the shame on others?' Allah inspired to him: 'When you committed the sin, they did not immediately rebuke you.'

Anas ibn Malik said that he went to 'A'ishah with another person, and the man said:' Mother of the believers, tell us about earthquake.'
She said: 'When the people get involved in adultery, drinking wine, playing with musical instruments, Allah gets angry in the heaven and says to the earth: Shake with them, if they repent and abandon their activities, leave them otherwise destroy them.'
The man asked: 'Mother of the believers, was it a punishment for them?'
She replied: 'It was rather an admonition and mercy for the believers and an example, punishment and Divine anger for the disbelievers.'
Anas said: 'I did not hear a Hadith after the Messenger of Allah, blessing and peace of Allah be upon him, which caused more happiness than this statement.'

---

[112] See Sh'ab al-iman of al-Bayhaqai (9428)
4. al-Bayhaqi (7595), Tabarani in Awsat (4390) see Majma' al-zawa'id (7: 270)

A report from the Prophet, Allah's blessing and peace be upon him, is as follows:

'The earth was shaken violently during the period of the Messenger of Allah, blessing and peace of Allah be upon him, and he put his hand on it and said:

"Keep calm because the time has not come yet."

Then he turned to his Companions and said:

"Your Lord is ordering you to pray for amend so try to please Him."

Then the earth has similar shaking again in the time of 'Umar ibn al-Khattab and he said:

'People, this tremor did not occur but due to something you have done. By the One in whose hand is my soul, if it happens again, I will not live in it with you.'[114]

In another report the earth was shaken violently in the time of 'Umar and he put his hand on it and said: 'What is wrong with you? What is wrong with you? If it were the time of Resurrection, it would have brought its news.' I heard the Messenger of Allah, blessing and peace of Allah be upon him, saying:

"When the Day of Judgement comes, there will remain no place at arm's length or span of hand's length but it will speak."

Safiyyah said:

'Madinah was shaken violently during the reign of 'Umar and he said:

'People, what is this? How quickly you brought something evil! If it happens again, I will not live with you here.'

Ka'b said:

'The earth is shaken when the evil deeds are done on the it; it shakes from the fear of the Lord Almighty that He may take notice of them.'

'Umar ibn Abd al-'Aziz wrote to the provinces:

'This tremor is a thing by which Allah expresses His unhappiness to the people, and I have written to the provinces asking people to go out on

---

[114] See Hakim (4: 516) It is not an authentic report.

such and such day in such and such month. If a person has something, he should give it in charity because Allah says:

"Certainly he is successful who purifies himself (by giving his wealth), and mentions the name of his Lord and prays." (87:14-15)

Say as Adam said:

"They said: 'Our Lord, we have wronged ourselves, if You do not forgive us and have mercy, we shall be lost." (7:23)

Say as Noah said:

"If You do not forgive me and have mercy on me, I shall be one of the losers." (11:47)

Say as Jonah said:

"There is no god but You, glory be to You, I was one of the wrongdoers." (21:87)

Ibn 'Umar reported that he heard the Messenger of Allah, blessing and peace of Allah be upon him, say:

"When the people withhold Dinar and dirham and do transactions with commodities, follow the tail of the cows and abandon the struggle in the cause of Allah, Allah will send affliction on them and will not remove it until they return to their religion."[115]

Ibn 'Umar said:
'I saw us when none of us considered himself more deserving to his Dinar or dirham than his Muslim brother and I heard the Messenger of Allah, blessing and peace of Allah be upon him, say:

"When the people withhold Dinar and dirham, conclude their sale with commodities, leave the struggle in the cause of Allah and hold the tails of the cows, Allah will send on them affliction from the sky and will not remove it from them until they return to their religion."

Hasan said:

---

[115] Ahmad (4825)

'Trial is no more than punishment from Allah Almighty for the people.'

Some of the prophets of the children of Israel looked at what Bukhtansar was doing to them and said:
'Because of what our hands earned that he was given power over us, who does not know You and have no mercy on us.'

Bukhtnasar said to Daniel; 'What gave me power over your people?' He replied: 'The severity of your sin and the wrongdoing of my people to themselves.'

Ammar ibn Yasir and Hudhayfah reported that the Prophet, Allah's blessing and peace be upon him, said:

"When Allah wills to afflict the servants with trial, He causes the children to die, makes the women barren, then the affliction comes and there remains no one deserving mercy."[116]

Malik ibn Dinar said:
'I read in some books of wisdom that Allah, the Most Glorious, says:
'I am the King of the kings, kings' hearts are in My hand; whoever obeys Me I make his ruler show mercy for him, and the one disobeys Me, I make him a trial for him. Do not keep your selves busy in abusing the kings, but turn to Me in repentance, I will show kindness to you.'[117]

Hasan reported the Prophet, Allah's blessing and peace be upon him, saying:

"When Allah wills good for a people he gives authority to their sensible people and their wealth to the generous ones of them; and when Allah wills evil to a people, He puts their affairs in the hands of stupid ones and their wealth in the hands of stingy ones."[118]

Qatadah said:
'Musa said: 'My Lord, You are in the heaven and we are on earth, what is the sign of Your anger from Your pleasure?' He replied: 'When I give power to your good people, it is the sign of My pleasure with you, and

---

[116] It is cited by Shaykh Albani in Daeef Al-Jami' as-Sagheer (1544)
[117] Tabarani in Awsat (2611), Abu Nu'aym in al-Hilyah (2: 388) see Majma' al-zawa'id (5: 248)
[118] Abu Dawud in Marasil. See al-Targhib (3: 382)

when I give authority to your evil men over you, it is the sign of My displeasure with you.'[119]

Al-Fudayl ibn 'Iyad said:

'Allah revealed to some prophets: 'when someone who knows Me disobeys Me, I give power over him to the one who does not know Me.'[120]

Ibn 'Umar reported that the Prophet, Allah's blessing and peace be upon him, said:

"By the One in whose hand is my soul, the Hour will not come until Allah raises rulers who will be lying and evil ministers, disloyal helpers, unjust assistants, disobedient religious preachers, their appearance will be like the monks while their hearts are more stinking than corpses, their desires are different. Allah will open for them a dusty dark sedition in which they will be trapped. By the One in whose hand is Muhammad's soul, Islam will be broken piece by piece until there will be no one to say: Allah, Allah. You must enjoin what is good and forbid what is evil or Allah will set as rulers over you the wicked ones of you who will subject you to the horrible torment. At that point your righteous people will call upon Allah but their prayer will not be answered. By Allah you must enjoin good and forbid bad or Allah will impose upon you the one who will not show mercy to your young ones or honour your elderly."[121]

Ibn Abbas reported that the Messenger of Allah, blessing and peace of Allah be upon him, said:

"No people give short measure and weigh less than required but Allah will stop sending rain to them. No people get involved in adultery but death will spread among them. No people get engaged in usury but Allah imposes madness upon them; no community starts killing one another but Allah will give power over them to their enemy. No people engaged in the act of the people of Lot but sinking down in the earth will happen to them. No people abandon enjoining what is good and forbidding what is bad but their deeds will not be raised and their prayer will not be answered."[122]

---

[119] Ahmad in Zuhd (277)
[120] Ibn Kathir cited it in his Tarikh (13: 81)
[121] Shajari in his Amaali Vol 2 P257 & 264
[122] See Tabarani in Kabir (10992), refer to Majma' al-zawa'id (3: 65) and al-Targhib (1: 271)

'A'ishah said:
'The Messenger of Allah, blessing and peace of Allah be upon hum, came to me while he was gasping. I knew from his face that something has troubled him. He did not speak, performed ablution and went out. I stuck to the apartment. He climbed the pulpit, praised Allah and extolled Him then said:

"People, Allah, the Most Glorious, says to you: 'Order what is good and forbid what is wrong before you call upon Me and I do not answer your prayer, you ask Me for help and I do not help you and you ask Me and I do not give you."[123]

Al-'Umari, the pious, said:
'Among the signs of your negligence of you soul and turning away from Allah is that you see something which Allah does not like and you go past it, you do not order or forbid concerning it out of fear of someone who does not have power to cause himself any benefit or harm.'
He also said:
'The one who abandons ordering what is right and forbidding what is wrong out of the fear of the people, the obedience will be taken away from him. If he tells his children or some of his slaves to do something, they would not fulfil their duty.'

Abu Bakr al-Siddiq said:
'People, you recite this verse and give it a wrong meaning:

"You who believe, you are responsible for your own souls; if anyone else goes astray it will not harm you as long as you follow the guidance" (5:105)

I heard the Messenger of Allah, blessing and peace of Allah be upon him, say:

"When the people see an unjust person and did not check him, it is very likely that Allah puts them all under His torment."[124]

Abu Hurayrah Reported that the Prophet, Allah's blessing and peace be upon him, said:

---

[123] Ahmad (6: 159), al-Bazzar (3304), Ibn Hibban (291)
[124] Ahmad (1: 2, 3), Tirmidhi (3057), Abudawud (4171), Ibn Majah (4005)

"When the misdeed is hidden it harms only the one who does it, but when it is committed openly and no attempt is made to stop it, it causes harm to the general public."[125]

'Umar ibn al-Khattab said:
'It is close that the towns are destroyed while they are flourishing.' He was asked: 'How could they be ruined when they are flourishing? He replied: 'When the wicked people dominate the righteous ones and the tribe is led by the hypocrites.'

The Prophet, Allah's blessing and peace be upon him, said:

"The wicked of my community will dominate the good of them to the extent that the believer will be lost among them as the hypocrites are hidden among us today."[126]

Ibn Abbas reported the Messenger of Allah, blessing and peace of Allah be upon him, said:

"There will come a time in which the heart of the believer will melt as the salt melts in water."

The asked: 'Why will it be so, Messenger of Allah?'
He replied:

"Because he sees abominable matters and is unable to change them."[127]

Jarir narrated that the Prophet, Allah's blessing and peace be upon him, said:

"No Community which is involved in committing sinful acts and those who are not involved are more in number and power and they do not change it, but Allah will destroy them all."[128]

Usamah ibn Zayd reported that the Messenger of Allah, blessing and peace of Allah be upon him, said:

---

[125] Tabarani in Awsat (4385) see majma' al-zawa'id (7: 2168)
[126] Ibn Adi in al-Kamil (7: 2647) it is a weak tradition.
[127] Ibn Abi al-Dunyal in al-Amr bi 'l-ma'ruf
[128] Ahmad (4: 364), Abu Dawud (4339), Ibn Majah (4008), Ibn Hibban (300) Tabarani (2382) al-Bayhaqi (10: 91)

"A man will be brought on the Day of Resurrection and thrown in the Fire. His intestines will come out and he will be going around it as a donkey goes around the millstone. The people of Hell will gather around him and say: 'So and so, what happened to you? Did you not use to enjoin us what is good and forbid what was wrong? He will say: 'Yes, but I asked you to do what is good and did not do it myself, and asked you to keep away from the evil and used to commit it.'"[129]

Malik ibn Dinar said:
A Rabbi from the children of Israel used to preach and admonish people of the favours of Allah, his house was attended by both men and women. One day he noticed that one of his sons was blinking at women, he said to him: 'Be careful my son, be careful my son!' He later fell down from his bed and his spinal cord was broken. His wife had miscarriage, and his children were killed. Allah revealed to their prophet: 'Tell the rabbi so and so that I will not produce any truthful person from his offspring. His anger for Me did not go beyond his saying: be careful my son!'[130]

Abdullah ibn Mas'ud reported that the Messenger of Allah, blessing and peace of Allah be upon him, said:

"Beware of the small sins because when they multiply they may destroy the person."

The Messenger of Allah, blessing and peace of Allah be upon him, gave an example, he said:

"It is like some people who camped in the desert, the overseer came and a man brought one piece of wood and another person brought another piece till they gathered big heap and lit a fire and cooked what they put in it."[131]

Anas ibn Malik said:
'You are doing things which are thinner than hair in your eyes and we used to consider them destructive.'[132]

Abdullah ibn 'Umar reported that the Messenger of Allah, blessing and peace of Allah be upon him, said:

---

[129] Bukhari (3267), Muslim (2989)
[130] Ahmad in Zuhd (1; 180)
[131] Ahmad (1; 402), Tabarani in Kabir (5872) and Saghir (2; 49), see Majma' al-za'id (10:190)
[132] Bukhari (6492)

"A woman was punished concerning a cat she tied till it died. As a result she went to Hell. She neither gave it the food or drink nor released it to find its food from the vermin of the earth."[133]

Hudhayfah was asked: 'Did the Children of Israel leave their religion in one day?'
He replied: 'No, but when they were commanded to do some thing, they did not do it and when they were asked to avoid something they committed it till they went out of their religion as a man comes out of his shirt.'[134]

A pious man said:
'Sinful acts are agent of disbelief as kissing is the agent of intercourse. Singing is the agent of adultery, gazing is the agent of passion and illness is the agent of death.'

Ibn Abbas said:
'O man involved in sin, do not feel safe from its evil consequences. What follows a sin is greater than the sin itself when you commit it. You have no shame from the one on your right and on your left (i.e. the angels). Your insistence on the sin is greater than the sin. Your laughing without being aware what Allah is going to do with you is more serious than the sin; your happiness when you succeed in indulging in sin is greater than the sin; your grief when you miss a sin is greater than the sin. You are scared from the wind when it moves the curtain of your door while you are involved in committing the sin and your heart does not shake from the sight of Allah is more serious than the sin. Woe to you! Do you know what was the fault of Job (Ayyub) which made Allah to afflict him in his body and destruction of his wealth? It was a poor man who sought his help against an unjust person to repel his injustice, but he did not help him and did not stop the unjust man from wrongdoing. So, Allah tried him with affliction.'[135]

Bilal ibn Sa'd said:
'Do not look at the triviality of the disobedience, but look at the one you have disobeyed.'[136]

Fudayl ibn 'Iyad said:

---

[133] Bukhari (3295), Muslim (2242)
[134] Abu Nu'aym in al-Hilyah (1: 279)
[135] Ibid (1: 324)
[136] Al-Zuhd (460)

'As much as the sin is little to you, it is big with Allah; and as much as you consider it big it is small with Allah.'

It is said that Allah revealed to Moses: 'Moses, the first person to die from My creatures was Iblis. He disobeyed Me, and I count anyone who disobeys Me among as dead.

Abu Hurayrah related that the Prophet, Allah's blessing and peace be upon him, said:

"When a believer commits a sin a black dot is imprinted on his heart. If he desists, turns to Allah in repentance and asks Him for forgiveness, his heart becomes clear. But if he continues that dot increases till it covers his heart. This is stain (*ra'n*) which Allah mentioned in his saying:

"No! But a stain has covered their heart because of what they were earning." (83:14)[137]

Hudhayfah said:
'When a person commits a sin a black spot is created on his heart till his heart becomes like dark black goat.'

Abdullah ibn Mas'ud reported that the Messenger of Allah, blessing and peace of Allah be upon him, said:

"People of Quraysh, you are the master of this affair as long as you do not disobey Allah. When you disobey Him, He will send over you someone who will chew you as this twig is chewed."
He was holding a twig and chewed it till it became solid white.[138]

Wahab said:
'The Lord Almighty said in one of the messages to the Children of Israel:
'When I am obeyed I am pleased, and when I am pleased I grant blessing and there is no limit for My blessing. On the other hand when I am disobeyed I get angry, and when I get angry I curse and My curse reaches the seventh generation of the person.'[139]

'A'ishah wrote to Mu'awiyah:

---

[137] Ahmad (2: 297), Tirmidhi (3334), Ibn Majah (4244), Hakim (2: 517), Ibn Hibban (1771)
[138] Ahmad (1: 458), Abu Ya'la (5024), Tabarni in Awsat (2516) See Majma' al-zawa'id (5: 192)
[139] Al-Zuhd (52)

'When a person commits disobedience of Allah, the people who praise him turn to disparage him.'[140]

Abu al-Darda' said:
'A man should be careful to be cursed by the hearts of the believers without knowing.' He said: 'Do you know how it happens?' He said: 'A man gets involved in the disobedience of Allah in secret, so Allah puts the hatred for him in the hearts of the believers and he is not aware of it.'[141]

Muhammad ibn Sirin was worried because he was under debt. He said: 'I know the cause of this worry; I committed a sin forty years ago so I suffer from it now.'[142]

There is fine point here concerning the sin many people misunderstand it. They do not see its impact immediately. The impact may be delayed and it is forgotten and the sinner feels that he is not going to be affected after that and the matter is as the poet has said in a line:
'When a wall did not produce dust in its fall then after falling there will be no dust.'

Glory is to Allah! How many people were ruined by this thought? How many favours were withdrawn and how much distress was caused!
There are many learned and distinguished people let alone the ignorant ones who are deceived by this assumption. The conceited man does not realise that the sin destroys even after sometime like the poison which produces its effect and like a wound healed by wrong and incorrect medicine erupts again.

Abu al-Darda' said:
'Worship Allah as though you see Him and consider yourselves among the dead, and remember that little that is enough for you is better than plenty that may lead you to cross the boundary.'[143]

A pious person looked at a boy and was enchanted by his beauty; he was visited in his dream and said: 'You are going to see its consequence after forty years'.

---

[140] Al-Zuhd (165)
[141] Al-Hilyah (1: 215)
[142] Al-Zuhd (2: 282), al-Hilyah (2: 271)
[143] Al-Zuhd (2: 56)

This is apart from the fact that the sin produces an immediate consequence without delay.

Sulayman al-Taymi said:
'A man commits a sin in secret and feels its disgrace upon him in the morning.'

Yahya ibn Mu'adh al-Razi said:
'I wonder from a reasonable person who prays: 'O Allah, do not make my enemies laugh at me,' while he is causing his enemies to laugh at him.'
He was asked: 'How is it?'
He replied: 'He disobeys Allah and on the Day of Judgement every enemy of him will laugh at him.'
Dhu al-Noon said:
'The one who betrays Allah in secret Allah will expose his secret in open.'

CHAPTER 3 - THE DESTRUCTIVE CONSEQUENCES OF SINFUL ACT

The sinful acts have many damaging and shameful effects known only to Allah, which cause harm to the body and the heart in the world and the Hereafter. Some of these are cited below:

1. Deprivation of knowledge

Knowledge is a light which Allah casts in the heart and the sinful act extinguishes that light.
When Imam al-Shafi'i sat before Imam Malik to learn and read something, Imam Malik was amazed by his excessive intelligence, brilliant brightness and perfect understanding. He said to him: 'I see that Allah has cast a light on your heart do not extinguish it by disobeying Him.'

Imam al-Shafi'i said in a couplet:
'I complained to Waki' about my bad memory and he advised me to keep away from sinful acts. He said that knowledge was a favour from Allah and Allah's favour is not given to a sinner.'

2. The deprivation of provision

The Prophet, Allah's blessing and peace be upon him, said:

"A person is deprived of provision due to a sin which he committed."[144]

As being conscious of Allah brings provision, being unmindful of Allah brings poverty. There is nothing certain to deserve the provision of Allah than keeping away from sinful acts.

---

[144] Ahmad (5:277)

3. Estrangement between the sinner and Allah

The sinner finds estrangement in his heart between him and Allah. It cannot be compensated by any joy. If all of the enjoyments of the world are put together, they will not be sufficient to remove that feeling of estrangement. This is something which is realised by the one whose heart has life. A person who is dead, injury is not going to cause him pain.

If the sins are the cause of this desertion, a sensible man has to avoid them. A man complained to some of the knowledgeable men about loneliness he found in his soul, and the knowledgeable man said: 'If it is the sins which causes you to feel estranged, then keep away from them and get comfort.'

There is nothing more painful to the heart than the estrangement caused by the sin. Allah's help is sought.

4. Alienation between the sinner and other people

This is created between the sinner and the people especially the righteous ones. He finds aversion from them towards him. As this feeling grows stronger his remoteness from them and from their company becomes solid and he is deprived of having benefit from them. He comes close to the party of Satan and far away from the party of the Merciful. This aversion grows strong to the extent of affecting his relation with his wife, his children and his relatives as well as between him and his soul, so you can see him estranged from his soul.

A man from the past said: 'I disobey Allah and feel the effect in the behaviour of my animal and my wife.'

5. His affairs become difficult for him

When a sinner embarks on his chosen path, (initially) he finds it difficult for him. It is as the one who has the fear of Allah, He makes his affairs easy for him, the one who neglects the essence of 'fear of Allah' finds that his affairs become difficult for him. How wonderful! A man finds the gates of goodness & benefits sealed for him due to his sins but he does not know why he has been afflicted.

6. A real darkness he feels in his heart

He feels the burden of sin as he feels the darkness of the deep dark night. The darkness of the sin in his heart becomes like the physical darkness for his eyes. Obedience is light and disobedience is darkness. As the darkness grows deeper his confusion increases till he succumbs to innovations, misguidance and destructive matters without realising. He becomes like a blind person who comes out in the darkness of the night walking alone. This darkness increases till it appears in the eye, then it covers the face and its darkness is noticed by everyone.

Abdullah ibn Abbas said:

'Good act has brightness in the face, light in the heart, expansion in provision, strength in the body and love in the hearts of the people; on the other hand an evil act has blackness in the face, darkness in the heart, weakness in the body, reduction in provision and hatred in the hearts of the people.'

7. The evil acts make the body and the heart weak

Evil deeds create weakness in the heart which is visible, and it continues affecting it till its life goes out completely. The weakness of the body comes from the weakness of the heart. The believer gets his strength from his heart. When his heart is strong, his body is strong. As for the wicked even if he is strong in body, he is the weakest one at the time of need. His strength leaves him when he is badly in need of it. Look at the strength of the bodies of Persians and Romans, how their strength left them when they were badly in need of it and the people of faith vanquished them by the power of their bodies and hearts.

8. The veil prevents the man from good deeds

Another bad effect of the misdeed is that it prevents from good deeds. It prevents the sinner from carrying out his duty and deters him from another duty and then from a third one and so on and so forth. In this way it deters him from many good acts each one of them is better for him than the world and what it contains. Its example is like a person who took a food which caused long illness and prevented him from many delicious meals. Allah's help is sought.

9. Reduction in life span

The sinful acts reduce the life span of the man and wipe out its blessing. Pious deeds increase the life span, on the opposite the evil deeds reduce the period of life.

Here there is dispute among the scholars concerning the increase or decrease in the period of life.

A group said that reduction in the life span of the guilty means disappearance and absence of its blessing. It is true, but it is only some of the effects of the sins.

Another group said that life is affected in reality as the provision is reduced. Allah, the Most Glorious, has made for the provision many reasons which affect its increase or decrease; in the same way there are many reasons to increase or decrease the age of a man.

They argued that it is not impossible for age to be increased or decreased for those reasons. The provisions, deaths, happiness and unhappiness, health and illness, wealth and poverty though all of them are by the decree of the Lord Almighty, yet He fixed them with causes which make them take effect by His will.

In some other people's opinion the impact of evil deeds in reducing the life span comes from the fact that the real life is that of the heart. For this reason Allah, the Exalted, declared the unbeliever dead without life as He said:

"They are dead not living." (16:21)

Life in reality is the life of the heart and the life of a human is only the period which he passes with Allah, the Supreme. This is the period of his life which is increased by good deeds, consciousness of Allah and righteous acts.

In short when a servant turns away from the obedience of Allah and gets involved in sinful acts, his real life is lost and he will see the consequence of it on the Day when he will say:

"Would that I had provided for this life to come! (89:24)

The man in this situation either has ambition for his interest of the world and the Hereafter or not. If he had no ambition, then all his life was ruined and wasted. If he has the ambition, his way is prolonged because of the obstacles, and the causes of good become hard for him due to his engagement in their contrary acts. It is the real reduction of his life period.

The core of the issue is that human has only life by devoting himself to his Lord, being pleased with His love and preference of His pleasure.

10. The evil produces other evils

The evil activities produce other evils and they grow to the extent that the servant finds it difficult to abandon and get out of them. Some early wise man has said: 'The retribution of the evil act is another evil after it, and the reward of pious deed is another good deed after it. When a person does a righteous work the one beside it says do me as well. When he does it, a third one makes similar request and so on so forth. In this way the profit is increased and good deeds are multiplied. The same is true about the evil acts till the good and evil deeds take roots and become permanent and inseparable qualities. If a pious person abandons good deed, his soul feels strained and the earth for its expansion is closed on him, and he feels like a whale which has been taken out of water till it is returned to it where it finds peace and delight.

Similarly if a criminal abandons his activities and starts doing righteous deeds, his soul is tightened, his chest is confined and he does not know what to do till he goes back to evil deeds. Many wicked people commit evil acts without feeling any joy or finding any motive, otherwise he would not feel distress by abandoning it. Abu Nuwas said in a line of his poem:
'I drank a cup with delight and had a second to treat it.'

Another poet said:
'My healing was by the same material which was the cause of my disease as the person drinking wine treats him by wine.'

A believer, who is accustomed doing good deeds, becomes fond of them, develops their love and prefers them till Allah, the Most High, sends by His mercy angels to him who give him support and encouragement and make him restless in his bed and his seat. The other person continues committing sinful acts, becomes fond of them, loves them and prefers them till Allah, the Glorious, sends the band of Satan who support him. The first man strengthened the forces of obedience by Divine supporters, who became his greatest helpers, and the second one got help by the band of disobedience and they became supporters against him.

11. Evil deeds weaken the heart

Evil deeds reduce the will power of the heart, and it is the most dangerous thing for a person. In this case the intention of the disobedience becomes stronger and the intention of the repentance becomes weaker and weaker and ultimately the thought of repentance goes out of the heart altogether. When his heart is dead, he is not interested in repentance. He seeks forgiveness and makes false repentance by the tongue but his heart is bent on evil act, firm on doing it and determined on it when he gets a chance. This is the most serious disease leading to perishing or self-destruction.

12. The heart loses the power of discernment

Defiance of the commands of Allah makes the heart unable to discern the ignominious nature of the evil acts. Involvement in sinful acts becomes a normal thing for him and he does not regard it repulsive from the people's seeing him doing it, and does not care about their criticism. It is the utmost shamelessness and full enjoyment of the sinners; one of them boasts of his crime and talks to those who do not know about his action that he did it. He says: 'So and so, I did such and such thing!'
This type of the person is unforgivable and the door of the repentance is closed in his face as the Prophet, Allah's blessing and peace be upon him, said:

"All my Community are going to be forgiven except those who commit sins openly. Doing openly includes that Allah covers a person but he exposes himself and announces: 'So and so, I did such and such thing on such and such day', he exposes himself while his Lord has covered his mistake."[145]

13. Every abominable act is inherited from one of the nations of the past which were destroyed by Allah.

Sodomy is inheritance of the people of Lot. Taking more and giving the dues less is the legacy of the People of Shua'yb. Atrocity and corruption on earth are the inheritance of the people of Pharaoh. Haughtiness and arrogance are the character of the People of Hud. A wicked man is committing the crime of one of these nations, who were the enemies of Allah.

---

[145] Bukhari (6069), Muslim (2990)

Malik ibn Dinar said:

'Allah revealed to one of the prophets of the Children of Israel: 'Tell your people: do not follow the behaviour of My enemies, do not put on the dresses of My enemies, do not use the mounts of My enemies, do not consume the food of My enemies lest you become My enemies like they are My enemies.'[146]

Abdullah ibn 'Umar reported that the Prophet, Allah's blessing and peace be upon him, said:

"I am sent with sword before the Hour till Allah alone is worshipped without any partner. My provision is made under the shade of my spear, and humiliation and disgrace are imposed on anyone who opposes my order. Whoever imitates a people he is one of them."[147]

14. The sinner loses his honour to Allah

Loathsome activities are the cause of the ignominy of the person to the Lord Almighty and he is dropped in His estimation.
Hasan Basri said:
'They were contemptible to Him so they disobeyed Him, if they had any honour, He would have saved them.'
When a servant is disgraceful to Allah, no one respects him as Allah Almighty has said:

"Anyone whom Allah disgraces no one can honour him." (22:18)

The people show respect to him outwardly for their need of him or for fear of his evil, but he is in their hearts the most despised and hateful person.

15. Being accustomed to evil

A man continuously commits sin till it becomes easy for him and insignificant in his heart. It is the sign of his destruction. A sin when it is small in the eyes of the servant it is big in the sight of Allah.
Ibn Mas'ud reported that the Prophet, Allah's blessing and peace be upon him, said:

---

[146] Al-Zuhd (2: 180)
[147] Ahmad (2: 50, 92)

"A believer sees his sins as thought he is under a mountain which may fall over him at any time while a wicked sees his sins like a fly which sat on his nose and he chased it and it flew away."[148]

16. The evil omen of the sin

The evil omen of the sin affects, apart from the culprit, other people and animals and due to his sin and wrongdoing he and others get burnt.

Abu Hurayrah said:
'The bustard (type of quail) die in its nest because of the wrongdoing of an unjust.'
Mujahid said:
'The beasts curse the children of Adam when the drought happens and rain is halted. They say that it was due to evil omen of the human.'
'Ikrimah said;
'The animals and insects even the beetles and scorpions say: 'We are deprived of the rain because of the misdeeds of the Children of Adam.'
The punishment of his sin is not enough and draws towards him the curse of those who had not done any evil.

17. Evil acts bring down disgrace.

The sins necessarily bring down disgrace; this is because the total honour lies in the obedience of Allah. Allah, the Most Supreme, said:

"Whoever desires honour; then to Allah belongs all the honour." (35:10)

It means that the person who desires honour he should seek it in the obedience of Allah; he will not get it except in His obedience.

One of the early pious men used to pray:
'O Allah, grant me honour by your obedience and do not cause me disgrace because of disobedience of You.'
Hasan Basri said:

---

[148] Bukhari (6308), Muslim (2744)

'No matter how much the mules clatter and the horse amble, the disgrace of the sin does not part from their hearts. Allah refuses but to humiliate the one who disobeys Him.'

Abdullah ibn al-Mubarak said in the following lines:

'I saw that the sins kill the hearts and persistence in them produces disgrace. In abandoning evil deeds are the life of the hearts and it is better for you to leave them. Was the religion spoiled except by the kings, evil Rabbis and priests?'

18. Misdeeds spoil the reason

The misdeed corrupts the reasoning faculty. Reason has a light and misdeed extinguishes its light and when its light is put out, it becomes weak and dwindles.

Some people said: 'No one disobeys Allah but his reason disappears.'

This is obvious because if his reason were present, it would stop him from committing sin. He is under the control of Allah and His power, and He is aware of his movement in his home on his bed, and His angels are witness over him watching him. The admonitions of the Qur'an warn him, the danger of death reminds him and the reality of the Fire frightens him. The good of the world and the Hereafter he is losing by committing sin is much less than the joy and delight he is going to gain. Will a man of correct intelligence ignore all that and not pay heed to it?

19. The sins seal over the hearts of the sinners

When the sins multiply the heart of the sinner is sealed and he becomes among the heedless ones. Allah said:

"No! The stain of what they used to do covered their hearts." (83:14)

Some people said that the reference was to sin after sin.

Hasan said:

'It is sin after sin until the heart becomes blind.'

Others said:

'When their sins became plenty their hearts were sealed.'

The basis of this is that the heart gets rusted by the disobedience. When disobedience increases, the heart becomes stained and it continues to grow till it becomes completely covered or heart is sealed. As a result the heart is covered by a veil and shield. If it happens after guidance and understanding, it turns over and the upper part becomes the lower, and his enemy gets power over him and drags him where he wants.

20. Evil deeds bring curse

The evil acts bring the sinner under the curse of the Messenger, Allah's blessing and peace be upon hum. He has cursed those who are involved in committing sins some of them are more serious than the others. For instance he cursed those who have tattoo marks and the one who made it, the one who gets false hair attached to her hair and the one who does it, the one who plucks the hair of the face and the one who does it.
He condemned the person who eats usury, the one who gives it, and the one who writes and the one who witnesses it.
He condemned the man who legalises a wife for her husband and the one for whom it was done.
He reproved the thief.
He reprehended the person who drinks wine, the one who supplies it, the one who makes it and the one who sells and the one who buys it, the one uses its price and the one who carries it and the one to whom it is carried.
He reproached the one who changed the signs of the earth and its paths.
He cursed the one who cursed his parents.
He disapproved the one who takes a living creature as an aim to shoot at by arrows.
He condemned men who display feminine manners and the women who display the male manners.
He reproved those who slaughter animals for other than Allah.
He damned the one who invented something new in religion or the one who gave refuge to an innovator.
He condemned those who make pictures.
He cursed the one who commits the act of the people of Lot.
He condemned the one who cursed his father or his mother.
He reproved a man who misled a blind person from the path.
He cursed the one who used an animal for intercourse.
He condemned those who branded cattle in its face.
He damned a man who caused harm to a Muslim or schemed against him.
He cursed the women frequently visiting the graves and those who take them as place for worship or light lamps over them.
He cursed a man who spoiled a woman against her husband or a slave against his owner.
He cursed a man who had intercourse with a woman in her backside.
He said that the angels curse a woman till morning who passed the night separately from of her husband.

He cursed the person who traced his ancestry to other than his father.

He told us that anyone who points to his brother with an iron tool the angels curse him.

He condemned anyone who used abusive language against the Companions.

21. Condemnation of Allah and His Prophet, Allah's blessing and peace be upon him, of particular categories of the people.

Allah condemned a person who spreads corruption on earth, severs his bond of relation and insults Allah and His Messenger, blessing and peace of Allah be upon him.

Almighty condemned those who hide the clear evidences and guidance which He revealed in His Book.

He condemned those who accuse the believing innocent unaware women of committing adultery.

He, the Glorious, condemned anyone who considers the way of the disbelievers better in guidance than the way of the believers.

The Messenger of Allah, blessing and peace of Allah be upon him, cursed a man who wears the dress of a woman and a woman who puts on the dress of a man.

He condemned the man who takes bribe, gives it and the one who acts as a middle man.

He cursed many other people and acts beside these.

If any evil act which is done by the agreement of its doer, it is condemned by Allah and is Messenger and His angels, and it is enough to be avoided.

22. Involvement in sinful acts is the cause of deprivation of the prayer of Messenger and the angels

The person who gets involved in sinful activities is deprived of the blessing of the Messenger, Allah's blessing and peace be upon him, and the angels. Allah commanded His Prophet to seek forgiveness for the believing men and women. He also said:

"Those angles who carry the Thrown and those who surround it celebrate the praise of their Lord and have faith in Him. They beg forgiveness for the believers: 'Our Lord, You embrace all things in

mercy and knowledge, so forgive those who turn to You and follow Your path. Save them from the pains of Hell and admit them, O Lord, to the lasting Gardens You have promised them, together with their righteous ancestors, spouses, and offspring: You alone are the Almighty, The All Wise. Protect them from all evil deeds: those who You protect on that Day from their Consequences of deeds, You have given them mercy. That is the supreme attainment." (40:7-9)

This is the prayer of the angels for those who turn to Allah in repentance and follow His Book and the Sunnah of His Prophet which are the only way of success. Others are not qualified for this prayer because they do not have those qualities. Allah's help is sought for.

23. The Punishments of the sinful deeds

They are many and are detailed in the Hadith collections. Samurah ibn Jundub reported:
'The Prophet, Allah's blessing and peace be upon him, very often used to ask his Companions:

"Did anyone of you see a dream?"

Then whoever Allah willed will relate his dream. One morning the Prophet, Allah's blessing and peace be upon him, said:

"Last night two persons came to me (i.e. in dream) and woke me up and said to me, 'Proceed!' I set out with them and we came across a man lying down, and behold, another man was standing over his head, holding a big rock. He was throwing the rock at the man's head injuring him. The rock rolled away and the thrower followed it and took it back. By the time he reached the man, his head returned to its normal state. The thrower then did the same as he had done before. I said to my two companions: 'Glory be to Allah! Who are these two persons?' They said: 'Proceed, proceed!' So we proceeded and came to a man lying in a prone position and another man standing over his head with an iron hook, and he would strike out the hook in one side of the man's mouth, and tear off that side of his face to the back (of the neck) and tear his nose from front to back and his eyes from front to back. Then he turned to the other side of the man's face and did just as he had done with the first side. He hardly completed that side when the first side returned to its normal condition. Then he

returned to it to repeat what he had done before. I asked my two companions: 'Glory be to Allah! Who are these two persons?'

They said to me: 'Proceed, proceed!' So we proceeded and came across something like an oven. In that oven there was much noise and voices. We looked into it and found naked men and women and a flame of fire was reaching to them from underneath, and when it reached them, they cried loudly. I asked them: 'Who are these?' They said to me: 'Proceed, proceed! We proceeded and came across a river red like blood. In that river there was a man swimming, and on the bank there was a man who had collected many stones. When the swimming man went near, he opened his mouth and the man on the bank threw a stone into his mouth and he went swimming again. Then the man would return to the bank and the same ordeal would be repeated. I asked my two companions: 'Who are these two persons?' They said: 'Proceed, proceed!

We proceeded till we came to a man with a repulsive appearance, the most repulsive appearance you have ever seen. Beside him there was a fire and he was kindling it and running round it. I asked my two companions: 'Who is this man?' They said: 'Proceed, Proceed!

So we proceeded till we reached a garden of deep green dense vegetation having all sort of spring colour. In the midst of the garden there was a very tall man and I could hardly see his head because of his great height, and around him there were children in such a large number as I have never seen. I asked my two companions: 'Who is this?' They replied: 'Proceed, proceed!'

So we proceeded till we came to a majestic huge garden greater and better than I have ever seen. My two companions said to me, 'Ascend up' and I ascended up. We ascended till we reached a city built of gold and silver bricks and we went to its gate and asked the gatekeeper to open it. It was opened and we entered the city and found in it men with one side of their bodies as handsome as the most handsome person you have ever seen, and the other side as ugly as the ugliest person you have ever seen. My two companions ordered those men to throw themselves into a river. It was a river the water of which was white like milk. Those men threw themselves in it and when they returned to us their ugliness had disappeared and they became in the best shape.

My companions said to me: 'This place is the Garden of Eden and that is your place.' I raised my eyes and I saw a palace like a white cloud. My two companions said to me: 'That palace is for you.' I said: 'May Allah bless you both! Let me enter it.' They replied: 'As for now you will not enter it, but you shall enter it one day.' I said: to them: 'I have seen many wonders tonight. What does all that which I have seen mean?' They replied: 'We are going to inform you: The first man you came upon whose head was being smashed with the rock, he symbolises the one who studies the Qur'an, then neither recites it nor acts according to its teachings, and sleeps neglecting the prescribed prayers. As for the man you saw his sides of mouth, nostrils and eyes were torn off from front to the back, he represents the man who goes out in the morning and tells lies that spread all over the world.

Those naked men and women you saw being burnt in the oven are the adulterers and adulteresses. The men and the women you saw swimming in the river and hit by the stone is the man who consumed usury. The ugly looking man you saw near the fire kindling it and going round it was Malik, the keeper of Hell. The tall person you saw in the garden was Abraham and the children around him are those who died on *fitrah*."

At this point some people asked the Prophet, Allah's blessing and peace be upon him: 'Messenger of Allah, what about the children of the polytheists?'

He replied: "And also the children of the polytheists."
The Prophet, Allah's blessing and peace be upon him, added: "My companions said that the men you saw half handsome and half ugly were those who mixed good and bad acts, but Allah forgave them."[149]

24. Evil activities are the causes of corruption

Another bad effect of the evil behaviours and wicked attitudes is that they cause variety of corruption devastation in water, air, farms, fruits and houses. Allah, the Most Exalted, said:

"Corruption has flourished on land and sea as a result of people's actions, so He may make them test the consequences of some of their own actions so that they may turn back." (30:41)

Mujahid said:
'When an unjust person gets power he works on spreading injustice and corruption, and as a result Allah withholds the rain, which causes the

---

[149] Bukhari (7047)

destruction of the crops and live stocks, and Allah does not like corruption. He read the following verse:

"Corruption has flourished on land and sea as a result of people's actions, so He may make them test the consequences of some of their own actions so that they may turn back." (30:41)

'Ikrimah said:
'Corruption has spread on land and sea, I do not say this sea of yours, but every town situated on water.'

Qatadah said:
'The land refers to the people of tents and the sea to the people of towns and country sides.'

I say:
'Allah, the Most High, has called the sweet water as sea, He said:

"The two bodies of water are not alike, one is palatable, sweet, and pleasant to drink, the other salty and bitter." (35:12)

'There is no sea in world stagnant with sweet water; it is only in flowing rivers. The salty sea is stagnant; Almighty called the towns on the banks of flowing water with the name of that water.'

Ibn Zayd said in the explanation of the verse: "Corruption flourished in the land and sea", that they are sins.
I say:
'He meant that sins are the cause of corruption which has spread. If he meant that the corruption which has spread is the sins themselves, then the *lam* in the verse will be the agent of consequence and justification. In the first case the corruption will mean the evil consequences and troubles which Allah creates on earth due to the involvement of the people in sinful activities. Whenever they start some sinful acts Allah creates punishment for them. Some pious man said:
'Whenever you start a sin, Allah will produce punishment for you.'

The obvious meaning of the verse indicates that corruption refers to evil deeds and their causes as Allah said:

"So that He makes them test the consequences of some their actions."

This is our condition; Allah has made us to test the consequences of some of our deeds. If He were to make us test the consequences of all our actions, He would not have left on the face of the earth any moving creature.

25. Other effects of the evil activities on land

Among the bad effects of the evil activities on earth are the calamities that occur on it like the earthquakes and sinking of the land and taking away its blessing. Allah's Messenger, Allah's blessing and peace be upon him, passed by the towns of Thamud and asked his Companions not to enter them except crying and forbade them to drink its water or drawing water from their wells. He ordered the flour, which was kneaded with their water to be given to the camels. The bad effect of the vicious activities of those people reached the water. In the same way the bad effect of the sins affects in reducing the yield of fruits and causing them damage.

Imam Ahmad cited in a Hadith that a grain of wheat the size of the stone of a date was found in the treasury of the Banu Umayyah, in a jar written on it: 'This is what grew in the time of justice.'[150]

Many of these calamities are caused by Allah because of the sinful acts of the people.
A band of the old people of the desert told me that they used to have the fruits bigger in size than they are now. Most of these tribulations which they suffered were unknown to them; they started in recent period.

26. The bad effect of evil activities on creation and forms

Allah's Prophet, blessing and peace of Allah be upon him, said:

"Allah created Adam and his height was sixty cubic, then the people continued decreasing till now."[151]

When Allah decides to cleanse the land from unjust, wicked and unfaithful people, He brings a devoted person from the progeny of His Prophet, Allah's blessing and peace be upon him, who will fill the earth

---

[150] Ahmad (2: 296), See Najma' al-zawa'id (5: 197)
[151] Bukhari (3148), Muslim (2841)

with justice as it was full of injustice. At that time the Christ will kill the Jews and the opposing Christians and establish the religion which Allah sent with His Prophet, blessing and peace of Allah be upon him. The earth will bring out its blessing and return as it was to the extent that a group of the people will eat and be satisfied by one pomegranate, and will use its peel for shade. A bunch of grapes will be a load of a camel and one she camel's milk will be enough for a group of people. This will be as the land become pure from the evil acts, and the results of blessing from Allah will appear after it was erased from disbelief and sins.

There is no doubt that the traces of the punishments which Allah sent on earth are existent and these acts are the remnants of those crimes. Allah's wisdom and natural procedure come together. So the great punishment was for the great crime and the light punishment for the light. This is how Allah decides among His creatures in the abode of *Barzakh* and the abode of retribution. Consider the work of Satan and his impact. When he came in contact with the servant and dominated him, the blessing of his life, his words and his provision was taken away, and his obedience did not work and blessing was taken away from every place he operated in obedience. It is also true about his abode of Hell; there is nothing of comfort, mercy or blessing.

27. Evil activities dispel the zeal of the heart

Another punishment of the evil acts is that the heart loses the zeal which is for its life and stability like the natural heat for the life of the whole body. The zeal and earnest concern are the heat of the heart and its fire that expels dirt and corrupt qualities from it, as the bellows cleanse the bad stuff of the silver, gold and iron. The noblest and highest ambitious person is the one who has earnest concern for him, his close people and general public. The Prophet, Allah's blessing and peace be upon him, was the most compassionate in intent for his Community, and Allah, the Exalted, is more vigilant than him as it is reported that he said:

"Are you surprised from the sense of honour of Sa'd; I am more jealous than him and Allah is more jealous than me."[152]

In another report he said:

---

[152] Bukhari (6846), Muslim (1499)

"Community of Muhammad, no one is more jealous than Allah that His slave or maiden commit adultery."[153]

He also said:

"No one is more respectful than Allah and it is due to this that He prohibited immoral acts open and hidden. No one loves excuse more than Allah and for this reason He sent the messengers giving good tidings and warning. No one likes praise more than Allah and for this reason He praised Himself."[154]

The Prophet, Allah's blessing and peace be upon him, combined in this Hadith the **jealousy which means disliking the immoral acts** and the love of excuse which requires perfect justice, mercy and kindness *(this is positive aspects of jealousy or envy unlike traditional notion of negativity)*. Allah, the Most Glorious, despite His jealousy loves His slave to apologise to Him and He accepts the apology of a person who turns to Him in apology. Almighty does not censure His servants for committing what He does not like to be done till He gives an opportunity for excuse. For this reason He sent His messengers and revealed His books to provide excuse and give warning.

This is the utmost nobility, kindness and extreme perfectness. Many human beings who have great feeling of jealousy rush out of their feeling to punish the offender without giving him a chance to make apology or to accept it. Many of those who accept excuses do it out of lack of jealousy; they extend the ways of excuses and consider what is not an excuse as excuse. Many of them take refuge in Divine Decree. All this is not appreciated at all.
The Prophet, Allah's blessing and peace be upon him, said:

"There are types of jealousy which Allah loves and others which He hates. The one He hates is jealousy without suspicion.[155]

The praiseworthy jealousy is the one joined with excuse. So it should be shown in the situation of jealousy and excuse be accepted in its place. If a person behaves like that, he is praiseworthy.

Bukhari (1044), Muslim (901)
[154] Bukhari (4634), Muslim (2760)
[155] Ahmad (5: 445), Abu Dawud (2659), Nisa'i (5: 78), Tabarani (1775) Ibn Hibban (295), Hakim (1: 417)

Since Allah has accumulated all the Attributes of perfectness in Him, He is more deserving of praise than anyone else. No one can praise Him as it should be done and as He had praised Himself. The jealous person is in conformity with his Lord in a quality of His Attributes, and a person who is in conformity with Allah in any of His attributes, it will lead him to Him, make him enter to His presence, bring him closer to His mercy and make him loved by Him. He, the Glorious, is Merciful loves the merciful, is Generous, loves the generous, is All Knowing, loves knowledgeable, is Powerful loves the resilient believer. The strong believer is more beloved to Him than a weak one. Almighty is diffident, loves the shameful, is beautiful and loves beauty; He is one, an odd number and love things or acts of worship in odd number.

Was it not that the evil acts produce in those who do them the opposite of these qualities and keep them away from them; it would have been enough as punishment. A thought turns into temptation which in turn becomes intention and when the intention becomes strong it turns into resolution which leads to action. After that it becomes intrinsic quality and firm disposition and takes root making to get out of it impossible, as he cannot get out of his inherent characters.

The point is that when the engagement of a person in sinful activities becomes frequent, it takes out jealousy from his heart concerning him, his family and general public. It becomes so weak that he does not consider an evil matter done by him or others reprehensible. When a man reaches this stage, he has approached his destruction.

Many such people do not only consider the evil acts as bad but encourage others to immoral acts and injustice, invite them and incite them and struggle to acquire those shameful things. For this reason the pimp is the most hateful creature of Allah and Paradise is forbidden for him. It is also true of those who consider injustice and aggression right and encourage others to get involve in them.

Now look how far the lack of jealousy can take a man! It will tell you that the basis of the religion is jealousy and the one who lacks it has no religion. Jealousy protects the heart and the parts of the body, and repels evil and immoral acts while lack of jealousy kills the heart and consequently the parts of the body also die, and the man is left without any source of defence.

The example of the jealousy in the heart is like the immunity that confronts and drives back the illness. Once it disappears the illness finds the suitable condition and sets in, and leads to death. Another example is the horns of the buffalo which it uses to defend itself and its young ones, if they are broken; its enemy finds opportunity to attack it.

28. The acts of disobedience take away the modesty

Another bad consequence of indulging in shameful activities is that the man loses his quality of modesty and shamefulness, which is the substance of the life of the heart. Modesty is the root of every benefit; when it goes away, every good goes away. The Prophet, Allah's blessing and peace be upon him, said:

"Modesty! all of it is good."[156]

He also stated:

"What the people have received from the words of early prophecy is: 'When you have no shame, do whatever you like."[157]

This statement has two explanations:
a) First that it is a threat and caution to mean that whoever has no shame will do whatever abominable things he wants. The quality that moves him to abandon them is shame, and once it has departed, there will be nothing to prevent him from getting involved in criminal activities. This explanation is given by Abu 'Ubayd.
b) The second meaning is that if you do not feel ashamed of Allah from doing a sinful thing, then you will certainly be inclined to perform it. A person is required to keep away from such deeds for which he feels ashamed of Allah. If he is not ashamed, then he will not hesitate to perform it. This is the explanation of Imam Ahmad.

According to the first explanation it will be a threat as it is in the statement of Allah:

"Do whatever you want." (41:40).
The second meaning is a permission and approval.

If it is said: Is there a way to take both explanations?
I will answer: 'No, even in the opinion of those who allow to use the joint word in all its meaning because the two meanings are incompatible with

---
[156] Muslim (37)
[157] Bukhari 3483)

one another. However consideration of one meaning will lead to consider the other one.

The aim is to say that sinful acts weakens the feeling of shame in a person, and he get out of it altogether to the extent that he does not care about the knowledge of the people about his evil acts. In fact many of them inform others of their evil deeds, and the cause of it is his deprivation of shame. When a person reaches this stage there remains no hope of his reform as it is said:

'When Iblis looks at his face he welcomes and says: 'I be ransom to the one who is not going to be successful!'

The word Haya', meaning shames and modesty, is derived from hayah, meaning life. The rain is called haya because it brings life to the land, plant and livestock. The life of the world and the Hereafter is known as haya'; anyone who has no shame is dead in the world and wretched in the Hereafter. Between the sins and lack of shame and jealousy there is attachment; each one of them requires the other and looks earnestly for it. Anyone who feels ashamed of Allah at the time of committing a sin will feel ashamed of His punishment on the Day he meets with Him; anyone who does not have shame from disobedience of Allah will not be ashamed of His punishment.

29. Immoral acts weaken the exaltation of the Lord Almighty

Another punishment of the immoral acts is that they reduce the glory and honour of the Lord in the heart of the person indulged in them.

The Lord's status in his heart is lowered whether he likes or not. If Allah's majesty and honour are strongly established in the heart of the slave, he would not dare to commit His disobedience. Some deceived person may say that he was encouraged on sin because of good hope and desire of His pardon, not because His greatness was reduced in his heart. It is a false assumption of the soul. Allah's greatness and His majesty in the heart of a person require him to respect what He has forbidden. This respect will act as barrier between him and committing sins. Those who venture on His disobedience do not appraise Allah as it is due. How can a person who takes His command and prohibition lightly appraise His power and glory and appreciate His majesty? It is utterly impossible and completely false.

It is enough for a sinner as punishment that Allah Almighty's glory is absent from his heart, His sacred ordinances lose their importance and His right is ignored.

Some of the punishment of this act is that Allah makes the person lose his honour in the hearts of the people who mock him as he took Allah's command lightly and attached no importance to it. In proportion to the love of Allah by the slave the people love him, and in accordance with his fear of Allah the people will fear him, and as much as he shows respect to Allah and His sacred ordinances the people will honour his sanctity. How can a person violate the inviolable ordinances of Allah and hope that people will not violate his sacred boundaries? How can he take the dues of Allah lightly and will not make him despicable to the people? Or how can he undermine the seriousness of the sinful acts and hope that the people will not undermine his position?

Allah, the Most Glorious, has indicated to this in His Book when He mentioned the punishments of the sins that He degenerated the evildoers because of their deeds,[158] covered their hearts and put seal over them,[159] He forgot them as they forgot Him,[160] caused humiliation to them as they disrespected His religion [161]and ruined them as they neglected His command.

Allah, the Exalted said in the verse related to the bowing down of the creatures to Him:

"Anyone Allah disgraces will have no one who can honour him." (22:18)

When bowing down was hard to them and they took it lightly and refused to do it, Allah disgraced them and there was no one to show respect to them. Who can honour someone who has been disgraced by Allah? Or disgrace the one whom Allah has honoured?

30. Rebellious acts cause Allah to forget the person

Among the consequences of the malicious activities is that it causes the slave to be forgotten by Allah. Almighty leaves such a person alone and

---

[158] The Qur'an (4: 88)
[159] Ch. 7: 101
[160] Ch. 7: 51, 59: 19

[161] Ch. 44;49)

gives Satan an opportunity to misguide him. It is the most serious destruction from which there is no escape. Allah, the Exalted, said:

"You who believe! Be mindful of Allah, and let every soul consider carefully what it has sent ahead for tomorrow; be mindful of Allah. Allah is well aware of everything you do. Do not be like those who forgot Allah, so Allah caused them to forget their own souls. They are the rebellious ones." (59:18-19)

Here Almighty commanded to be mindful of Him and forbade His believing servants to be like those who being neglectful forgot Him. He told that the punishment of anyone who forgets Allah is that He makes him to forget himself i.e. He makes him forget his interests and the means of saving him from His punishment. He becomes also unaware of what can bring him the eternal life and take him to the perfect joy, pleasure and comfort of that life. Allah made him forget all that as a punishment of his forgetting the greatness and fear of Him and carrying out His commands. You will find a disobedient person neglecting the benefits of his soul, and damaging them. He follows his low desire and his affairs are ungoverned. His benefits of the world and the Hereafter were lost and he overlooked his eternal happiness and exchanged it with the least joy which was like the cloud of summer or the imagination of fantasy. It is said in a line of poetry:
'It is like dreams of sleep or vanishing shadow; a man of reason is not deceived by such things'

The severest punishment for a person is to forget his own soul, neglect its benefits, lose its share and portion from Allah and sell it with deception, disgrace and small price. He surrendered the one who was indispensable and essential for him and took instead what he was in no need of him. It is said:
'Everything you lose you have a substitute, but if you lose Allah, there is no substitute for Him.'

Allah compensates for anything other than Him; there is no compensation for Him. He is sufficient for everything and there is nothing which can be sufficient for Him. He gives shelter against anything but nothing can give shelter from Him. He protects from everything and there is nothing which can protect from Him. How can then the servant forsake the obedience of Him, even for the twinkling of an eye, who is like that? How can he forget to remember Him and neglect His affairs and as punishment forget his soul, and cause it loss and does great injustice to it? The servant did not wrong his Lord, but wronged himself; his Lord did not wrong him, but it is he who wronged his soul.

31. Evil deeds are the cause of expulsion from the circle of Sincerity

Another bad consequence of the evil acts is that the miscreant is expelled from the circle of sincere people and is deprived the benefits of them. When the faithfulness comes in direct contact with the heart, it prevents it from evil deeds. This is because a man, who worships Allah as though he sees Him, is doing it because His remembrance, love fear and hope have dominated his heart and he becomes as though he is watching Him. This phenomenon obstructs his way to the thought of evil deeds let alone to commit them. When he gets out of the circle of the sincerity he loses the company of Allah and His chosen fellows. He is deprived of their pleasant life and perfect enjoyment.

Now if Allah decides to show favour to him, He will retain him among the circle of the general believers. However, if he indulges in such misdeeds that take a person out of the circle of faith, he is removed from that circle as well. The horrible misdeeds which damage the faith of a person are mentioned by the Prophet, Allah's blessing and peace be upon him, in the following Hadith:

"No adulterer commits adultery and remains believer when he is doing it, No one drinks wine and remains believer when he is drinking it, no thief steals and remains believer while he is involved in stealing and no one snatches a noble material which people watch when he is doing it remains believer. So, beware, beware; and repentance is still available."[162]

32. Mischievous acts cause the loss of beneficial things

A person who is dispossessed of the company of the believers and the good defence of Allah loses every superior result which Allah has arranged for the faith. There are about hundred qualities each one of them is better than the world and what is in it. Some of them are listed below:

1. The mighty reward as He said:

---
[162] Bukhari (2475), Muslim (57)

"Allah will give the believers a mighty reward." (4:146)

2. Protection from the evils of the world and the Hereafter. Allah, the Most High, said:

"Allah defends those who believe." (22:38)

3. The prayer of the angels and the carriers of the Throne for their forgiveness. Allah, the Exalted, said:

"Those Angels who carry the Throne and those who surround it celebrate the praise of their Lord and believe in Him. They beg forgiveness for the believers." (40:7)

4. Support of Allah for them and the one who is supported by Allah will never face humiliation.

"Allah is the ally (patron) of those who believe." (2:257)

5. Allah orders the angels to strengthen those who believe. He said:

"Your Lord revealed to the angels: I am with you, strengthen those who believe." (8:12)

6. They will have high ranks with their Lord, forgiveness and generous provision as the Lord has said:

"They will have high positions with their Lord, forgiveness and noble provision." (8:4)

7. To them belongs power as Almighty said:

"The power belongs to Allah, His Messenger and the believers but the hypocrites do not know." (63:8)

8. Allah in the company of people of faith as He said:

"Allah is with the believers." (8:19)

9. High position in the world and the Hereafter. Almighty said:

"Allah will raise up, by many degrees, those of you who believe and those who have been given knowledge." (58:11)

10. Allah will give them double share of His mercy, and make a light in which to walk and forgiveness of their misdeeds. (57:28)

11. He will grant them love by loving them and making them loved by His angels, His prophets and His righteous servants. (19:96)

12. Safety from fear on the Day when the fear will be intense as He said:

"The one who believed and does good deeds for him there will be no fear or grief." (6:48)

13. They are those who have been favoured and He ordered us to pray to Him every day seventeen times to guide us to their path.[163]

14. The Qur'an is guidance and healing as He confirmed:

"Say it is guidance and healing for those who believe, and those who do not believe their ears are heavy, they are blind to it. Those are being called from a distant place." (41:44)

15. The aim is to ascertain that faith is the cause of every advantage, any benefit in the world and the Hereafter is the outcome of the faith. On the other hand every evil and calamity in the world and the Hereafter is the result of not having faith. How can a person do something which may take him out of the circle of the faith and create a barrier between him and the faith? However, by making mistake he is not going to be expelled from the circle of the general Muslims. If he persists on sins, there is a danger that it may stamp on his heart and he is driven out of Islam completely. This explains the extreme fear of the early Muslims as one of them said: 'You fear sins and I am afraid of disbelief'.

33. Defiant attitudes cause weakness in the march of the heart to Allah

Another serious consequence of the involvement in wrong actions is that it slows down the speed of the journey of the heart to Allah and the life to come. It hampers its move, hinders it and disrupts its walk and does not let it proceed to Allah any further. Sins, instead turn the heart away from

---

[163] The reference is to the opening chapter, which is read in every prayer and which includes the o supplication: "Guide us to the right path, the path of those whom You have favoured."

Allah and in backward direction. Sin in this way creates a veil before a person who is about to reach his destination, hinders the marcher and reverse the seeker. The heart moves to Allah by its power and when it is affected by sins that power, which takes it ahead become weak. If it is removed totally, he will be detached from Allah completely, and it will be hard to set it right. Only Allah can help!

Evil deed either causes the death of the heart or makes it dangerously ill or reduces its energy. This process continues till it reaches the stage of eight things from which the Prophet, Allah's blessing and peace be upon him, used to seek refuge of Allah. They are: worry and grief, incapacity and laziness, cowardice and stinginess, overwhelming of debt and overpowering of men.[164] Every two of them are linked as pair. Worry and grief are linked together. If a mishap affecting the heart related to something in future, it produces worry; and if it is caused by a past matter, it produces grief.

Incapacity and laziness are joined together. When a slave fails to reach the causes of good and success, then if is caused because of his inability, it is incapacity; and if it is the result of lack of the intention, it is laziness. In the same way cowardice and stinginess are associated together. If the lack of help of others is due to the body, it is cowardice; and if it is connected with wealth, it is stinginess. The same can be said about the pair of overwhelming of debt and overpowering of men. If the domination of others over him is legal, then it is overwhelming of debt and if it is unjust, it is overpowering of men.

The aim is to assert that the sinful acts are the strongest causes for these eight categories as they are the powerful causes of the troublesome affliction, being subject of misfortunate, evil decree and mockery of the enemies. They are also the main causes of the removal of the favours of Allah, turning off welfare provided by Him, sudden revenge and all His angers.

34. Evil acts take away the favours and bring misfortune

Another consequence of the evil acts is that they cause the removal of the favours and bring misfortunes. No favour is taken away from a person but because of a sin, and he is not afflicted by misfortune but because of a sin, and no trouble is removed but by repentance as Ali ibn Abi Talib said:

---

[164] See Bukhari (6369), Muslim (2706)

'No misfortune comes but because of sin and no tribulation is removed but by repentance.'
Allah, the Most Glorious, said:

"Whatever misfortune befalls you, it is because of what your hands have done, and He forgives much." (42:30)
(This is) because Allah would not change a favour He had conferred on a people unless they changed what was within themselves." (8:53)

Here Allah informed that He does not change a favour He conferred on a person unless he changes what is within himself by changing the obedience of Allah with disobedience; gratitude changed to ungratefulness and the causes of His pleasure changed to causes of His anger. When a servant changes from within, his condition is changed, an appropriate requital, and your Lord is not unfair to the servants.
If after that the servant replaces the evil act with good one, Allah will change the punishment with wellbeing, and disgrace with respect. He, glory is to Him, said:

"Allah does not change the condition of a people unless they change what is in themselves, when He wills harm on a people, no one can ward it off, and apart from Him, they have no protector." (13:11)

In some Divine saying Allah says:
'By My honour and majesty, none of My servants is on the path I like then changes to what I dislike, but I will change what he likes to what he dislikes. On the other hand, none of My servants moves from what I dislike to what I like but I change what he dislikes for what he likes.'

A poet has rightly said:
'If you have a favour, take care of it because the evil deeds take away the favours.
Protect it by the obedience of the Lord of the people; the Lord of people is quick in taking revenge.
Keep away from wrongdoing as much as you can; the wrong done to the people is extremely disastrous.
Travel with your heart among the people to see the result of those who had done wrong.
These are their houses after them as witness on them without any doubt.
There was nothing more damaging for them than injustice and it was the cause of their downfall.

How many gardens, palaces and high buildings they left behind! They went into Hell and lost the favour and what they had turned into a dream.'

35. Vicious acts are the cause of fear and terror of the heart

Another harmful result of the sinful activities is that Allah casts terror and fear in the heart of the sinner. You do not see him but terrified and scared. Obedience is the great fortress of Allah; when someone enters it, he becomes safe from the torment of the world and the Hereafter. The one who gets out of it is surrounded by dangers from every side. Anyone who obeys Allah, the sources of fear turn for him into the sources of safety, and the one who is involved in disobeying Him, his places of safety turn to the areas of scare. You will find a sinful person shaking like the wings of a bird. If the wind shakes the door, he says: 'the search has come'. If he hears footsteps, he fears that a danger is approaching. He thinks that every shout is against him and every misfortune is heading toward him. Anyone who has the fear of Allah, He will protect him from everything, and anyone who does not have fear of Allah; He will make him scared of everything.

36. Great alienation in the heart

Another distressful result of the evil deeds is that it casts severe estrangement in the heart of the evil doer. He finds himself alienated. He is alienated from his Lord and from the people and feels strange to himself. As the sins multiply, his estrangement increases. The bitterest life is that of those who feel lonely and scared, and the most pleasant life is that of those who are in company of others. If a sensible person pays attention and compares the joy of offensive act with its outcome in the form of fear and estrangement, he will realise the bad condition and loss of his work. He sold the comfort of obedience and its sweetness for the loneliness of disobedience, and now faces the fear and harm of it.

The secret of the matter is that obedience produces nearness to the Lord, glory be to Him. The nearer the person is to Allah, his intimacy grows stronger. The sinful act causes remoteness from the Lord, and the more a person is moved away from Him, his loneliness increases. This explains the situation of a man who feels estrangement between him and his enemy even if he is around and close to him, and finds intimacy and closeness between him and the one whom he loves even though he may be far away from him.

The cause of desolation is barrier and as the barrier gets thicker the desolation grows intense. Heedlessness results in desolation and worse than it is the desolation of disobedience and greater than it is the desolation of disbelief and association of partners with Allah Almighty. You will not see anyone who is connected with any of the aforementioned matters but he feels strangeness according to his involvement in it. The strangeness covers his face and his heart, and he is alienated from the people and people are away from him.

37. Indulgence in evil deeds turns the heart from uprightness

Another consequence of getting involved in evil deeds is that it turns the heart away from its health and uprightness to illness and crookedness. It become ill and does not benefit from foods in which lies his life and recovery. The impact of sins on the hearts is like the effect of illness in the bodies. The sins are the disease of the hearts and its cure; as a matter of fact its cure lies in abandoning the sins. The travellers to Allah are unanimous that the hearts do not get their desired goal until they reach their Patron, and they do not reach their Patron unless they are sound and healthy, and they will not be sound and healthy until their disease becomes their cure which is only possible by opposing their desire. Their desire is their disease and the cure lies in abandoning it; if the disease takes root, it may kill or bring near to death.

As a person who restrains himself from base desires Paradise will be his home, thus his heart in this home will be in a present Paradise. The pleasure of the people of it is not similar to any other pleasure, the difference between his joy and the joy of other people is like the difference between the joy of the world and that of the Hereafter. This is a matter which is known only to those who have experienced this and that. Allah informs His slaves:

"The righteous will be in bliss, and the wicked will be in Hell." (81:13-14)

Do not think that the words of Allah apply to the bliss and punishment of the Hereafter only. It is in all three homes: the home of the world, the place in Barzakh and the home of the permanent abode. In all these homes the good ones will be in bliss and the wicked in Hell. Is the pleasure anything except the comfort of the heart, and the torment is only the torment of the heart? Which torture is more severe than the fear, worry, grief, dejection of the chest and turning away from Allah and the Hereafter, and disconnection from Allah and the Hereafter and attachment with others? Anything a person is fond of and loves it besides Allah; it will subject him to terrible torment. Anyone who loves other than Allah will be tormented three times in this home. He is in torture before he gets it; when he gets it, he is tortured with fear of its being snatched and loss. This will cause him worry and embitterment and variety of mishaps. When it is taken away from him, his suffering becomes harder for him. These are three types of torture in this home.

As for the Barzakh he will suffer from the pain of departure without the hope of returning, and also from pain of losing the great bliss because of engaging in opposite of it and the pain of removal from Allah and the pain of regret that cuts the liver into pieces. The worry, sorrow, regret and grief work in their souls as the insects and worm work in their bodies. Their work in the souls is lasting and will continue till Allah returns them to their bodies. After that the torment moves to another type which is more disastrous and painful. Where is it from the pleasure of the one whose heart is dancing in happiness and association with his Lord? He is in great desire for Him, comfortable with love of Him and relaxed in His remembrance.

It is so enjoyable that some of them say at the time of his death: 'O delight!' Another says: 'Poor the people of the world! They got out of it and did not enjoy the pleasant life of it, and did not test the gratifying matter of it.'

Another says: 'If the kings and sons of the kings notice the comfort we are in, they will fight us with swords for it.'

Another one says: 'There is a Garden in the world, if a person did not enter it, he did not enter the Garden of the Hereafter.'

How unfortunate is the man who sold his expensive share with the lowest price and was duped in this transaction! It is amazing that you have a commodity which Allah is going to purchase and pay in price the Garden of Restfulness. The agent who is the middle man for the transaction of sale and the guarantor from the purchaser is the Messenger, Allah's blessing and peace be upon him, but you sold it with despicable rate. A poet says:

'If this is what a man does to himself, then who is going to honour him after that?'

Allah, the Most High, said:

"Whoever Allah disgraces there in no one to honour him. Allah does what He wills." (22:18)

38. Activities of disobedience obscure the power of the perception of the heart

Another damaging result of the defiant actions is that they block out the mental capacity of the heart, blot out its light, close the ways of learning and screen the sources of guidance. Imam Malik said to Imam al-Shafi'i, when he noticed signs of intelligence in him:
'I see that Allah, the Exalted, has cast light on you, do not put it off by the darkness of sinful acts.'

This light continues losing its power and fading away, and the darkness of the sin become stronger till the heart becomes like the deep dark night. The result is that the man falls in perilous ditch without noticing. He becomes like a blind person who goes out in the night on a path full of dangers and risks. What a plight of safety! What a quick perish!
Then that darkness becomes strong and passes from the heart to other parts of the body, and a black veil covers the heart in line to its power. When he comes to die it moves to the Barzakh and the grave is filled with darkness, as the Prophet, Allah's blessing and peace be upon him, said:

"These graves are full of darkness for their people and Allah gives light to them by my prayer."[165]

When the Day of Return comes and the people are gathered, that darkness appears clearly on their faces which everyone can see. The face turns black like charcoal. What a punishment which cannot be compared with all the joys of the world from the beginning to the end! How regrettable it is for a man who troubled himself, exhausted and remained miserable for a while which was just an hour of dream! Allah's help is sought.

---

[165] Muslim (956)

39. The evil deeds degrade the soul

Another punishment for the evil deeds is that they degrade, subdue, disgrace the soul and reduce its value till it becomes the lowliest and meanest thing; while the obedience makes it grow, develop and advance. Allah, the Most Supreme, said:

"The one who purifies his soul succeeds, and the one who corrupts it fails." (91:9-10)

The meaning is that the one who struggled to raise his soul and put it on high state by obeying the Lord is successful, and the one who diminished, degraded and reduced it was at loss. The sinner buries his soul in sinful acts, hides its place and conceals himself from the people to escape the bad result of his work. In this way he has reduced himself, became insignificant in the sight of Allah and disgraceful to the public. The good deeds and righteous works give honour to the soul and raise it high till it becomes the noblest, biggest, highest and most purified, though it is the meanest, smallest and most despicable thing to Allah. With the humiliation of the soul a person achieves the honour, eminence and distinction. The souls are reduced by the disobedience of Allah, and they are raised high, given honour and good status by the obedience of Allah Almighty.

40. Misdeeds put the evil doer under the control of Satan and his desire

One of the terrible effects of the evil deeds is that the sinful person is always in the control of Satan and prisoner of his base desires. He is imprisoned and enchained. No prisoner is in worse condition than a prisoner who is arrested by his worst enemy, and no prison is tighter than the prison of lust and no shackle harder than the shackle of desire. How then such a person can proceed to Allah and the Hereafter whose heart is confined, locked up and detained? How can he take a step further? When the heart is confined all kind of calamities surround it from every side. The heart is like a bird, as it goes high, it is away from calamities and disasters; when it comes down it is attacked by them. It is reported:

"Satan is the wolf of man."[166]

---

[166] Ahmad (5: 233, 243), Tabarani in Kabir (20: 344) See Majma' al-zawa'id (2: 23)

As a goat which has no protector and is surrounded by wolves is quickly killed, in the same way when a servant has no protector from Allah, his wolf will definitely kill him. If he has a protector from Allah by being mindful of Him, there will be a protection from Allah and a strong fortress between him and his wolf. It also will provide him with shelter from the torment of the world and the Hereafter. When the goat is near the shepherd it will be safer from the wolf, and when it is away from him, it will be closer to perish. It is saved when it is close to the shepherd because the wolf attacks the goat which is separated from the herd and away from the shepherd.

The basis of all this is that when the heart is away from Allah, the calamities will reach him quickly, and when it is close to Allah, the disasters will be away from him. Being away from Allah has degrees some of them are harder than others. Negligence keeps the heart away from Allah, and the distance of the disobedience is greater than the distance of negligence, and the distance caused by innovation is more serious than the distance of disobedience, and the distance caused by hypocrisy and association of partners with Allah is far more dangerous than all these.

41. Evil deeds cause decline of the rank of the evildoer in the sight of Allah and the people

Sinful deeds result in the loss of rank, dignity and honour of the sinner with Allah and the general public. The noblest person to Allah is the one who is most conscious of Him, and the closest one is the one who is the most obedient of Him. According to the obedience of a person his rank is decided with Allah. When he disobeys Him and violates His commands, he is dropped in His estimation. He drops his respect from the hearts of His slaves. When he loses his status to the people and becomes disgraceful to them, they treat him accordingly. He ends in living among them most terrible life being unknown, miserable and without any position. He has no respect and is deprived of happiness and delight. It is because the loss of reputation and status and rank produces every worry, grief and sorrow, and deprives of any happiness and delight. How can this pain be compared with the joy of the disobedience if it were not for the intoxication of the base desire?

The greatest favour of Allah to a person is to have good reputation among the people and enjoy the respect of them. He is singled out, for this reason, His prophets and messengers for the honour He did not give to others. Almighty said:

"Remember Our servants Abraham, Issac and Jacob, all men of strength and vision. We caused them to be devoted to Us through their sincere remembrance of the final home. (38:45-46)

Almighty says that He gave them special rank and good, name with which they will be known in this world. It is the good name which Abraham asked Allah to grant him. He said:

"Give me good name among the next generation." (26:84)

Almighty said about His prophets and their offspring:

"We granted Our grace to all of them, and gave them a noble reputation." (19:50)

He said to His Prophet, Allah's blessing and peace be upon him,:

"We raised your reputation high." (94:4)

The followers of these prophets get a share of that rank in line with their obedience and faithfulness, but those who go against them will lose that rank in accordance with their work.

42. Evil acts disparage the person

One of the scandalous results of the abhorrent acts is that they take away the good names and commendable reputations from the person involved in them and give him the titles of disgrace and humiliation. The titles of believer, righteous, kind, conscious of Allah, obedient, repentant, pious, cautious, honest, worshipper, fearful, remembering Allah much, pleasant, acceptable and like them. Instead he is called wicked, disobedient, opponent, wrongdoer, corrupt, evil, disagreeable, adulterer, thief, murderer, liar, unfaithful, sodomite, breaker of the bonds, cheater and so on. These are the titles of defiant people. How bad it is to be called with bad names after accepting faith. It causes the anger of the Lord, and entrance into the Fire and life of humiliation and disgrace.

The first group is the names which produce the pleasure of the Merciful and cause entrance into the Gardens and high rank for the one named with them on the rest of mankind. If the punishment of the disobedience was no more than deserving those bad names and their results, it would have been enough to be rejected by the reason. On the other hand, if there was no more reward of obedience than deserving the good names, there would have been enough reason to follow the right path. But there is no preventer to what He gives, and no giver of what he withholds, and no one to bring close who He keeps away and no one to keep away those whom He brings close.

"Whoever Allah disgraces, there is no one to honour him; indeed Allah does what He wills." (22:18)

43. Offensive acts reduce the power of reasoning

Another damaging result of the sinful acts is that they affect the reasoning faculty by reducing its ability. You will not find two intelligent persons, one of them faithful to Allah and the other disobedient but the comprehension of the faithful one will be wider and more perfect, and his thought more sound, his opinion appropriate and mostly correct. This is why the Qur'an addresses the people of reason and understanding. Allah said:

"Be mindful of Me, you who have understanding." (2:197)

"Be mindful of Allah, people of understanding, so that you may prosper." (5:100)

"Only those with understanding take heed." (2:269)

There are many other examples.

How can a man be full of wisdom when he disobeys the One who has control over him and he lives in His house, and he is fully aware that He is watching him and observing his movements? He disobeys Him while he is not hidden from Him, and uses His favours to do what makes Him angry. He prompts every moment His wrath over him and invites His curse upon him. He is involved in deeds that push him away from Him and drive away from His door. His acts make Him to turn away from him, desert him, leave him alone with his enemy and drop him from His rank, and deprive him of His comfort and pleasure. His disobedience keeps him away from achieving the comfort of his eye by getting close to Him, enjoying His company and looking at His Face with the group of His allies, and much more aspects of honour which He will grant to His friends and multiple punishments which He has prepared for those who disobey Him.

What type of reason is that which induces to prefer the delight which stays for an hour, or a day or a period then vanishes as though it was a dream over the lasting joy and great success? He loses the delight of the world and the Hereafter and if he did not have that amount of reasoning which will be used against him to condemn him, he would be considered among the insane people. The insane may be better than him and safe in consequence. This is one aspect. On the other hand the evil deeds also affect the reason of the evil doers in his life. This lack of understanding is common among the people and it is not easy to know the inferiority of the reason of the sinner to the reason of the faithful. However, insanity manifests itself in many ways.

It is amazing, if the reasons are used rightly, they will realise that the source of acquiring delight, joy, satisfaction and pleasant life is in experiencing the pain of the work for His pleasure. Suffering and all torments are in His wrath and displeasure. If He is pleased, one will gain comfort of his eyes, happiness of the souls, life of the heart, joy of the spirits, and delight of the life, joy of living and pleasant time. If one atom's pleasure of paradise is compared with all the pleasures of the world, it will be greater than it. Moreover, if a small share of it is achieved by the heart, it will not accept the world and what is in it as compensation for it. Still he enjoys his share of the worldly materials better than the enjoyment of the luxurious people; his enjoyment is free from the grief, sorrows, worries and challenges. He as a matter of fact has achieved two kinds of delight and is waiting for two others greater than these two though he faces during this many troubles. Allah said:

"If you are suffering hardship, so are they, but you hope to receive something from Allah for which they cannot hope." (4:104)

There is no god but Allah! How little is the understanding of a man who sells the pearl in exchange of dung and filth! He exchanged the company of those whom Allah has shown favour from among the prophets, truthful ones, martyrs and righteous people with the company of those who Allah has been angry with and cursed them and prepared for them Hell which is evil destination.

44. Acts of defiance cause separation between the servant and his Lord

Another terrible consequence of the offensive acts is that it severs the relations between the slave and his Lord, the Glorious and Blessed. When this relationship is broken every source of good is cut off and the sources of evil become operative. How can a man receive any success or any comfort and peace from whom the sources of good have been cut off, and the relation between him and his Patron whom he cannot dispense with for twinkling of an eye are severed? He has lost the causes of good, and the sources of evil have surrounded him. He has been joined with his worst enemy who adopted him, and his patron deserted him. No soul knows what sorts of pain and suffering is hidden in this rift.

One of the pious men said:

'I saw the servant dropped between Allah, the Exalted, and Satan. If Allah turns away from him, Satan takes over him, and if Allah takes over him, Satan gets no way to him. Allah said:

"And when We said to the angels, "bow down before Adam," they all bowed down, except for Iblis. He was one of the Jinn and disobeyed his Lord's command. Are you going to take him and his offspring as your allies instead of Me, even though they are your enemies? What a bad exchange for the evildoers!" (18:50)

Allah, the Glorious says to His worshippers: 'I honoured your father, raised his status and made him superior over others, and ordered My angels to bow down before him as a sign of honour and reverence. They obeyed My order but My enemy and his enemy refused and disobeyed command and rejected to obey Me. How is it suitable for you after that to take him and his offspring as allies instead of Me? You obey him to reject My command and make him an ally against My pleasure when he is the worst enemy of yours? I commanded you to take him as enemy but you took him as an ally. Anyone who befriends the enemies of the king, he and his enemies will be in the same position. It is because the friendship and intimacy are not complete without taking the enemies of the friends as enemies and befriending his allies. To side with the enemies of the king and claim that you are his ally is unacceptable. Thus, in case the king's enemy is not your enemy as well, but if he is in reality your enemy and the enmity between you and him is greater than the enmity between the goat and the wolf, then it is more serious. It is not proper for a reasonable man to take his enemy and the enemy of his Patron and Supporter beside whom he has no supporter.

Allah, the Exalted, has drawn attention to the ignobility of this friendship by saying:

"He (Satan) is your enemy." (18:50)

He also pointed out to the ignobility of his act saying:

"He defied the command of his Lord." (18:50)

It is clear that his enmity of his Lord and his enmity to us both are enough cause of taking him as an enemy. From where then came this friendship? How it was exchanged? Bad is the exchange for wrongdoers. It is very likely that under this address there is a kind of fine admonition and it is that Allah says: 'I took Iblis as My enemy when he refused to bow down before Adam with My angels. I made him My enemy for the sake of you, and you repaid this enmity by making a contract of friendship between him and you!

45. Mischievous acts eradicate the blessing of the religion and the world

A very serious damaging result of the evil acts is that they eradicate the blessing of the life, blessing of the provision, and the benefit of knowledge, deeds and obedience. In short, they annihilate the blessing of the religion and the world. You will not find more unfortunate in his life and religion and the world than a person who disobeys Allah. The blessing of the earth was erased by the disobedience of the people only. Allah, the Glorious and Blessed, said:

"If the peoples of the towns had believed and been mindful of Allah, We would have showered them with blessings from the heavens and earth." (7:96)

He also said:

"If they had stayed on the right way, We would have given them abundant water to drink, a test for them." (72:16-17)

"The slave is deprived of the provision for a sin he committed",

Said the Messenger, Allah's blessing and peace be upon him.[167]

He, peace be upon him, said:

"The Pure Spirit (Gabriel) has cast in my heart that no one is going to die until he takes his full share of the provision. So, be conscious of Allah, and be moderate in struggle. What is with Allah cannot be gained without His obedience, and Allah has put the comfort and happiness in satisfaction and certainty, and put the worry and grief in doubt and dissatisfaction."[168]

The report cited by Imam Ahmad in his book *'al-Zuhd*[169] has been mentioned earlier in which Allah says:
'I am Allah; when I am pleased, I bless and there is no limit for My blessing; but when I am displeased I curse and My curse reaches the seventh generation.'

The expansion of the provision and deeds is not by their great number; neither is the length of age by abundance of months and years but the blessing in them.

It has been said earlier that the life span of a person is the one he lives, and there is no life for the one who turns away from Allah and gets engaged with others. The life of the animals is better than his life. It is because the life of a human is by the life of his heart and soul, and the life of the heart depends on the recognition of its Creator, and it is also the result of His love, and His worship only. It also depends on turning to Him, getting peace in His remembrance and gaining satisfaction in being close to Him. Whoever misses this life he has missed all the good even if he tries to get it with the big price. The whole world is not a substitute for this life. Everything which a person misses he has a substitute, but when he misses Allah nothing can compensate for Him.
How can an inborn poor be substitute for an innate Self-Sufficient, an incapable for the Powerful, the dead for the Living who is not going to die and the created for the Creator? How can the one whose existence and everything of his comes from other be equal to the One whose self-sufficiency, life, perfectness, generosity and mercy are an innate character of His essence? How can a man who does not own the smallest amount

---

[167] Ahmad (5: 277) it has passed earlier.
[168] Abu Nu'aym in al-Hilyh (10: 277)
[169] P. 52

be a match to the One who holds the kingdom of the heavens and the earth?

Disobedience of Allah is the cause of the ruin of the blessing of provision and the life because Satan is given control over evil deeds. He has power to affect the people concerning involvement in sinful activities, and anything connected with Satan its blessing is stamped out. That is why mention of the name of Allah is ordered at the time of eating, drinking, putting on dress, riding and having intercourse. The name of Allah brings blessing and it drives away Satan, and blessing given by Allah Almighty cannot be done away. Anything which is not for the sake of Allah, its blessing is dropped. Only He, the Most High, has power to bless. All blessing comes from Him and anything attributed to Him is blissful. His speech is blessed, His Messenger is blessed, His believing slave who is beneficial to His creature is blessed, His sacred house is blessed, and His quiver on earth i.e. Syria, is the land of fortune. Almighty described it with blessing in six verses in His Book.[170]

It is He who grants blessing and there is nothing blessed but is related to his Lordship, love and pleasure. The whole universe is related to His creation and Lordship. Anything He kept away from Himself whether objects, speeches or deeds, has no blessing in it; and anything which is close to Him is blessed in accordance with its closeness.

Opposite of blessing is curse, so any land Allah cursed or any man He cursed or any act He rejected are the farthest from benefit and blessing; and anything connected with them in any way also lacks blessing. Almighty cursed His enemy Iblis and drove him away, so anything which comes from his side is condemned by Allah according to its connection with him.

For this reason evil deeds work in eradicating the blessing of life and provision, knowledge and deeds. Any time which is passed in the disobedience of Allah, or any money which is spent in sin, or any physical or moral act or position of knowledge or act which was used in deeds which Allah does not like – all of it is going against the servant. He will gain only from his life, money, strength, status, knowledge and works when they are used in the obedience of Allah. There are people who live in this world hundred years or so and their life is not counted ten years or less. In the same way a man may have treasures of gold and

---

[170] See the chapters (41:10; 7:137: 17:1; 2171; 21:81; 34:18)

silver piled up high, but in real sense his money is no more than a thousand dirham. The same can be said about rank and knowledge.
The Prophet, Allah's blessing and peace be upon him, said:

"The world is condemned and its materials are condemned as well except the remembrance of Allah and what He loves, and a man of knowledge or the one who is involved in learning."[171]

In another report:

"The world is damned and what is in it is damned except for the things which are for Allah."[172]

Allah's help is sought, on Him is the trust.

46. Evil works are the cause of humiliation

One of the disgraceful results of the evil works is that they bring down the miscreant to a lower status after he was prepared to be among the upper class. Allah, the Exalted, has divided His creature into two categories: upper and lower. He made '*Illiyin*' the abode of the upper class and the lowest of the low the abode of lower class. He raised the people who obey Him high in the world and the Hereafter, and lowered those who disobeyed Him in the lowest level. He made the people of His obedience the most honourable people with Him and the ones involved in wrongdoing the meanest of the creature. He decreed honour for former and disgrace & humiliation for latter. It is reported that the Prophet, Allah's blessing and peace be upon him, said:

"I have been sent with sword before the Hour, and my provision is made in the shade of my spear, and humiliation and disgrace are decreed for those who violate my order."[173]

As a man commits a sin he goes down to a low degree and continues going down till he reaches the lowest place. When a person, on the other hand, does a good deed, he goes high one degree and continues going up till he becomes among the upper class. A person may face during his life ascending from one side and descending from the other. The one which

---

[171] Tirmidhi (2322), Ibn Majah (4112)
[172] Abu Nu'atm in al-Hilyah (3; 157, 7: 90)
[173] Ahmad (2: 50)

dominates he becomes one of them. Someone who went up hundred degree and came down one degree is not like the one who is opposite of him.

There is a serious misunderstanding among the people. A person may go down far deep farther than the distance between the east and the west and the distance between the heaven and the earth. In such a case his ascendance a thousand degree will not be enough to compensate for that one descending. The Prophet, Allah's blessing and peace be upon him, said:

"A person utters a word without giving it any consideration, falls because of it in the Fire farther than the distance of the east and the west."[174]

Which ascendance can be parallel to this descending? Going down is a must for human being, however, some people's fall is due to negligence. When he recovers from it, he returns to his previous status or even higher than that according to his alertness. Some other's fall is due a permissible act which he does not intend to use for carrying out a duty to Allah. When he returns to the obedience, he may return to his previous status and may not return to that, it is possible that he may go higher if he had stronger will. He may have weak will or his earlier will may return.

There are others who get down because of a sin minor or major. Such people require in order to reach their previous status to make the sincere repentance and true penitence.

The people dispute about the question whether a man will return to the status he was in after repentance on the basis that repentance wipes out the traces of the sin and makes it as though it was not committed? Or he will not return to same status because the repentance works in cancelling the punishment, as for the status which he missed is not going to be achieved by him. This is explained in the following way: He was ready by engaging in obedience in the period he committed the sin for another rise and go up by all his previous deeds. His example is like earning of a man every day with the total wealth he has; when the money increases the profit also increases. In the period of the sin he climbed up and gained profit of his total wealth. When he resumed the work, he started going up from lower point while before that he was only going up and up. There is big gap between the two levels.

---

[174] Bukhari (6478), Muslim 92988)

This can be explained further by another example: there are two men who climb up two endless stairs and both are equal, then one of them went down even one step then resumed his ascendance, it is clear that the person who did not go down will be higher than the one who descended one step.

Shaykh al- Islam Ibn Taymiya passed a reasonable judgement between the two men. He said:
'It is certain that among the repentant is the one who returns to a higher status, and some who return to the same status and some who does not return to his previous status.'

I say:
'This depends on the power or strength of the repentance and the change which the sin has produced in him. He experienced humbleness, humility and devotion, and the sin produced in him caution and fear of Allah and made him cry from the awe of Allah. These things sometimes are strong and make the repenting man reach a higher status than he was on, and he becomes better than he was before committing the sin. Sin in the case of this person is a mercy because it wiped out from him the disease of self conceit and purged from his soul his confidence and arrogance. It made him submit his face of humility and humbleness on the doorstep of his Master and Patron, and realise his status. It also showed him his need and obligation to the protection of his Master and Patron, and to His forgiveness and mercy. It took out from his heart the pride of obedience, and curbed him from raising his head high in arrogance and considering himself better than others. It put him before his Lord among the sinner and offenders, with his head down, ashamed, scared and afraid considering his good works little and regarding his sin big. He realised his shortcoming and failing and became certain of his Lord's perfectness, praise and fulfilment.
Any favour he receives from Allah he considered it too high for himself and regards himself far less than it and not being qualified for that. Any misfortune or trouble he experiences he regards himself deserving much more than that and feels that his Patron has been kind to him as He did not treat him in accordance with his offence or more than that. The punishment he deserved was heavier than the capacity of solid mountains let alone this weak and powerless slave. The sin no matter how small it is against the Great and there is nothing greater than Him, Big and there is nothing bigger than Him and Glorious and there is no being to match His glory or His beauty. He is the One who grants all big and small favours therefore to confront Him with disobedience is the most abominable and horrible matter. To encounter the great, supreme and most honourable

people with such attitude is regarded by every believer and disbeliever an unacceptable matter.

The lowest and basest man is the one who confronts them with ignominious acts. Then how it will be with Supreme holder of the heavens and the earth, the King of the heavens and the earth, the Lord of the heavens and the earth? Were it not that His mercy overwhelms His wrath, and His forgiveness outstrips His punishment, the earth would have pounded to dust with the one who encountered Him with what was not suitable. Were it not for His clemency and forgiveness the heavens and the earth would have been crushed because of the sinful acts of the people. Allah, the Exalted, said:

"Allah keeps the heavens and earth, from vanishing; if they did vanish, no one else could stop them. Allah is Most Forbearing, Most Forgiving." (35:41)

Consider the end of the verse by two beautiful Names of Him namely 'Forbearing and Forgiving'. You will notice that if not for His forbearing from the criminals and His forgiveness of wrongdoers, the heavens and earth would not have remained stable.
He, the Most Powerful, said about some aspects of the evil acts of His slaves:

"It almost causes the heavens to be torn apart, the earth to split asunder, the mountains to crumble to pieces, that they attribute offspring to the Lord Merciful." (19:90)

Allah, the Glorious, expelled our parents (Adam and Eve) from Paradise for one single offence they made by violating His prohibition. He, the Most High, cursed Iblis and drove him away from the realm of the heavens and earth for only one sin he committed by rejecting His command. But we, the foolish ones, are as a poet says:
'We join one sin with the other and hope for the high status of Paradise with everlasting delight. We know that He expelled the parents from His high realm for only one sin.'

The aim is that the slave may be after repentance in a better position than he was before the sin, and achieves higher rank. The sin may weaken his will, affects his determination and makes his heart ill, and in this case his repentance may not be strong enough to return him to the previous healthy status. However, it is possible that the illness is treated and health returns as before and he resumes similar deeds and returns to his previous status. All this when his going down was caused by disobedience, but if it was for a matter affecting his belief like doubts, suspicion and hypocrisy, then there is no hope for the person to rise up except by renewing his faith.

47. Offensive actions make the offender target of all the people

Another damaging effect of offensive acts is that they give power to every creature over the offender, which did not have this opportunity. So, Satan becomes bold and causes him harm and whispers to him and frightens him. He misguides, causes worry and makes him forget the One in whose remembrance lies his interest and forgetting Him leads to loss. In this way Satan gets an opportunity to drag him successfully to the disobedience of Allah Almighty. Even the devils among the humans cause him harm as much as they can. His family, servants, children and neighbours and even the animals hurt him.

A pious mans said:

'I disobey Allah, and see its effect in the behaviour of my wife and my animal.'

The people in authority use their power against him and if they deal with him in justice, they would execute the punishment of Allah on him. His soul as well becomes bold on him and becomes difficult for him to control. If he wants it to do good deeds, it does not comply with his order and does not listen to him, but on the contrary leads him to matters in which lies his destruction, whether he likes or not. It is because the obedience is the fortress of the Lord, the Glorious and Blessed, whoever enters it becomes among the safe people. When a person gets out of the fortress the way layers and others ambush him. In accordance with his misdeeds will be the attacks of these forces on him, and he will have no way to beat them. It is the remembrance of Allah, His obedience as well as charity, guiding the ignorant, ordering what is good and forbidding what is bad are the sources of prevention, which defend the slave. They act as the power which resist the illness and counter it. When the power is reduced the symptom of the sickness dominates and causes death. The slave needs something to defend him.

The causes of evil and good are engaged in battle and the triumph is for the more powerful. If the side of righteous deeds is strong, the defence will be strong. Allah defends those who believe; and the belief consists of statement and actions. The defence will be indeed according to the power of faith. Allah is help is sought.

48. Acts of disobedience betray the person at the time of need

One of the terrible consequences of sinful acts is that they desert the sinful person at a time when he is in desperate need. Every person is in need of knowing what is useful or harmful in his life and the life to come; the most learned of the people is the one who knows these things in detail. The most skilful and tactful is the one who has control over his soul and desires and uses them in what is beneficial for him, and holds them back from what is harmful. The people's knowledge, their power and their ranks are different in this respect. The most discreet person is the one who is well learned about the causes of the happiness and misfortune; and the most successful is the one who prefers the good over the bad, and the most unlucky is the one who does the opposite.

Acts of disobedience let the sinner down when he is in extreme need of acquiring this knowledge, and putting the dear and lasting share above the despicable and expiring lowly share. His sins bar him from perfecting this knowledge and from getting engaged in what is suitable and more beneficial for him in both houses. When he faces a trouble and needs to get out of it, his heart, and soul and the limbs desert him. He becomes like a man who has a sword covered with rust and stuck in its shield in a way that when he tries to pull it, it does not come out. In this situation an enemy appeared to him with the intention of killing him, he put his hand on the handle of his sword and tried to pull it, but it did not come out, the enemy took him in surprise and got hold of him.

The heart gets rusted by sins and exhausted by illness. When there is need to fight an enemy with it, it does not work. The servant fights and confronts and proceeds with his heart, the limbs are subservient to it, but when the heart has no power to defend what the limbs can do?
The peaceful soul also is spoiled by base desires and evil acts and becomes weak, but the commanding soul becomes stronger. The more strength it gains other becomes weak, and the power and dealing remain with the commanding soul. His peaceful soul may suffer death without any hope of life. It will be dead in the *Barzakh* and not living in the Hereafter in a useful manner, rather its life will be only to receive the pain.

The aim is that when the servant is affected by hardship or trouble or mishap, his heart, tongue and limbs deceive him and turn him away from what is useful for him. The heart does not move to have trust in Allah, to turn to Him in penitence and show humility and dejection before Him. His tongue does not cooperate in remembering Him; if he remembers with his tongue the heart and tongue do not come together in this exercise. If he repeats the words of remembrance or prays, his heart will not be alert and attentive. If he wants his limbs to assist him with some good deeds which can protect him, they will not obey him and do not help him.

All this is the effect of sins and evil deeds. He is in this situation like a ruler who had soldiers to defend him, but he neglected them, ignored and disregarded them and cut off their maintenance, then wanted them, when the enemy ambushed him, to come to his defence without any power.

There is something more serious and dangerous, and it is that his heart and tongue desert him at the time of death and moving to Allah. He may be unable to say the words of witness, as it has been seen with many people to the extent that they were asked to say: 'There is no god but Allah', but he said: oh, oh I cannot say it!

Another person was said to say, 'There is no god but Allah', and he said, 'Shahrukh' and passed away.

Another person was asked to say the word of Tawhid, and he said: 'Some women saying one day after being exhausted, 'Where is the way of the bath of Minjab?' and he died.

Another when asked to say, 'There is no god but Allah', started singing: tatna, tantana' till he died.

Another man said when he was asked to say it: 'How is it going to benefit me when I did not leave any sin but I did it. He died without saying it.

Someone else said when he was asked to say it: 'How is it going to save me when I know that I never performed a prayer for Allah', and he did not say it.

Another person said in reply: 'I do not believe in what you are saying', he did not say it and died.

Another person said: 'Anytime I want to say it my tongue gets dumb.'

Someone who was present with a beggar at the time of his death told me that he continued saying: 'a penny for the sake of Allah, a penny for the sake of Allah!' till he died.

A trader told me about one of his relatives that he was with him at the time of his death and people tried to tell him to say: 'There is no god but Allah', and he said: 'This piece is cheap, this is a good bargain, this is such and such', till he died.

Glory is to Allah! How many such scenes people have come across! What is hidden from the conditions of those who were on the verge of death is greater and more important to teach a lesson!

Consider when Satan can get control over a person when he is in full control of his understanding and perception, and the devil drags him in disobedience of Allah according to his wish, makes his heart forget the remembrance of Allah and blocks his tongue from mentioning Him and his limbs from the acts of obedience; then what will be the case when his strength dwindles and his heart is busy in the agony of the death? At that point Satan gathers all his strength and brings out all the sources he can in order to achieve his goal. It is the last moment and Satan becomes more active at this time while the man is weakest. How can he escape from him? This is the moment.

"Allah gives firmness to those, who believe in the firmly rooted word, both in this world and the Hereafter, but He leaves the evildoers astray. Allah does whatever He will." (14:27)

How can a man whose heart Allah has blocked from His remembrance and he follows his desire be helped by Him for the good end? The one whose heart is far away from Allah, the Exalted, is kept away from it. He is unmindful of Allah, worshipping his desire, captive of his lust, his tongue is dry from the remembrance of Almighty and his limbs are busy from doing good deeds and engaged in His disobedience. It is unlikely that such a person be helped to good end. The fear of the end has broken the backs of the righteous people, but it looks as though the evildoers have taken signature of safety!

"Have you received from Us solemn oaths, binding to the Day of Resurrection, that you will get whatever you yourselves decide? Ask them which of them will guarantee this." (68:39-40)

A poet said:

'O the one who feels safe despite his evil deeds, have you received a signature of safety with you?
You combined two things together, feeling of safety and running after desire while only one of them is enough to destroy a person.
The righteous people have walked on the path of fears and you are not going to walk on it.
You neglected planting at the time of putting the seed out of stupidity, then how are you going to reap when the people will collect their harvest?
The most amazing thing in you is that you are averse of the everlasting abode because of a life you are going to leave.

Are you crazy, by Allah, or are cheated in transaction which you will soon realise?'

49. Evil acts blind the heart and weaken its insight

One of the damaging effects of the evil deeds is that they blind the heart; if they don't blind, then they weaken its insight. It has been mentioned earlier that sinful acts necessarily affect the understanding of the heart. When the heart becomes blind and weak, it is unable to realise the work of guidance and its power to lead the man to the right path fades, and it fails to guide others as well according to its weakness of insight and power. **The perfection of human revolves on two principles: (a)** to distinguish the truth from falsehood and **(b)** choosing the truth. The differences of the people in ranks with Allah, the Exalted, in the world and the Hereafter are according to their differences in these two matters. These are the matters which Allah, the Glorious, has praised His prophets for. He said:

"Remember Our servants Abraham, Issac, and Jacob - all men of strength and vision." (38:45)

They had strength in fulfilling the truth, and they had vision of religion. Almighty described them with having perfect knowledge of truth and perfectly fulfilling it. The people in this regard are of four categories:

1. The first are those who are the noblest among the creatures of Allah.
2. Those who are opposite of them; they have no vision of religion and no power to fulfil its due. They are majority of the people, seeing them is the thorn in the eye and fever of the souls and the illness of the hearts. They crumble in the towns, raise the prices and their company produces only shame and disgrace.
3. Those who have vision and knowledge of truth but they are weak and lack power to fulfil the due and call others to it. This is the condition of the weak believer while the strong believer is better and dearer to Allah.
4. Those who have power and determination but they have little vision of religion. They are almost unable to differentiate between the friends of the Merciful and the allies of Satan. They regard every black object a date and every white thing as fat. They consider swelling as fatness and useful medicine as poison.

They are not suitable for the leadership in religion. It is only the first category which is entitled for that. Allah, the Glorious, said:

"We raised leaders among them, guiding by Our command when they became patient and then firmly believed in Our signs." (32:24)

Almighty informed that these people achieved leadership of religion by patience and certainty. These are the people who have been chosen by Allah, the Most High, from the group of losers. He swore by the time, which is the period of the losers and successful ones that other than these are among the losers. He said:

"By the time, man is in loss, except for those who believe, do good deeds, urge one another to the truth, and urge one another to steadfastness." (103:1-3)

They did not stop at the knowledge of truth and showing steadfastness on it, but went ahead by urging one another, encouraging and inciting on it. When other people beside them were losers, it becomes clear that sins and misdeeds blocks the vision and makes them unable to understand. His power and determination becomes weak and he has no patience. Sometimes his perception turns upside down and sees false as true and true as false, good as bad and bad as good. He reverses in his walk and turns from his journey to Allah and the Hereafter to the resting place of the improper souls, which had agreed with the worldly life. He has found peace in it being neglectful of Allah and His signs, and abandoned making preparation for meeting with Him.

If there was no other punishment for the sins beside this, it was enough to call the man to be away from them and to abandon them. Allah is to be turned to, for help.

The righteous deeds fill the heart with light, make it clear and polish it; they give it power and make it firm. As a result it becomes like refined mirror in its brightness and clearness and is filled with light. When Satan approaches it, its light chases him in the form of clearly burning flames, which shoot the eavesdropping devils. Satan is scared of this heart much more than the fright of the goats from lion. A man with this powerful heart knocks down Satan and makes him fall on the ground. The band of devils gathers around him and asks one another: 'What is the matter with him?'

It is said: 'A human has struck him. He has been affected by an evil eye of a human. Is this heart comparable to a heart which is dark from every side and filled with various desires? Satan has taken this corrupt heart as his abode and prepared it for his resting. In the morning he greets the man and says: 'You be ransom by a companion who is not successful in his world or his life to come! Satan says to him:

'I am your partner in the world and on the Day of Resurrection, and you are my partner in every place.

If you end up in the abode of misfortune, I and you are together in trouble and disgrace.'

Allah, the Most High, said:

"Whoever turns away from the revelations of the Lord of Mercy, We assign an evil as a comrade for him. They bar them from the right path, and they think that they are well guided. When such a person comes to Us, he will say (to his comrade): 'If you had been as far away from me as east is from west. What an evil comrade! (It will be said to them): You have done wrong. It will never benefit you that Day, when you have wronged, that you are together partners in the punishment." (43:36-39)

Almighty said that anyone who turns away from His remembrance, which is His Book that He revealed to His Messenger, and he averts, and closes his eyes from it, and his understanding is blocked from contemplating and knowing the message of Allah, Almighty will assign a Satan for him as a punishment for his aversion from His Book. The devil will be his permanent comrade and will not part from his company whether he is at home or on journey, he becomes his ally and associate. What a wicked ally! What a wicked associate!

Almighty also informed that Satan diverts his companion and friend from the way which leads to Allah and to His Paradise, but the misguided and deluded person thinks that he is on the path of guidance. When the two partners meet on the Day of Resurrection, one of them will say to the other: 'I wish that there was distance between me and you like the distance between east and west! You were bad companion for me in the world. You misguided me from the path of guidance after it came to me and prevented me from the truth and deluded me till I perished, and today you are the wicked comrade for me.

When an afflicted person is joined by others, he feels little bit of consolation and comfort; Allah said that it would not work in the case of those who are put together in punishment. The comrade will not gain any rest or any comfort by the punishment of his partner, though the mishaps in the world when become general becomes sort of solace as al-Khansa' said about her brother Sakhr:

'If there were not many people around me crying on their brothers, I would have killed myself.
They are not yelling on people like my brother, but I console myself by their moaning.
Sakhr, I am not going to forget you till I part my life and enter my grave.'

Allah, the Most Glorious, deprived the people of the Fire that much of comfort by saying:

"It will never benefit you this Day, when you have wronged, to have partners in punishment." (43:39)

50. Sins are support against the human for his enemy

Another painful punishment for the sinner is that his sins give support to his enemy against him. They are like army giving help to the devil to fight him. Allah, the Exalted, tried this man with an enemy who does not part with him at any moment. He is a companion who does not leave him or ignore him. He and his forces see you from where you do not see them. He exerts his efforts to trick him and does not spare any scheme through which he can cause him harm. He gets support against him from his tribe of the devils of Jinn and Satan of the humans. He has set nets for him and devised havoc for him. He extended traps around him and set snares and wires around him. Then he called his aids: 'Take your enemy and the enemy of your father; he should not escape you! It should not happen that he gets Paradise and you end up in Hell, his share is mercy and yours is curse. You are aware of what I and you suffered from disgrace and rejection and being thrown away from the mercy of Allah. It was all because of him. So make effort to make them our partners in this tribulation as the company of their righteous people has eluded us.
Allah, the Exalted, told us all this about our enemy and advised us to be careful and prepare ourselves against his tricks.

When Allah Almighty knew that Adam and his children have been tried with this enemy and he has got power over them, He strengthened them with armies and troops to combat him. He also aided their enemy with troops and soldiers to fight them. Almighty established the field of Jihad in this world for the whole period of life, which is in comparison to the Hereafter like a single breath. He, the Glorious, purchased from the believers their souls and their wealth in return for the Garden. They fight in the way of Allah, and kill and are killed. He affirmed that it was a promise confirmed in His noblest Books, the Torah, the Gospel and the Qur'an. He also said that there is no one more faithful to his promise than Him, glory is for Him! Then He ordered them to be glad with this transaction, if someone is interested in realising the value of it, he should look at the purchaser and at the price given in it, and the One on whose hand the transaction has been concluded. Which success is greater than this? Which trade is more profitable than it?

Then Allah, the Exalted, affirmed this matter by saying:

"You who believe, shall I show you a bargain that will save you from painful torment? Have faith in Allah and His Messenger and struggle for His cause with your possessions and your persons – that is better for you, if only you knew – He will forgive your sins, admit you into Gardens below which streams flow, into pleasant dwellings in the Gardens of eternity. That is the supreme triumph. He will give other things that will please you: Help of Allah and imminent breakthrough. (Prophet), give good tiding to the believers." (61:10-13)

Allah, the Exalted, did not give power to Satan over His believing servant, who is the most beloved creature to Him, but because the struggle is the dearest thing to Him. People involved in struggle are the highest in rank and closest to Him. Allah Almighty gave the banner of this battle to the cream of His creatures and attached it to their hearts which is the place of His recognition, love, servitude, sincerity, trust in Him and turning to Him. Almighty assigned the responsibility of this battle to it, and supported it with the forces of angels who do not part with them. He said:

"He has assigned for each person angels before him and behind, watching over him by Allah's command." (13:11)

These angels succeed one another, when one of them goes another takes his place. They support him, enjoining him what is good, encouraging him and remind him of the promise of Allah and say: 'It is only the patience of an hour which will result in the comfort for ever.'

Allah, the Glorious, sent another support to the believer in the form of His Revelation and His Speech. He sent His Messenger and revealed to him His Book. This supplied them with strength after strength, and support upon support, help upon help and force after force. He aided them with the power of reasoning as a minister and manager; and with knowledge as advisor and counsellor. He further supported them with faith to consolidate them and give support, and with certainty to clear the reality of the matter so that he sees what Allah has promised His allies and His party for the struggle against His enemies. The reason arranges the natter of His troops; knowledge guides them to the tactics of the battle and its strategic positions; faith provides them with the strength and patience, and certainty makes them advance and launch real attacks.

Almighty provided further support to the man engaged in this war by physical and moral forces. He appointed the eye his vanguard, the ear his reporter, the tongue his spokesman, the hands and the feet his aids. Furthermore, He made His angels and the carriers of His Throne seek forgiveness for them, and ask Him to save them from the evil deeds and admit them in Paradise. Almighty undertook Himself their defence and announced: They are My party, and the party of Allah is sure to succeed. He said:

"They are the party of Allah, and certainly the party of Allah is successful." (58:22)

He said: They are My troops, **"and the troops of Allah are going to be victorious." (37:173)**

Almighty taught His obedient servants the tactics of this war and struggle, and put them in four words, and said:

"You who believe, be steadfast, endure, be stationed, and be mindful of Allah, so that you may succeed." (3:200)

The duty of this struggle will not be fulfilled without these four qualities. The person will not be able to be steadfast unless he watches the enemy and guards the heart lest the enemy enters it. He is also required to guard the front of enemy's confrontation and combat. When he watches his enemy, he needs another matter which is to take up position which means to guard the frontiers of the eye, the ear, the tongue, stomach, the hand and the leg. These are the areas through which the enemy enters and roams around and spoils anything he has power on it. Keeping position means to guard these frontiers and not to leave them abandoned to give the enemy an opportunity to enter through them.

The Companions of the Messenger of Allah, may Allah's blessing and peace be upon him, who were the best of the people after the prophets and the messengers and more watchful of Satan, left the position they were ordered not to leave on the day of Uhud, and the enemy entered from it and the result was what it was.

The pillar of all these three matters on which they stand is consciousness of Allah, the Great. The steadfastness, endurance and positioning will not work without consciousness of Allah, and it in itself is not found without steadfastness.

Now look at yourself the meeting of the two troops and combat of two armies, how it is in your favour sometimes and against you another time. The king of the disbelievers comes with his armies and troops and finds the heart sitting in its fortress on his kingdom, his orders are carried out by its supporters and its troops are surrounding it fighting and defending its territory. The enemy does not get a chance to attack unless he stirs up some of his commanders and troops against him. He asks which one is the closest and most intimate person to him? He is told that it was the soul. He orders his aids to enter from the side of its desire. He says to them; 'Look at the objects of its desires and love, try to make promises and incite desires in it, print the image of its beloved in it in its sleep and waking. When it finds comfort in it and relaxes, throw on it the hooks and snares, then drag it to your side. If you succeed in attracting the heart and it becomes under your control, you have taken the frontiers of the eye, the ear, the tongue, the mouth, the hand and the leg. Firmly hold position on these fronts. Once you entered the heart you will be able to kill it or arrest it or injure it badly. Never abandon these fronts and do not let any contingent get access through them to the heart; it will kick you out of it. If you are overpowered, make effort to weaken the contingent and make it unable to reach the heart. If it reaches it, it will be weak and will not be able to do anything.

When you hold control on these fronts it prevent the front of the eye from making its look contemplative, but make it amusement and attraction and pastime. If it eavesdrops to take a lesson, spoil it by the look of negligence, attraction and desire. This will be closer to him, more attractive and lighter. Take hold of the front of the eye. Through it you can achieve your aim. I did not corrupt the children of Adam with anything more effective than looking. I sow with it the seed of desire in the heart, then water it with the false hopes, and continue making promise and arousing desire till his intention becomes strong. After that I drag him to get out of the protection. Do not, therefore, neglect this front, and spoil it as much as you can. Make its matter easy for him and say to him: What value has the look which calls you to glorify the Creator and contemplate on His unique creation while the beauty of this form which has been created so that the one who looks at it can argue for His Power! Allah has not created your eyes in vain, and He did not create this form to barricade it from looking. If you find that the man is lacking intelligence and understanding, tell him: 'This form is a manifestation of the Truth and presentation of Him'. In this way invite him to the unity of the existence. If he shows resistance then tell him to believe in fully or partly incarnation. Do not agree from him in less than that. He will be from among the brothers of the Christians. Preach him of decency, modesty, engagement in worship and keeping away from the world. Hunt through him the ignorant people. He is the closest of my deputies and biggest of my soldiers; rather I become his soldier and among his troops.

(Iblis continues giving instructions to his gang)

Then block the front of the ear and do not allow anything to enter it, which may spoil your work. Try your best to make sure that nothing but falsehood enters through it. Falsehood is light on the soul and considered sweet and good by it. Choose the sweetest and most charming words for the reasons and mix them with what is appealing to the souls. Speak the word, if you find the man paying attention to it, mix it with others similar to it. If you see that he appreciates something, speak about it constantly. Be careful and do not let anything of the words of Allah or His Messenger or sincere people enter from this front. If you are overpowered in this matter and something of good entered through it, obstruct his way to understand it or contemplate or think about it and get lesson from it. Do it by putting something contrary to it or by terrifying it and frightening him by putting in his mind that it is a very difficult matter and a very heavy burden, you should not bother about it. You can present it to him by reducing its importance and inspiring him that it is better to engage in something higher than this, and more difficult and strange for the people, tell him that everybody is involved in it. The truth is neglected and its promoter is subject of enmity of the people, what is more useful should be adopted etc. In this way you may put in his heart falsehood. Try to put it in his heart in any acceptable and easy form, and present the truth in a detestable and difficult shape.

If you are interested in understanding it, look at the Devils from among the humans how they put commanding what is good and forbidding what is evil in the form of futile talks, following the mistakes of the people, indulging in unbearable problems and creating sedition among them, etc. They present following of the Sunnah and description of the Lord Himself in the form of anthropomorphism, comparison and descriptive designation. They consider Allah's being above His creature and establishing Himself on His Throne and being separate from His creature as confining Him to a place. They regard His descending to the lowest sky and calling: 'Who is there to ask Me, so that I can give him' as movement and change. They name what He has described for Himself as hand and face limbs and parts of the body. They call His acts accidental and His Attributes contingent, then they deny those characters which He has mentioned for Himself. They put in the minds of ingenious and less prudent people that attaching those Attributes which the Book of Allah and the Sunnah of the Messenger, Allah's blessing and peace be upon him, have said leads to this result. They try to present this denial of the Attributes in the form of purification and magnification. Many people of less understanding accept a thing in a word and reject it in another word. Allah, the Exalted, said:

"And thus We assigned for every prophet an enemy – devils from mankind and Jinn. They suggest alluring words to one another in order to deceive." (6:112)

Allah called their words alluring, which is falsehood as the speaker decorates and embellishes as much as he can, then puts it to the ears of the listener who is deceived.

The aim is to say that Satan has taken position at the front of the ear and does not allow entering it except what is detrimental to the person, and does not allow anything useful to go through it. If something useful enters without his choice, he spoils it.

(Iblis continues giving instructions to his band)

Take position in the matter of tongue because it is very important. Make it utter things which are harmful for him and not useful. Endeavour to stop it from saying anything useful for him like remembrance of Allah, seeking forgiveness from Him, reciting His Book, giving sincere advice to His servants and passing the beneficial knowledge to other. There are two great matters in this matter, anyone of them you get, will be useful to you:

1. To utter false words, the one who speaks false words is one of your brothers and the biggest soldier and helper among you.
2. Keeping silence from speaking truth. The one who keeps quiet from truth is a dumb brother of yours whereas the first one is speaking brother. The second brother may be more useful for you. Did you not

hear the saying of the advisor: 'The one who speaks false word is speaking Satan, and the one who keeps quiet is a dumb Satan?

Keep hold of your position on this front and make sure that he does not speak truth or refrains from falsehood. Encourage him by every means to utter futile words and frighten him from speaking truth.
Remember my children that I destroy the children of Adam by the tool of the tongue, and brought them down on their faces in the Fire. How many people I grabbed from this front and killed them and injured and made prisoners!
I give you an advice to remember it. One of you should utter through the tongue of your mate from the human being and let the other appreciate it, be amazed and like it and ask his brother to repeat it.

Join your forces and support one another against the human; enter to them through every door and wait for them at every lookout post. Did you not hear my swearing to their Lord when I said?

"Because You have put me in the wrong, I will lie in wait for them all on Your straight path: I will come at them, from their front and their back, from their right and their left – and You find that most of them are ungrateful." (7:16-17)

Do you not see that I sat on every path for the children of Adam? When I miss a path I sit on another till I achieve my objective in full or in parts. Their Messenger has given them warning about it saying:

"Satan sat on every path of the son of Adam: he sat on the path of Islam and said: 'Are you going to embrace Islam and abandon your and your fathers' religion?' He sat on the path of emigration and said: 'Will you emigrate and leave your land and your heaven?' The man did not listen to him and emigrated; then he sat on the path of Jihad and said: 'Will you take part in Jihad and killed, and your wealth will be divided and your wife will be married?"[175]

In this way you should sit on every path of good deeds. When one of them intends to give out charity, try to stop him from it saying: 'You want to give out your money and remain like this beggar, and you and he become equal? Did you not hear what I put on the tongue of a man who was asked by another for charity: 'This is our wealth if we give it to you, we become like you?'

---

[175] Ahmad (3: 483), al-Nisa'i (6: 21), Ibn Hibban (4593), Tabarani (6558)

Sit down on the path of the pilgrimage and say to the intending pilgrims: 'The road is full of dangers and hardship; the traveller is subject to losing his life and possession.' In this way sit down on the rest of the paths of good deeds and discourage people from them and describe their difficulties and risks. Then take position on the ways of evil deeds and beautify them in the eyes of the children of Adam and present them in attractive forms. Use women as the biggest tool to delude them. Approach them from their side; they will be very helpful in your job.

Do not forget the front of the hands and feet; try to stop them from holding anything harmful to you or proceeding to something detrimental to your cause.

Remember that the greatest help in stationing yourselves on these positions will come from making the evil commanding soul (نفس الامّارة) your ally. Help it and get help from it, strengthen it and get strength from it, and fight with it against the tranquil soul (نفس المطمئنة). Spare no effort in crippling it and destroying its power. This will be possible only by cutting off its sources; when its sources are cut off and the sources of the evil commanding soul becomes strong and it comes under your control, dislodge the heart from its fortress and get it out of its kingdom. Install in its place the evil commanding soul; it will command what you like and desire and will not bring about what you dislike. It will not go against anything you advise it to do; when you suggest something it will set out to do it promptly. If you sense that the heart is trying to return to its kingdom, and you wish to be safe from it, contract marriage between it and the soul. Beautify the soul and decorate it and present it to the heart in the most possible attractive shape of a bride and say to it: 'Enjoy the taste of this union and relish the company of this bride. You had tasted the bitterness of the war and encountered the pain of stab of spears and blow of the sword. Compare this delight of this peace with the bitterness of that war. Let the war end; it is not the matter of one day but it is a continuous war linked with death, and your strength cannot sustain a permanent war.'

My children, take support from two great soldiers with them, you will never be defeated:

The **first** is the soldier of negligence. Try to make by all means the hearts of the children of Adam neglectful of Allah, the Most Glorious, and the Last Home. There is nothing more effective in achieving your goal than that. When the heart is unmindful of Allah, the Exalted, you will have access to it and a chance to misguide it.

Second is the soldier of desires. Beautify them in their hearts and present them in attractive shape in their eyes; then launch attack with these two soldiers. There is nothing more successful in the children of Adam than these two. Seek help of negligence in the matter of desires, and help of desires in the matter of negligence. Join them among the neglectful and then use them on the men involved in remembrance. One person cannot overcome five; with the neglectful there are two Satan which make the number four and the Satan of mindful becomes the fifth. When you see a group of people coming together on what is harmful to you like the remembrance of Allah or discussion of His command, prohibition and His religion and you fail to disperse them, seek help of their kind worthless humans, bring them close to them and disturb them by them.

In short, prepare for your works champions, and thrust yourselves on every man from the door of his desire and longing. Support him on them and help him to achieve them. If Allah has ordered them to exercise patience and endurance against you, and to take position on the front to combat you; then you as well undertake patience, endurance and hold position against them. Grab every opportunity against them at the time of lust and anger, you may not find a better opportunity against the sons of Adam than in these two conditions.

Remember that there will be someone who is in the control of passion; his control over the anger is weak and can be overpowered. Take him from the side of craving and leave the side of anger aside. You will find others who are under the control of anger, do not leave the way of desire for them and do not abandon its front. Anyone who cannot control himself at the time of anger, he is very likely not to control himself at the time of anger from the side of craving. Join his anger and craving, mix one of them with the other. Seduce him to the lust from the side of anger, and to the anger from the way of lust.

Remember that you have no stronger weapon against the human being than these two weapons. I was able to get their parents out of Paradise from desire, and cast enmity among their children through anger. By it I cut off their blood relations, shed their blood, and it was the cause for one of the sons of Adam to kill his brother.

Know that the anger is a flame in the heart of the son of Adam, and desire is a fire which is roused from his heart. The fire is extinguished by water, prayer, remembrance and glorification of Allah. Do not give the son of Adam any chance to make ablution and perform prayer when he is angry or craving. This will extinguish the fire of anger and desire in him. This was instructed by their Prophet. He said:

"Anger is a flame in the heart of the son of Adam. Do you not see his eyes become red and his jugular veins are swelled? When one of you feels that, he should perform ablution."[176]

He also said to them:

"Fire is put out by water."[177]

Allah has commanded them to seek help against you by patience and prayer. Obstruct their way to it and make them forget it; seek help against them by lust and anger. The most effective and forceful weapon of you against them are negligence and following the lust. The strongest weapon of them and the most impregnable fortress against you are remembrance of Allah, and disobedience of the desire. When you notice a man going against his desire, run away from his shade and do not go near him.

The point is that evil deeds and sins are weapon and reinforcement which a man supplies to his enemies. By them he helps the enemies against himself; they fight him by his weapon and get support against him. It is the extreme ignorance. It is said in the following line:
'Enemies cannot harm an ignorant man as much as he harms himself.'

The amazing matter is that the servant endeavours to humiliate himself and claims that he is doing well to him. He makes effort to deprive himself from the highest honour and status and thinks that he is trying to bring him good luck. He takes pain in humiliation and polluting his soul and feels that he is working for its promotion and raising its rank.

Some pious people used to say in his sermon:
'There are many who disgrace their souls and think that they are honouring them, they cause humiliation to them and think that they are raising them up, he belittles them and feels that he magnifies them, and he destroys them and thinks that he is fulfilling their dues. It is enough as ignorance that a man is with his enemy against himself, and causes by his actions much harm which his enemy was unable to do.'

---

[176] Ahmad (3: 19, 61), al-Bayhaqi in Sha'b al-iman (20289)
[177] Abu Dawud (4784), Ahmad (4: 226)

Allah is the only source of help!

51. Sinful acts are cause of forgetting self

Another devastating result of the evil deeds is that they make the slave to forget himself, and when he forgets his soul, he neglects it, destroys and ruins it.

If it is said: 'How can a person forget his soul? If he forgets his soul, what can he remember? What is the meaning of forgetting oneself?

It will be said:

'Yes, he forgets his soul regrettably. Allah, the Great, said:

"Do not be like those who forgot Allah, so He made them forget their own souls. They are real defiant." (59:19)

Almighty punished those who forgot Him in two ways:

One, He forgets them.

Two, He makes them forget themselves.

Allah's forgetting the slave means that He ignores him, abandons and leaves him alone and neglects him. His ruin is closer to him than the hand is to the mouth. As for making the man to forget himself it denotes that Almighty makes him forget his high fortunes and the causes of his soul's happiness, success and welfare and the matters which lead to its perfection. He makes him to forget, the do not pass to his thought, he does not remember and does not show interest in them. He also makes him to forget his faults and shortcomings and never thinks about removing them and reforming himself. Almighty also makes him to forget the illnesses of his soul and heart and the pain caused by them. He does not move to remove the symptoms and the disease which ultimately lead to his ruin and perish. He becomes sick weakened by illness, which is taking him to death. He does not realise his illness and does not bother to cure it. This is the most severe punishment of all the people high and low.

Which punishment is more devastating than the condition of a man who neglects and ignores his soul, forgets its interests , suffering, treatment and the causes of its happiness, success, welfare and everlasting life in the permanent delight?

Whoever pays attention to this issue will come to realise that the most of the people have forgotten themselves and caused the loss of their share from Allah. They have sold them for a cheap price with a loss. This will appear to them at the time of death, and will appear more clearly on the

Day of Resurrection. On that Day the servant will realise that he was duped in the transaction he made for him in this home. He was cheated in the trade he entered for the life to come; everyone involves in trade in this world for his next life.

The losers are those who believe that they have gained profit by purchasing the life of this world and its delight for the joy of the Hereafter and its pleasures. They squandered the pleasant materials of the worldly life, enjoyed them, and were pleased and content with them. They endeavoured to acquire them and got busy in selling, buying, and got engaged in trade, and sold the later for sooner, credit for cash and absent for available. They said that it was the scrupulousness. One of them said: 'Take what you see and leave what you heard of. How can I sell what is present and seen in this life for an absent commodity in another life beyond this?'

This is the result of the weakness of the faith and power of the motive of desire and love of the present, and following the others in this trend. Most people are involved in this trade of loss, about them Allah said:

"They are the ones who have bought the life of this world at the price of the Hereafter, so the punishment will not be lightened for them, nor will they get any help." (2:86)

Almighty also said:

"Their trade did not reap profit and they were not rightly guided." (2:16)

When the Day of mutual neglect comes, their loss in this trade will be clear and their souls will shatter in painful regret.

The people of the profit sold the vanishing for the lasting, contemptible for precious, and small for great. They said: 'What is the period of this world from the beginning to the end so that we sell our share of Allah Almighty and the next life for it?' What a person gets in this short period is in fact like a dream of slumber, which has no relation with the abode of permanency. Allah, the Exalted said:

"On the Day He gathers them together, it will be as if they have stayed (in the world) no longer than a single hour, and they will recognise one another." (10:45)

"They ask you about the Hour, saying, 'When will it arrive?', but how can you tell that? Its time is known only to your Lord; you are only sent to warn those who fear it. On the Day they see it, (and) it

**will seem they lingered (in this life) an evening or its morning."
(79:42-46)**

**"On the Day they see what they had been warned about, it will
seem to them that they lingered no more than a single hour of a
single day. This is warning." (46:35)**

**"How many years were you on earth? They will say: 'We stayed a
day or a part of a day, but ask those who keep count.' He will say:
'You stayed but a little, if you had only known.' (23:112-114)**

**"When the trumpet is   sounded and We gather the sinful,
sightless, they will murmur with one another, 'You stayed only ten
days – We know best what they say – but the more perceptive of
them will say: 'Your stay was only a single day." (20:102-104)**

This is the reality of this world when the Day of Judgement comes. When
the evildoers come to know that their stay in the world was brief and
there was a home beside this one, which is the lasting home and the place
of permanent remaining they will realise that it was the biggest loss to
sell the everlasting house for the vanishing one. That Day the profit of
their trade and the amount of what they bought will become clear to them.
Everyone in this world is involved in trade, selling and buying.
The Prophet, Allah's blessing and peace be upon him, said:

**"Everyone goes out in the morning, sell his soul, he either release it
or destroys it."[178]**

Allah, the Glorious, aid:

**"Allah has purchased the persons and possessions of the believers
in return for the Garden – they fight in the way of Allah, they kill
and are killed – this is a true promise given by Him in the Torah,
the Gospel and the Qur'an. Who could be more faithful to his
promise than Allah? So be happy with the bargain you have made,
that is the supreme triumph." (10:111)**

This is the first payment of the price of this trade, so get involved, O poor
ones. The one who is unable for this price there is something else; if you
are among those who belong to this group of traders, pay the price.
Allah has said:

---

[178] Muslim (223)

"(The believers are) those who turn to Allah in repentance, who worship and praise Him; who fast, bow down and prostrate themselves; who order what is good, forbid what is wrong and observe Allah' limits. Give glad news to such believers." (10:112)

"You who believe, shall I show a bargain that will save you from painful torment? Have faith in Allah and His Messenger and struggle for the cause of Allah with your possessions and your persons that is better for you, if only you knew." (61:10-11)

The point is that sins make the person forget his share from this profitable trade, and keep him busy in losing business; and it is enough as torment. Allah's help is to be sought.

52. Sins eliminate present and future pleasures

One of the devastating punishments of the wicked acts is that they eliminate the existing bounties and barricade the way of incoming favours. In this way the acts of disobedience terminate the existing bounties and cut off the way of incoming ones. Allah's favours are preserved only through His obedience and they are acquired by doing His prescribed duties. Allah, the Most High, has fixed cause and effect for everything: a cause which brings them and a disaster to destroy them. He has made the cause of His favours His obedience, and the disastrous cause to prevent them are sinful acts. When Allah wishes to preserve His grace for a servant, He inspires him to take care of it by obeying Him, and when He wishes to take it away from him, He leaves him alone and he gets involved in disobedience.

The amazing thing is that the servant knows it by experiencing it in himself and others, and by hearing the news of the people who lost the favours of Allah by disobedience of Him. Yet he insists on committing the sins as though he is excluded from this rule or ruled out from this general principle. It seems that he feels that this matter is applicable only to other people but not to him, and it is for the rest of people and not for him! Which ignorance is more far reaching than this! Which wrongdoing is above it! The judgement belongs to Allah, the Most High, the Great.

53. Offensive works keep the angels away from the offender

One of the destructive consequences of the offensive acts is that angels keep away from sinner, his friend and the most useful and sincere person whose closeness is the cause of happiness for him. That is the angel who has been assigned to him. Instead his enemy gets a chance to come close to him. It is Satan who is the most deceptive creature and most harmful for him. When the slave disobeys Allah Almighty, the angel runs away from him according to the seriousness of the disobedience till he goes away a long distance in case the one, who lies.

It is narrated in a report:

'When the slave tells a lie the angel goes away one mile from him due to the bad smell of it.'[179]

If the angel gets away for one lie, what will be his distance for what is more offensive and more repugnant than that?
Some early pious man said:
'When a male commits a sin with a male, the earth cries out to Allah, the angels run away to their Lord and complain the gravity of the act they saw.'
Another early righteous person said:
'When a person enters the morning the angel and Satan rush to him. If he remembers Allah, glorifies and praises Him, the angel kicks Satan away and makes the man his friend. If he starts his day in other way, the angel deserts him and Satan takes charge of him.'
The angel continues coming closer to the servant till he gets power, judgement, control and obcdicncc for him; the angels then adopt him in his life, at the time of his death and the time of his resurrection as Allah, the Exalted, has said:

"Those who say, 'Our lord is Allah,' and take the straight path towards Him, the angels come down to them and say: 'Have no fear or grief, but rejoice in the good news of Paradise, which you have been promised. We are your allies in this world and in the world to come'." (41:30-31)

---

[179] Tirmidhi (2039), Abu Nu'aym in al-Hilyah (8: 197). It is a weak tradition.

The angel who takes charge of him is the most sincere, the most helpful and the most caring for him. He gives him support, teaches him, strengths his heart and helps him. Allah, the Most Glorious, said:

"When your Lord revealed to the angels: 'I am with you, give the believers firmness." (8:12)

The angel says to him at the time of his death:
"Do not be scared and do not grieve and get good tiding of what will please you."

He also keeps him firm with the firmly rooted word at a time when he will be in great need in this worldly life, at the time of death and at the time of questioning in the grave.

There is no one more helpful for the servant than the angel who keeps company with him. He is his companion when he is awake, sleeping, in his life, at the time of his death and his grave. He is the companion in his loneliness, a friend in his privacy, talks to him in secret, fights against his enemy and defends him by supporting him against the enemy. He promises and gives him good news and encourages him to confirm the truth. It is said in a report:

'The angel has a visit to the heart of the son of Adam and Satan has a visit to it. The angel gives good news and the belief of the promise; Satan gives the news of evil and denying of the truth.'[180]

When the angels becomes closer to the servant, he speaks on his tongue and puts right word on it; when he goes away from him, Satan comes close and speaks on his tongue and put lies and indecent words on it. It is noticed that the angel speaks on the tongue of the man and Satan speaks on the tongue of the other.

It is reported in a Hadith:

"Tranquillity speaks on the tongue of 'Umar."[181]

When one of the people heard a good word from a righteous man he said: 'It is the angel who put this on your tongues, and when he heard

---

[180] Tirmidhi (2988), Ibn Hibban (997), Abu Ya'la (4999) Al-Bayhaqi in Shu'ab (4187) The chain is weak
[181] Ahmad (1: 106)Tabarani (9: 184) See Majma' al-zawa'id (9: 67)

something bad, he would say that it was put on his tongue by Satan. The angel casts truth in the heart and puts it on the tongue whereas Satan casts falsehood in the heart and puts it on the tongue.

So the evildoer's punishment is that his work turns away from him his supporter whose closeness and friendship bring happiness to him, and brings his enemy who is the cause of his distress, corruption and destruction close to him. The angel defends the servant and repels from him any foolish man who abuses him and acts immorally. It happened in the presence of the Prophet, Allah's blessing and peace be upon him, when two people engaged in dispute and one of them started using foul language against the other while he was silent. Then he spoke some words to reply the man. The Prophet, Allah's blessing and peace be upon him, stood up and left. He said: 'Messenger of Allah, when I replied the man some of his words, you left? The Prophet, Allah's blessing and peace be upon him, said:

"An angel was defending you, but when you spoke against the man, Satan came in; I was not to sit with Satan."[182]

When a Muslim prays for the benefit of his Muslim brother in absence, the angel says *Amen* on his prayer and says: 'You also get similar to that.'[183]

When a man completes reading the opening chapter, the angels say *Amen* on his prayer.[184]

When a sincere Muslim who follows the way of Allah and His Messenger's Sunnah, commits a sin, the carriers of the Throne and the angels around it seek forgiveness for him. When a believer goes to bed having ablution an angel passes night in his dress; whenever he wakes up in the night, the angel seeks forgiveness for him.[185]

So the angel of the believer defends him, fights and repels attacks against him. He also teaches him, makes him firm and encourages him. The man is required not to misbehave with him, cause him harm and try to repel him because he is his guest and neighbour. When treating with honour a human guest and doing good to the neighbour are requirement of the

---

[182] Ahmad (2: 436), Abu Dawud (4896) The story is connected with Abu Bakr al-Siddiq.
[183] Muslim (2732)
[184] Bukhari (780), Muslim (410)
[185] Ibn Hibban (1051), al-Bazzar (288). See Najma' al-zawa'id (1; 226)

faith, then what do you think about honouring the noblest guest and best neighbour and most righteous one. When the person treats the angel unfairly and immorally in any way, he prays Allah against him and says: 'May Allah do not repay you well!' He prays for his welfare when he honours him and behaves in a nice way.

Some of the Companions said: 'There are people with you who do not part with you, so honour them and be ashamed of them.'
No one is more despicable than the one does not feel ashamed from the honourable and high ranking being, and does not respect him and show reverence to him. Allah, the Glorious, pointed out to this point in the following verses:

"Over you stand watchers, noble recorders who know what you do." (82:10-12)

It means that you should feel ashamed from these noble watchers, show respect to them and be careful to be seen by them in acts which you do not like to be seen by them. The angel feels offended from what the human being is offended. When a human feels offended from the one who does immoral act and openly disobeys Allah even though he himself be involved in similar act, then what do you think about the hurt of the noble recorder angels? Allah's help is sought!

54. Rebellious acts lead to destruction in the world and the Hereafter

Another destructive result of the disobedient activities is that they manifest the causes of perish of the servant in this world and the Hereafter. Sins are diseases when they take root, they kill. As the body does not remain healthy without nourishment which can preserve its strength, and expulsion of evil vices and spoiled components which will kill the man if left unattended, and an antidote which can protect the body from taking what is harmful and injurious; in the same way the life of the heart will not be safe without the nutritious amount of faith and righteous deeds that can preserve its strength. It is also in need of sincere repentance to expel the corrupt and spoiled materials, and in need of antidote to protect its health and keep it away from what is harmful for it. *Taqwa*, consciousness of Allah, includes all these three matters, if anything is missing, the consciousness will be reduced accordingly.

When it is clear then it should be noted that sins are opposed to these three items; they produce the harmful conditions, cause corruption to stop the antidote from working and prevent the evacuation by the sincere repentance. Look at an ill body which had gathered the spoiled components and the causes of illness, which are not taken out. How can it survive and preserve its health? A poet said:

'You protected your body by antidotes for fear of pain. It was more appropriate for you to protect it from the Fire by keeping away from sins.'

Anyone who preserves the strength by obeying the orders, and applies the antidote by keeping away from the forbidden acts, and gets the spoiled materials out by sincere repentance, he has chosen the path of good deeds and run away from the evils. Allah's help is sought.

CHAPTER 4 - PRESCRIBED PUNISHMENT OF SINS

4.1 Sinful acts have legal punishments

If the aforesaid punishments do not have any impact on your heart, remind yourself of religious legal punishments which Allah and His Messenger have assigned for the crimes. For instance cutting off the hand for stealing the value of three dirham, cutting the hand and leg for plundering the possession and persons of innocent people, striking by lashes the one who accuses a chaste person of adultery and lashing eighty strokes someone who drank wine. There are other punishments for other crimes like stoning to death a man who had committed adultery, this punishment was reduced in the case of unmarried person and he is to be lashed hundred lashes and to be banished from his home to strange land for one year. If a slave commits this crime with a close relative, he is to be killed. The same applies to the man who leaves an obligatory prayer or uttered a word of disbelief. The Messenger ordered to kill a man who had intercourse with a male like him together with the man with whom he committed the crime. He commanded to kill a man who committed this crime with an animal together with the animal itself. He was determined to burn the houses of those who kept away from the prayer in congregation and many other punishments which he prescribed for crimes. He decided them by his wisdom in accordance with the motives of the crimes and deterrents from them.

If the deterrent was natural, and there was no natural motive for the crime, he was content with declaration of its prohibition and sort of admonition without prescribing any punishment like eating excrement, drinking blood and eating carrion.

Where there was innate motive he assigned the punishment according to the gravity of its bad impact and the natural motive. Since the innate desire for adultery is one of the most powerful one, its punishment was the most horrid killing, and the easiest punishment for it was the severest beating by lashes in addition to banishment from the town for one year. The crime of sodomy contained both causes so its punishment was death at any rate. The motive of the crime of theft was strong and its harm great, the hand was to be cut off. Consider the Legislator's wisdom in severing the limb which was used in committing the crime when he decided to spoil the hand and the foot of the robber. He did not rule cutting off the tongue of the one who accused chaste person because the evil effect of it was more than the crime, so he ruled causing pain to his whole body by striking by lashes.

If someone asks: 'Why did he not spoil the organ of the adulterer which he used in committing the crime?'
It will be said: He did not do it for the following reasons:
First, its impact was more than the evil of the crime; it would lead to eliminate the offspring and subject it to annihilation.
Second, the private organ is a hidden limb, its cutting off will not lead to achieving the objective of the punishment, which is to deter and warn other criminals unlike cutting of the hand.
Third, only one hand is cut off, he has another hand which he can use, but there is only one organ of recreation.
Fourth, the joy of the adulterer was felt by all the body, it was better to include the whole body in punishment rather to punish one particular part. This shows that the punishments of the Shari'ah are perfect, very reasonable and more appropriate for the objective.
The point is that the sins either have the religious punishment or decreed one; Allah may combine them together for someone or remove altogether from the one who turns to Him in repentance and reforms his behaviour.

4.2 Punishments are religious and decreed

The punishments of the criminal acts are two types: religious or decreed. If the religious one was implemented, the decreed one will be erased or made lighter. Allah, the Exalted, is not going to join the two punishments for a person unless one is not enough to eliminate the cause of the crime and did not remove the problem. If the religious punishments are neglected, they will remain in decree, which may be harsher than the religious one or less than that. But it will be comprehensive where the religious punishment is particular. Allah, the Most High, does not assign religious punishment except in the case of a man who committed the crime or was cause of it.

As for decreed punishment it is general and particular. When the sin is hidden it does not harm but the person who did it, and when it is committed openly, it harms everyone. When the people notice the abominable act and do not join together in stopping it, it is likely that Allah, the Most Sublime, embraces them all in His punishment. It has been earlier indicated that Allah Almighty has fixed the religious punishment in accordance with the damage caused by the sin and the motive of the self. He has divided them into three categories: killing, cutting off the part and lashing. He assigned killing for disbelief and what is close to it like adultery and sodomy because this damages the religions and corrupts the families and human race.

Imam Ahmad said:
'I do not know any sin more serious than adultery after killing. He quoted in support the report of Abdullah ibn Mas'ud who asked:
'Messenger of Allah, which is the greatest sin?' He replied:

"That you assign partner to Allah while He has created you."

I asked: 'then which one?'

He replied:
"That you kill your child for fear that he will eat with you."

I then asked:
'Which one is next?'

He said:
"That you commit adultery with the wife of your neighbour."[186]

Allah, the Glorious, confirmed it in the following verse:

"Those who do not invoke with Allah another deity or kill the soul which Allah has forbidden, except in pursuit of justice, and do not commit adultery" (25:68)

The Prophet, Allah's blessing and peace be upon him, mentioned from each category the highest one to make his answer agree with the question of the Companion. He asked about the most serious sins, the Prophet replied with what included the greatest of all the categories. The most offensive type of association is to assign a partner to Allah. The most atrocious kind of killing is to kill one's own child with fear that he will join the father in his food and drink; and the most heinous type of the adultery is to do it with the neighbour's wife. The crime of the adultery becomes more serious with violating the right of the person involved. Adultery, therefore, with a woman who has a husband is more horrid than committing it with a woman who has no husband. The former contains violation of the right of the husband and connecting a lineage with him, which does not belong to him. There are other harms in this and for that

---

[186] Bukhari (4477), Muslim (86)

reason committing adultery with a woman who has a husband is more horrendous than doing it with a woman who has no husband. When the husband of the woman is his neighbour, add the misbehaviour with the neighbour and harming him with the most serious offence. It is the biggest destructive act. It is reported that the Prophet, Allah's blessing and peace be upon him, said:

"Anyone whose neighbour is not safe from his atrocities will not be admitted into Paradise."[187]

There is no bigger atrocity than committing adultery with the wife of the neighbour.
If the neighbour happens to be his brother or relative, the sin of severing the bond of relation is added and the sin becomes multiple.
If the neighbour was away to fulfil the duty of Allah like prayer, search of knowledge or struggle for the cause of Allah, the sin becomes more serious. The person who committed adultery with the wife of a person who was away in the jihad will be held up on the Day of Resurrection and the victim will be said to take from his good deeds as much as he wished. The Prophet, Allah's blessing and peace be upon him, said:

"What do you think?"

That is what do you think how much of his good deeds will remain when Allah orders the wronged to take from it? This will happen on the Day when everyone will be in great need of one good deed, and the situation will be that the father will not leave the son, nor will a friend leave his friend any right which was due to him.

If the woman is a relative of him, the crime of severing her relation is added. If the man involved in illicit act is married the crime is more serious; and if he is an old man, his crime is more offensive. This person is one of those whom Allah will not speak to on the Day of Resurrection, will not purify them and for them is severe punishment.[188]
If this crime was committed in sacred month or sacred city or at a time which is respected by Allah like the times of the prayers and times of granting of the supplication, the gravity of it becomes more. Consider the seriousness of the sins and their gravity in sin and punishment according to these factors. Allah's help is to be sought.

---

[187] Muslim (46)
[188] See Muslim (107)

4.3   Theft is the cause of spoiling the wealth

Allah, the Most Glorious, had fixed the punishment of cutting hand of the thief for spoiling the wealth. It is difficult to avoid a thief because he takes the money secretly, makes hole in the house and enters it in other ways beside the doors. He is like cat and snake which break in without you noticing it. The damage of stealing is not repaired by killing the thief or by lashing him, so the best way to repair it is to cut off the part which he used in committing the crime. Lashing was prescribed for disrupting the reasons and shattering the honour by false accusation.

The legal punishments designed by Allah Almighty revolve around these three categories as the penalties also revolve around three categories: freeing a slave, which is the highest one, feeding the poor and fasting.
Allah, the Exalted, divided the crimes into three categories:
One for which He fixed a punishment. In this He did not assign any penalty, the punishment was considered enough.
For the second category he did not fix a punishment but fixed a penalty for wrong actions like having intercourse in daytime during Ramadan, having intercourse while in the condition of Ihram, *Zihar* i.e. declaring the wife as mother, killing by mistake, breaking the oath, etc.
The third category is the one in which there is no punishment or penalty. It is of two kinds:
One in which the deterrent is natural like eating filth, drinking urine or blood.
The second is that the damage of which is less than the damage for which a punishment is fixed like gazing, kissing, touching, talking and stealing one penny, etc.

He fixed expiations in three categories:

1. Something which was originally permissible then was forbidden and someone did it when it was forbidden like having intercourse in the condition of Ihram and fasting and intercourse during menstruation or confinement, unlike intercourse in anal. Some jurist joined it with intercourse during menstruation, which is not correct. It is not allowed in some period rather than other; it is like sodomy and drinking intoxicants.

2. The second category is where a man makes a vow for Allah, or takes an oath for Him and makes something forbidden for the sake of Allah, then wants to legalize it, Allah has ruled to legalize it by expiation. This expiation is not going to erase the sacredness of it as some jurists

think. The breaking may be obligatory or recommended or permissible. The expiation is to release the man from what he had vowed.

3. The third category is to rectify what is missed like the expiation of the killing by mistake and the expiation of hunting by mistake: all this is for rectification while the first category is for prevention and the second is for legalizing what the contract had forbidden.

The prescribed punishment and chastisement cannot be joined in a crime. If there is a prescribed punishment, it will be implemented; otherwise chastisement will be enough. Similarly, the prescribed punishment and expiation cannot be combined together. Any crime for which there is a prescribed punishment there will be no expiation, and any fault which has expiation there will be no punishment.

Whether chastisement and expiation can be combined in a case for which there is no prescribed punishment?
There are two views:
In the case of having intercourse during Ihram and fasting and intercourse during the period of menstruation there is expiation but it is said that chastisement is also required because the sacredness of the rule is tempered. Some other people said that there was no chastisement and expiation will be enough; it will restore the damage.

4.4 The decreed punishments are related to the heart and to the body

The decreed punishments are two types: one which affects the hearts and the souls, and the other which concern bodies and possession.
The ones which affect the heart are of two kinds:
One is pains that the hearts feel; and the second is to cut off the materials with which its life and wellbeing are attached. When these sources are suspended their opposites will take place. The punishments of the hearts are the hardest one and they are the root of the punishment of the body.
This punishment increases and grows stronger till it passes from the heart to the body as the pain of the body passes to the heart. When the soul leaves the body the matter sticks with the soul and at that time the punishment of the heart becomes obvious. This is what is known as the punishment of the grave, and its relation to the *Barzakh* is like the punishment of bodies to this life.

4.5 The physical punishments are of two types: worldly and in the life to come

The bodily punishments are of two types: one in this world and the other in the next world. Their severity and duration are in line with the damages caused by the sins. There is no evil in the world except the crimes and their punishments. The word evil includes all that, and its root is the evil of the soul and bad deeds. These are two bases from which the Prophet, Allah's blessing and peace be upon him, used to seek refuge in his sermon. He said:

"We seek refuge in Allah from the evils of our souls and misdeeds of our deeds."[189]

Misdeeds are from the evils of the soul, so all the evil comes from the evil of the soul; misdeeds are its results and outcomes.

There is disagreement in the meaning of "from the evils of our deeds". Does it mean the evils from our deeds; or it means from the punishments of our deeds, which are unpleasant?

The second explanation is supported by the fact that seeking refuge may include all the evils as the evils of the soul produce evil deeds which lead to the unpleasant punishments. He indicated by the evils of the souls the bad deeds produced by them as they come from them. Then he mentioned the end of the evil which is the bad deeds, which lead to the punishments and pains. Thus this seeking refuge included the basis of the evil, its result and end.

Among the prayer of the angels for the believers is:

"Protect them from all evil deeds: those You protect on that Day from (the punishment of) evil deeds, You have shown mercy to them." (40:9)

It is shown that what is required on that Day is protection from the punishments of the evil deeds.

If it is said that the angels prayed to Allah to protect the believers from the torment of the Fire, which means protecting them from the evil consequences, which shows that they asked Almighty to protect them from the evil deeds, and the angels prayer will be like what the Prophet,

---

[189] Ahmad (1: 432), Abu Dawud (2118, Ibn Majah (1892) al-Bayhaqi (7: 146)

Allah's blessing and peace be upon him, sought refuge from. The word "on that Day" does not pose a problem because the request is the protection of evils of the misdeeds on that Day, which are the evil deeds themselves.

It will be said in reply that protection from the evils is two types:

1. Protection by giving support against doing them;
2. Protection from their recompense by forgiving, which will result in removing the punishment. The verse included the request of both matters.

Consider what this information about angels includes: their praise for belief and righteous deeds and by doing favour to the believers through seeking forgiveness for them. They sent before their seeking refuge, their soliciting Allah Almighty by His vast knowledge and great mercy. His vast knowledge embraces His knowledge of their sins and their causes. He knows that they are weak from keeping away from misdeeds because their enemy and their souls have control over them, their desires also dominate them in addition to the alluring materials of the world. Almighty knows them from the time He originated them from the earth and when they were foetuses in the wombs of their mothers. He knew in advance that they will necessarily disobey Him, and He loves forgiving and pardoning and other areas of His vast knowledge which no one can comprehend except Him.

The span of His mercy requires that He will not let any believer from among the people who believe in His oneness and love Him to perish. His mercy is vast and only wretched people will be excluded from it. There is no one more unfortunate than a man who was not covered by His mercy, which covers everything.

Then the angels asked Allah Almighty to forgive those who return to Him in repentance. They are the ones who follow His path, which leads to Him and that is comprehended by His knowledge, His love and His obedience. These are the people who repented from what He dislikes and followed the ways He loves. The angels further asked Almighty to save these believers from the torment of the Fire, and admit them into Paradise which He had promised them together with their parents, offspring, and spouses who have followed the path of belief. Although He, glory be to Him, does not break His promise, yet He has attached His promise with some reasons, among them is the supplication of the angels in this respect. It was due to His mercy that He helped them do good deeds, and He made His angels pray for their admission into Paradise.

He informed us that the angles said at the end of their supplication:

"You are indeed the Almighty, the Wise." (2:129)

They said it to confirm that the source of this bounty and its cause and objective came from His perfect power and absolute knowledge. Might refers to perfect power, and wisdom refers to absolute knowledge. With these two qualities He decides what He wishes, enjoins, forbids, rewards and punishes. Actually these two qualities are the origin of creation and commandment.

In short the punishments of crimes are divided into religious and decreed. The decreed ones are either concerned with the heart or the body or both of them. There are punishments in the *Barzakh* after death and on the Day when the bodies will be raised. Anyway the crime is not left without punishment, but due to his ignorance the slave does not realize the punishments he is passing through. He is like the drunk, intoxicated or sleeping person who does not feel the pain. When he wakes up and comes to his senses, he feels the pain. The punishments are made as a result of the sins like burning is for the fire, splitting for breaking, drowning for water and the bodies by poisons and the diseases for the causes producing them. Sometime the harm comes immediately after the crime, and sometime it is delayed for a little or long period as the disease comes late from its cause or with it. A slave makes mistake in this situation, when he commits a crime and does not see its effect after that. He does not realize that it works slowly as the poisons and harmful materials work slowly. If the person rectifies by medicine and antidotes, he recovers, otherwise he is proceeding to ruin. If this is the condition of one crime which was not rectified by something, what will be the case of crime after crime every day and every hour?
Allah's help is sought.

4.6 Punishments which Allah has assigned for criminal acts

Now call to mind some of the punishments which Allah, the Exalted, has assigned for crimes. They may be coming to you, so prepare yourself to avoid those evil acts in order to be safe from them. I am citing some of the punishments to you, which are enough for a man of reason. These are:

1. Setting seal on the hearts and ears, and covering the vision by veil.
   The Lord sets locks on the hearts, and covers them with crust, and

seals them, turns their hearts and eyes away, comes between a man and his heart. It may be that He makes the heart neglectful of the remembrance of the Lord, makes him forget himself, and does not wish to purify the heart, but to make it closed and suffocated as if the person is climbing to the skies. He turns the heart from the truth and increases its illness, makes it fall back and turns it upside down and it remains in that condition. Imam Ahmad reported that Hudhayfah ibn al-Yaman said: 'Hearts are four types: an empty heart with a brilliant lamp, it is the heart of the believer; a closed heart which is the heart of the disbeliever; an inverted heart which is the heart of a hypocrite; and a heart which is pulled by two factors: the one of belief and the other of hypocrisy, and it will be inclined towards a dominant force.'

2. Another punishment is to hold the person back from the obedience and to make him unable to fulfil the duties.

3. Another punishment is to make the heart deaf and unable to listen to the truth, dumb unable to speak what is right and blind which cannot see the truth. The relation between the useful truth and the heart becomes like the relation of the ear and the sounds, the eye of the blind and colours, and the tongue of the dumb and speech. It makes clear that blindness, deafness and dumbness belong in reality to the heart and subsequently to the limbs as Allah said:

"It is not the eyes that are blind, but the hearts which are within the breasts." (22:46)

The sense is not negation of the physical blindness, because Allah said;

"There is no blame on the blind." (24:61)

"He frowned and turned away when a blind person came to him." (80:1-2)

The meaning rather is that the complete blindness in fact belongs to the heart and it is correct to reject the blindness of the eyes in the sense that of denying its perfectness and power as the Prophet, Allah's blessing and peace be upon him, said:

"The strong man is not the one who knocks down others, but the one who controls himself at the time of anger."[190]

---

[190] Bukhari (6114), Muslim (2609)

He also said:

"Poor is not the one who goes from house to house and is satisfied by one morsel or two, the poor is the one who does not beg people and is not known to be given charity."[191]

There are many other examples. The point is that one of the punishments of the sinful acts is that the heart of the sinner is made blind, deaf and dumb.

4. A further punishment is to make the heart sink in the ground as a place is sunk in ground with all it has. The heart is sunk to the lowest of the low while the man does not feel. The sign of sinking is that it continues roaming around the low, filthy and base things, as the heart which Allah has raised high and brought it close to Him wanders around the Throne.

5. Another punishment is to put it far away from the pious and good deeds and noble acts, words and moral behaviours. Some early scholars said; 'These hearts are wandering around, some of them wander around the Throne, and some roam around the lavatory.'

6. Furthermore the heart is transmuted and its form is transformed. So, it becomes like the heart of the animals in behaviour, acts and nature. Some of them are transformed in the form of the pig because of their rigorous resemblance to it, others are transformed in the forms of the dog, donkey, snake, scorpion or other animals. Sufyan ibn 'Uyaynah explained the following words of Allah:

"There is no creature that crawls on the earth or bird that flies with its wings but they are communities like you." (6:38)

Sufyan said: 'Some people have the manners of ferocious beasts, some have the behaviour of the dogs or pigs or donkeys. There are those who adorn in their dress as the peacock adorns itself by its feather, yet there are some who are idiots like donkeys, and some who prefer others over themselves like the cock, some who like to be intimate and friendly with others like the pigeon, others are malicious like the camel, others are all good like the sheep, others like the wolves and some like fox cunning and dodgy. Sometimes Allah, the Exalted, compared the people of ignorance and transgression with donkeys, other times with dogs and cattle. This resemblance of inner side becomes so strong that it becomes obvious in outer features, which is noted by the people of reason. It appears in the acts seen by everyone,

---

[191] Bukhari (1479), Muslim (1039)

and continues to grow in ugliness, and in the end Allah changes their forms. This is complete transformation where the man's shape transmuted to the shape of the animal as it was done with the Jews and others, and Allah will do it with some people of this community by transmuting them to monkeys and pigs. Glory be to Allah! How many hearts are turned upside down but these people do not realize? How many hearts are transmuted and how many of them are sunk in the ground? How many people are deceived by the praise of others; how many are deluded by the covering of Allah; and how many enjoying the favours of Allah upon them? All these are punishments and disgrace but the ignorant people falsely believe that they are sign of honour.

7. Another truthful reality is that Allah schemes against those who boast to scheme, deludes those who insist to be self-deluded, mocks those who arrogantly mock and turns the heart of one who chooses to deviate and go astray.

8. Another punishment is to turn the heart upside down so the person sees the false as truth and the truth as false, good as bad and bad as good. He causes corruption and thinks that he is reforming things in order, prevents people from the way of Allah and thinks that he is calling them to it. He bargains for misguidance instead of guidance and thinks that he is guided and follows his desire and claims that he is following the orders of his Master. All this is among the punishments of the crimes which affect the hearts.

9. Another punishment is that the heart is screened off from the Lord in the world and biggest screening will be on the Day of Resurrection as Allah, the Exalted, has said:

"No! Their hearts are encrusted with what they have done. No! On that Day they will be screened off from their Lord." (83:14-15)

The sins have barred them from crossing the distance between themselves and their hearts; they failed to reach them in order to see what can put them in order and purify them, and what can corrupt and spoil them. They failed to cross the distance between their hearts and their Lord. So the hearts did not reach Him and failed to succeed with His closeness and honour, and to have the comfort of the eyes and pleasure of the soul. The sins became a veil between them and their hearts, and between them and their Lord and their Creator.

10. A further punishment is to suffer from great hardship in the world and the *Barzakh* and torment in the Hereafter. Allah, the Glorious, said:

"Whoever turns away from My remembrance will have a life of great hardship, and We shall raise him blind on the Day of Resurrection." (20:124)

The hard life has been interpreted as the torment of the grave. No doubt it is a hard life, but the verse includes more than that. Almighty attached the hard life to turning away from His Remembrance. The slave will experience the hardship of life according to his attitude even if he enjoyed all kinds of pleasures in the world. His heart will suffer from loneliness, humiliation and regrets which shatter the hearts. They are hidden from him by the intoxication of the desires, passion, the love of the world and power. The intoxication of the wine is not added to it, but the intoxication of these things is greater than the intoxication of the wine. A man intoxicated by wine comes to sense where as the man intoxicated by the desire and love of the world never comes to sense until he is amongst the dead. The hard life is inevitable for the person who turns away from the Remembrance of Allah, which He revealed to His Messenger, Allah's blessing and peace be upon him, in this world, in the *Barzakh* and on the Day of Resurrection.

The eye does not have comfort, the heart does not have peace and the soul does not relax except with its deity and the object of worship that is truth. Any deity beside Him is false. Whosoever's eye is comfortable with Allah, all eyes will find comfort in him; and whoever's eye has no comfort with Allah, his soul will be shattered in regret for the world. Allah, The Exalted, made the pleasant life for the one who believed in Him and performed righteous deeds. He said:

"Whoever, male or female, does good deeds and has faith, We shall give him a pleasant life and reward him according to the best of what he has done." (16:97)

Almighty has guaranteed for the people of faith and good deeds the reward of pleasant life in the world and the best reward on the Day of Resurrection. Such people will have pleasant life in both worlds and they will remain alive in them.
Similar to that are the following sayings of Allah:

"For those who do good deeds there is good reward in the world, and their home in the Hereafter is far better." (16:30)

"Ask your Lord for forgiveness, then turn back to Him. He will grant you wholesome enjoyment until an appointed time, and give His grace to everyone who has merit." (11:3)

So, the righteous people attained the delight of the world and the Hereafter, and gained pleasant life in both worlds. The pleasure of the soul, happiness of the heart and its delight, joy, relaxation and being protected from the prohibited desires and false doubts are the real pleasure. There is no relation for the pleasure of the body to it. Someone who had tasted this joy said:

'If the kings and their sons were to know what we are in, they would have fought us with swords.'

Another said:

'Some periods pass in the heart in which I say: 'If the people of Paradise are in conditions like this, then they are in real pleasant life.'

Another person said:

'There is a Paradise in the world like the one in the Hereafter, whoever entered it, entered that Paradise, and someone who could not enter it, he did not enter the Paradise of the Hereafter.'

The prophet, Allah's blessing and peace be upon him, pointed out to this Paradise saying:

"When you pass by the meadows of Paradise, graze in it."
They asked: 'What are the meadows of Paradise?'
He replied:
"They are the circles of remembrance."[192]
He also said:
"Between my house and my pulpit is a meadow of Paradise."[193]

Do not think that the statement of Allah, the Supreme:

"The righteous will be in bliss and the wicked will burn in the Fire." (82:13-14)

Do not think that it applies only to the Hereafter. The righteous are in bliss in all three homes and the wicked are in trouble in all three places. Which pleasure is more gratifying than the righteousness of the heart, purity of the breast and knowledge and love of the Lord Almighty, and working according to His order? The real life is the life of the devoted

---

[192] Tirmidhi (3509), Ahmad (3: 150)
[193] Bukhari (1195, 6588, 7335), Muslim (1390)

heart. Allah, the Exalted, praised His friend Abraham for having devoted heart and said:

"Abraham was of the same faith when he came to his Lord with devoted heart." (37:83-84)

Almighty quoted him saying:

"On the Day no wealth or children can help but the one who comes with devoted heart." (26:88-89)

The devoted heart is that which is safe from association of partners to Allah, rancour, spite, hatred, envy, greed, arrogance and love of the world and power. It is, thus, protected from every evil that keeps it away from Allah. It is safe from every doubt about His information, and every desire that defies His command. It is free from any intention that competes with His will and from any cause that cuts it off from Allah. The devoted heart is in Available Paradise in the world, in the *Barzakh* and in the Hereafter. Its devotion will not be complete until it is free from the following five things:

i.   Association which is opposed to unity,
ii.   Innovation that contradicts the Sunnah,
iii. Desire which counters the command,
iv.   Negligence which bars the remembrance and
v.   Longing which is opposed to sincerity and devotion.

These five are barriers from Allah, and under each of them there are many categories which include unlimited units.
Hence, the servant is in great need to ask Allah to guide him to the straight path. There is nothing else which he needs more, and which is more helpful to him.

The straight path includes knowledge, actions and leaving out many open and secret matters which he faces every now and then. The servant may be aware of the details of the straight path and he may not be. What he does not know may be more than he knows; among what he knows there may be matters which he is capable of it and there may be some which is beyond his capacity. However, it is the straight path even if he is unable to follow it. Among the matters he is capable there may be something which he wants to do and some which he has no wish to do it out of laziness and indifference or for some other reasons. What he wants to do he may do it or may not do it; and what he does may be with sincerity or without it; and what he does with sincerity he may follow it or may not; and what he follows he may be firm on it or turn his heart away from it. All this more or less is going on in the life of a slave.

Human by himself cannot be guided to it, but when he is left with his nature, he may be barred from all that. This is the setback which Allah made the hypocrites suffer from because of their evil acts, and He returned them to their natures and the ignorance and wrongdoing on which they were created.

The Lord Almighty is on the straight path in His decree and fate, His command and prohibition. He guides whoever He wishes to the right path by His grace and mercy, and puts guidance where it suits; and turns away from the straight path whoever He wishes by His justice and wisdom for the object not being suitable for that. When the Day of Resurrection comes, He will set for His slaves a straight path to which He will guide them. He is permanently on the straight path.

He set a straight path of His command for His slaves and called them all towards it, in order to complete His proof and establish His justice. He guided whoever He wills to walk on it as a grace and bounty from Him. He always maintains His straight path by virtue of His justice. When the Day of meeting with Him comes, He will set a straight path for His slave to reach His Paradise. He will turn away from it the one who turned away from it in the world, and will keep on track the one who was striving for it in the world. He created the light for those who believed in their hearts, in Him and His Messenger and that he brought a clear light shining brightly ahead of them and to their right in the darkness on the Day of Congregation. He guarded their light for them till they crossed as He protected their faith till they met with Him. In the meantime He extinguished the light of the hypocrites when they were in great need of it as He extinguished the light in their hearts in the world.

He put the deeds of the disobedient on both sides of the bridge in the form of hooks and spikes to grab them as they were kept away from following the right path in the world. He made the degree of their speed and running in accordance with their speed and running to it in the world. He allocated a pool for the believers to drink from it according to their following His religion in the world, and deprived those who were averse to His religion and rules in this world.

Now look at the life to come clearly and consider the wisdom of Allah in both worlds, you will definitely learn that the world is the field of the Hereafter and the positions of the people as regards success and failure in it is according to their position in this world as regards faith and the righteous deeds. Help comes from Allah. The greatest punishment of the crimes is to get out from the straight path in the world and the Hereafter.

4.7 The punishments of the sins vary according to the acts

Since the crimes are different in their levels and degrees of damage, their punishments are also different accordingly in the world and the Hereafter. We are, with the help and support of Allah, going to explain it in a brief comprehensive section. We start by saying:

As a principle the crimes are of two types:

i.   Neglecting what is commanded and
ii.   Committing what is prohibited

These are two evils with which Allah tried the fathers of the Jinn and the humans.
Both crimes are divided as regards their places externally to the limbs and internally to the heart. They are also divided according to their relation to the right of Allah and the right of His creature. As a matter of fact any right of the creature include His right, yet it is called the right of the creature because it becomes obligatory by their demand and is dropped by their decision.

Then these crimes are further divided into four categories:

1. Angelic,
2. Satanic,
3. Beastly and
4. Animalistic

The **Angelic crimes** are to adopt the qualities of Lordship which is not appropriate for a man such as greatness, pride, might, force, sublimity, subjugation of the creature etc. This includes association of partners with the Lord Almighty, which is of two types:

i.   Association of partner in His Names and Attributes and
ii.   Taking other deities beside Him

There is another form of association in dealing with Him. This last may not necessarily be a cause for admission into the Fire though it will ruin the deeds in which another being was joined with Allah.

This category is the most serious crime, and includes speaking about Allah without knowledge concerning His creation and command. Whoever is involved in this crime, he has competed with Allah, the Glorious, in His Lordship and Kingdom, and has set up a rival to Allah. This is the gravest sin concerning Allah, and no act will be useful with it.

The **Satanic crimes** are those which emerge from the acts of Satan like envy, transgression, deceiving, duping, cheating, scheming, urging to commit sinful acts, alluring them to people, preventing from the obedience of Allah and exposing it as bad thing. It also includes introducing innovations in His religion and calling people to innovation and misdeeds.

This category is next to the first one in corruption though its damage is less.

The **Beastly crimes** are embodied in aggression, anger, shedding blood, torturing the weak and incapable people. It leads to hurting the mankind and doing injustice, and hostility.

The **Animalistic crimes** are greed, craving to fulfil the desire of the belly and the private part. This leads to committing adultery, stealing, usurping the wealth of orphans, niggardliness, avarice, cowardice, anxiety, impatience etc. This category embraces most crimes of the people as they are unable to commit the beastly and angelic crimes, they proceed to other sins from it. It drags them to beastly crimes then to Satanic ones then to competition with Allah in Lordship and association in His oneness.

If someone pays proper attention to this, he will realize that sins are the doorstep of association and disbelief and competition with Allah in His Lordship.

CHAPTER 5 - CATEGORIES AND CAUSES OF SINS

5.1   Major and minor sins

The Qur'an, the Sunnah and the consensus of the Companions, their Followers and the leading Muslim scholars stated that the sins are major and minor. Allah, the Exalted, said:

"If you avoid major sins which you are forbidden, We will remove from you the minor misdeeds and admit you through a noble entrance." (4:31)

"Those who avoid major sins and immoralities except for small ones." (53:32)

The Messenger, Allah's blessing and peace be upon him, said:

"Five daily prayers, Friday prayer to the next Friday and (fast of) Ramadan to the next Ramadan are sources of eliminating the sins committed between them provided the major sins are avoided."[194]

These good deeds which wipe out the sins have three levels:

1. They are unable to eliminate the minor sins due to their weakness and lack of sincerity and failure in fulfilling their dues, like the weak medicine which falls short of combating the disease due to fault in its quantity and quality.
2. They are able to resist the minor sins but do not reach the level of wiping out the major ones.
3. The wipe out the minor sins and still retain some power to eliminate some of the major ones as well.

Consider this point; it will remove from you many problems.
The Messenger of Allah, blessing and peace of Allah be upon him, said:

"Should I not tell you the most serious of the grave sins?"

They said: 'Indeed, tell us, Messenger of Allah.'
He said:

---

[194] Muslim (233)

"To associate partner to Allah, disobedience of parents and false witness."[195]

He also said:

"Avoid seven destructive acts."

They asked: 'What are they, Messenger of Allah?'

He replied:

"Association of partner with Allah, magic, taking life which Allah has forbidden except for just cause, consuming the property of the orphan, consuming usury, running away from the battle field and accusing chaste, unaware believing women."[196]

He was asked: 'Which crime is the gravest with Allah?'
He replied:

"To assign a partner with Allah while He created you."
'Then which one?' He was asked.
"To kill your child with the fear that he will eat with you", he replied.
'Then which one is the next?'

He replied:

"To commit adultery with the wife of your neighbour."[197]

Allah revealed confirmation of this in the following verse:

"They are those who do not invoke any other deity beside Allah, do not take the life which Allah has made sacred except in pursuit of justice and do not commit adultery." (25:68)

The scholars are in disagreement concerning the major sins. Are they confined in any number? There are two opinions. Those who said that they were limited disagreed in their numbers:
Abdullah ibn Mas'ud said that they were four.
Abdullah ibn 'Umar said they were seven.

---

[195] Bukhari (2653), Muslim (87)
[196] Bukhari (2766), Muslim (89)
[197] Bukhari (4477), Muslim (86)

Abdullah ibn 'Amr ibn al-'Aas said they were nine.
Some other people said they were eleven, and some said they were seventy.

Abu Talib al-Makki said:
'I collected them from the words of the Companions and found four of them to be in the heart: association of partners with Allah, insistence on disobedience, despair of Allah's mercy and feeling secure from the plans of Allah. Four are connected with the tongue and they are: giving false witness, accusing chaste women, disastrous swearing and practicing sorcery. Three are connected with the stomach, and they are: drinking wine, consuming the wealth of the orphan, and consuming the usury. Two of them are connected with the private part namely adultery and sodomy. Two are connected with hand and they are murder and theft. One is concerning the feet and it is running away from the battle field. One is connected with the whole of the body and it is treating the parents unkindly.'

Those who did not limit them to a particular number, some of them said that anything which Allah, the Glorious, prohibited in the Qur'an is a major sin and what the Messenger of Allah, blessing and peace of Allah be upon him, prohibited is a minor one.

A group of them said:
'Any act which is forbidden and connected with curse, anger or punishment is a major sin, and that which is not connected with it is a minor one.'
Another view is that acts for which there is prescribed punishment in the world or threat in the Hereafter are among the major sins, and those which are free from this are minor ones.
It is also said that anything which is prohibited by religions is a major sin and the one which is forbidden by some religion and not others is a minor one.
It is also said that any act which Allah and His Messenger cursed its culprit is a major sin.
It is said that all those matters which are mentioned from the beginning of the Chapter four to the verse 31 which reads:

"If you avoid the grave sins you have forbidden, We will wipe out the minor ones for you."

Those who did not divide the sins into major and minor said:

'All the criminal acts are major because they embody boldness and disobedience of Allah and opposition of His command. As regard the One whose command has been disobeyed and His prohibition has been violated all the misdeeds are necessarily major sins and they are equal in this respect.'

They further said:

'It is clarified by the fact that the sins do not harm Allah, the Exalted, and He is not affected by them. As such no one of them is bigger than other as far He is concerned. So the common factor in it remains His disobedience and violation of His commands, and in this there is no difference between one evil act and the other.'

They went on:

'The damage of the evil acts is based on the boldness and intrusion on the right of the Lord, the Blessed and exalted. Therefore, if a person drinks wine or has illicit intercourse with a woman without believing it to be prohibited, he would have gathered between the ignorance and the evil of committing a prohibited sin. However, if he did it while he believed its prohibition, he would be committing one of the two evils, and he would deserve to be punished not the first one. It shows that the effect of the crime is based on the boldness and intrusion.

It makes clear that committing evil includes taking the command of the Lord who is to be obeyed and His prohibition lightly and underrating the violation of His order. There is no difference between a sin and other in this regard.'

They said further:

'The servant is not required to look at the severity and insignificance of the evil itself, but should look at the status and greatness of the one he has disobeyed and violated His order. There is no difference between an evil and another in this case. If a great powerful king orders one of his slaves to go on an errand to a far away town, and orders another to be engaged in a job next to the house, and both of them disobeyed and did not carry out his order, they will be equal to him in guilt and losing their status.'

They said:

'For this reason the sin of someone who did not perform pilgrimage from among the residents of Makkah and the one who did not attend the Friday prayer while he lived next to the mosque is greater to Allah than the crime of a person who neglected them from a far place. It was more important to one of them than it was to the other. If a person had two hundred dirham and did not pay zakat of it, and another had two million and did not pay zakat, they will be equal in sin of neglecting what was obligatory for them. They may face equal punishment if each one of them insisted on withholding the zakat of his wealth, whether the money was plenty or little.

5.2 Allah Almighty has created the creation for declaring His Oneness and worshipping Him alone

This issue is illustrated in the following way:
Allah, the Exalted, sent His Messengers, revealed His Books and created the heavens and the earth in order to be known and worshipped alone. He made the religion wholly for Him, and obedience belongs to Him and call should be made to Him. He has stated this in many places in the Book:

"I did not create the Jinn and humans but for My worship." (51:56)

"We did not create the heavens and the earth and what is between them but with truth." (15:85)

"It is Allah Who created seven heavens and similar number of earth. His command descends between them, so you should realize that Allah has power over all things and that Allah's knowledge encompasses everything." (65:12)

"Allah has made the Ka'bah – the Sacred House - a means of support for the people, and the Sacred Months, the sacrificial animals including the garlanded. That is so you may know that Allah has knowledge of all that is in the heavens and earth and that Allah is fully aware of all things." (5:97)

Allah Almighty told in the previous verses that the purpose of the creation and command was to know Allah with His Names and Attributes and to worship Him alone without associating any partner with Him. It was also intended that the people uphold justice, which is the balance on which the heavens and earth are established. He, glory be to Him, said:

"We sent Our messengers with evidences and revealed with them Book and balance so that people may maintain their affairs with justice." (57:25)

In this verse Almighty declared that He sent His Messengers and revealed His Books so that people uphold justice. The biggest justice is to declare the oneness of Allah. It is the basis of the justice and its foundation opposite of it is association of partners with Him, which is injustice. Allah, the Exalted, said:

"Association of partners with Allah is the greatest injustice." (31:13)

Association (shirk) is the greatest injustice while declaration of oneness (Tawhid) is the greatest justice. Anything which is in contradiction with this purpose is the gravest sin. Its grading will be in line with its contradiction in degree. On the other hand any matter which is in agreement with this purpose is the most important, obligatory and most essential requirement of the religion.

Consider carefully this principle and follow it in learning the details of the religion, you will be able to understand the wisdom of the Most Just of the judges and the Most Knowledgeable of the learned in all that He assigned as compulsory duties on His servants or forbidden them. It also will indicate the degrees of the good deeds and evil acts.

Since association of partners with Allah Almighty was in direct contradiction with this objective, it was absolutely the gravest sin. Allah, the Most High, has forbidden Paradise to any person involved in association. He allowed the followers of Tawhid to kill him take his wealth and capture his family as slaves. It is due to his failing in the duty of acknowledging His Lordship and neglecting it. Allah has decided not to accept any act from a man who associates with Him a partner. His intercession is not to be granted and his supplication in the Hereafter is not to be answered and his misdeeds are not to be forgiven. Such a person is the biggest ignorant, he assigned a partner to Allah from among His creation. It is the extreme ignorance and great injustice. However, he did not cause harm to his Lord, but he wronged himself.

There is an issue here: that a man associating partners with Allah has in mind the expression of the honour of the Lord, the Blessed and Exalted. He thought that because of His greatness He could not be approached but through intermediaries and intercessors as was the case with kings of the world. So, the polytheist did not intend to underrate the honour of the Lord but aimed at His exaltation. He said: 'I worship these intermediaries so that they bring me closer to Him and guide me and make it easy for me to come to Him. Almighty is my objective; and these are only intermediaries and intercessors. How can this be the cause of the anger and wrath of Him, glory be to Him, and the person will be cast in the Fire to abide in it forever, and deserve his colleagues to be killed and their women and wealth be taken?

There is another question related to this: that, is it possible for Allah, the Exalted, to allow His worshippers to approach Him through intermediaries and intercessors, so its prohibition will be based on the Shari'ah or it is abominable in the reasons and instincts which makes the Shari'ah to ordain a rule about it, and the Shari'ah's ruling was to affirm its ignominy established in the instincts, and reasons and consider it more serious than any other evil matter, and for this reason it was not to be forgiven out of the rest of the crimes? Allah said:

"Allah will not forgive association of partners with Him, and may forgive anything less than that." (4:48)

Contemplate on this question and put your mind and heart together to find answer for that. Do not consider it little because by this the difference will be made between the polytheists and believers, those who have knowledge of Allah and those who are ignorant, and the people of Paradise and the Fire.

5.3   The *shirk*, association of partners with Allah

We say to clear the matter knowing that the help and support come only from Allah, and from Him we seek help and right path; if He guides someone no one can send him astray, and the one He misguides no one can put him on the right path; there is no one to withhold what He grants and no one can grant what He withholds.

Association of partners with Allah is of two kinds:
One which is related to the essence of the Lord and His Names, Attributes and acts;
and the one which is connected with His worship and His governing of things. It is *shirk* even the person involved in it believes that there is a partner with Allah in His essence or attributes or actions.

The first type of *shirk* is of two kinds:
The first one is to deny the actions of Allah, which is the most offensive. It is like the *shirk* of Pharaoh who said:

"What is the Lord of the worlds?" (26:23)

Allah says that he said to Haman:

"Pharaoh said: 'Haman, build me a tall tower so that I may reach the ropes that lead to the heavens to look for the God of Moses. I am convinced that he is lying." (40:36-37)

Association of partners and denial of actions are inseparable. Every person who associated partner is denying the actions of Allah and every denier of the action is committing association. Association in principle does not lead to the denial, it is possible that a person who associates partner with Allah is asserting the existence of the Creator and His Attributes but he disregards the right of the oneness (Tawhid).

The basis of shirk and its foundation is denial of Attributes. It is of three types:

1. Denying the relation of the object with its Creator and maker;
2. Denial of the Creator, the Exalted, from His perfectness by denying His Names, Attributes and Actions;
3. Denying His right of declaration of oneness by keeping away from his duty of recognition.

To this category belongs the *shirk* of the group of pantheism who say that there is no creator or created. There are no two different things, but the Pure Truth is the created one himself. It also includes the shirk of the atheists who believe in the eternity of the world and that He never was nonexistent. He was from eternity and never ceased to be. All the incidents, according to them, are attached to causes which required their creation; they call them intellects and souls. It also includes the shirk of those whose deny the Names, Attributes and actions of the Lord, the Sublime, from among the extremist Jahmiyyah and Qaramitah. They do not attribute any name or attribute to Him, but make the creature more perfect than Him because the perfection of the essence is due to its names and attributes.

The second type of the shirk is the act of the one who takes another deity beside Allah, and does not deny His Names and Attributes or His Lordship. It is like the Christians who consider Him one of the three; they take the Christ one god and his mother another one.

To this category belongs the shirk of the Magians who attribute the good incidents to the light and the evil incidents to the darkness. It also includes the shirk of the Qadariyyah who claim that a man creates his acts and they are produced without the will of Allah and His power and wish.

For this reason they are considered semi-Magians. In this category comes the act of the person who disputed with Abraham concerning his Lord:

"when Abraham said, 'my Lord is the one who gives life and causes death,' he said, 'I give life and death." (2:258)

He put himself equal to Allah claiming that he gives life and death. Abraham challenged him by saying that Allah brings the sun from east, why don't you bring it from the direction of west. It was not change of the discussion as some people say but to force him to accept the proof if his claim was true. It also includes the belief of those people who consider the heavenly stars as managers of the affairs of this world as it is the religion of the Sabi'ah. It also includes the act of the worshippers of the sun and the fire and other objects. Some of them claim that the object of their worship is the real God; some of them go the extent of claiming that he is the biggest God. Others believe that he is one of the gods and when a person devotes him wholeheartedly to him and dedicates himself to his worship, he will take care of him and protect him. Others believe that his lower god will bring close to the higher one, and this one to his superior till he reaches Allah, the Exalted. Sometimes the number of gods in between increase and sometimes decrease.

5.4   Shirk in worship

Association of others with Allah in worship is easier than the above mentioned categories. It is because it comes from those who believe that there is no deity beside Allah, and no one is capable of causing harm or bringing benefit or has power to give and withhold except Allah. There is no one worthy of worship except Almighty and no Lord apart from Him. But they do not dedicate to Allah in dealing with Him and worshipping Him. They work sometimes for the benefit of themselves, sometimes for seeking worldly benefit and another time for seeking position, rank and status with the creature. They have portion of their work for Allah, and some portion for their soul and benefit, and another portion for Satan and some for the people.

This is the condition of many people. It is the association about which the Prophet, Allah's blessing and peace be upon him, has said:

"Shirk, (association of partners with Allah), is more hidden in this community than the crawling of the ant."

The Companions asked: 'How can we get rid of it, Messenger of Allah?'

He replied:

"Say: O Allah, I seek refuge with You from associating any partner knowingly with You, and seek forgiveness from what I do not know."[198]

Showing off is all *shirk*, Allah, the Glorious said:

"Say, I am only a human being like you, to whom it has been revealed that your God is One. Anyone who expects meeting with his Lord should do good deeds and not associate in the worship of his Lord anyone." (18:110)

It means that as He is the only one God, there is no other god beside Him, so worship should be exclusively for Him. He stands alone in being God so He must be singled out for worship.
The righteous deed is that which is free from show off and done according to the Sunnah.
'Umar ibn al-Khattab used to pray:
'O Allah, make all my deeds righteous, and purely for Yourself. Do not make any share for anyone in it.'[199]

This association in worship spoils the reward of the deed; the person may be punished if the deed was obligatory. His deed is null and void and as such he will be punished for abandoning an obligatory duty. Allah, the Exalted, has commanded to worship Him with devotion and sincerity.
He said:

"They were ordered to worship Allah alone, sincerely devoting their religion to Him as people of true faith." (98:5)

So anyone who was not sincere in his worship has neglected what he was ordered; he did what he was not asked, and therefore his deed is not right and it will not be accepted. Allah said in a Divine Hadith:

"I am not in need of the partners at all; so anyone who does a deed and associates with Me another person, his deed will be for the one he associated with Me. I am free from it."[200]

---

[198] Ahmad (4: 403), Tabarani (Awsat: 4940) See Majma' al-zawa'id (10: 226)
[199] Ahmad in Zuhd (118)
[200] Muslim (2985)

This association can be either forgiven or not to be forgiven, big or small. The big one is either serious or more damaging. However, nothing of it is going to be forgiven. In this category comes association of partners with Allah in love and glorification. To love a creature as due to Allah is the type of association which Allah, the Glorious, will not forgive. Allah said about it:

"There are some who choose to worship others besides Allah as rivals to Him, loving them with the love due to Allah. But those who believe have greater love for Allah." (2:165)

The people committing this association will say to their gods when they are put together in Hellfire:

"By Allah we were clearly misguided when we made you equal with the Lord of the worlds." (26:97-98)

It is well known that they did not make them equal to the Lord almighty in creation, giving provision, causing death or giving life, power and sovereignty, but put them together with Allah in their love, dedication, submission and being humble to them. This was the greatest degree of ignorance and injustice. How can the dust be considered equal with the Lord of the lords? How can the slaves be equal with the One who holds the lives of everyone in His Hand? How can a total destitute, essentially powerless, needy in himself who owns nothing but nonexistence be equal with the One who is originally free of need, has infinite power whose freedom, power, kingdom, generosity, kindness, knowledge, mercy and full perfectness are part of His essence?

Which injustice is more horrible than this? Which judgement is more false than this when the One who has no match is equalled with His creature? Allah, the Exalted said:

"Praise belongs to Allah who created the heavens and the earth and made the darkness and the light; yet the disbelievers set up equals to their Lord." (6:1)

The disbeliever regarded the One who created the heavens and the earth and made the darkness and the light equal to the one who has no power to give and atom's equal from the heavens and the earth for himself or others. Is there any more unjust behaviour and more horrid injustice than this?

5.5 Association of others with Allah in deeds and words

Association in worship is followed by association of partners with Allah in deeds, words, intentions and purposes. The examples of the association in deeds are bowing down in prostration to other than Allah, circling (i.e. in Tawaf) around buildings other than His House, shaving of head to show humbleness and respect to others, kissing the stones besides the black stone which is the right hand of Allah on the earth, kissing the graves and prostrating before them. The Prophet, Allah's blessing and peace be upon him, has cursed those who take the graves of the prophets and righteous people as places of prayer. How then will be the position of those who take graves as idols and worship them besides Allah?

The Prophet, Allah's blessing and peace be upon him, said:

"Allah has cursed the Jews and the Christians because they took the graves of their prophets as mosques."[201]

He also said:

"The worst people will be those who are alive when the Hour comes, and those who take the graves as mosques."[202]

He also said:

"The people before you used to take the graves as mosques. Beware! Do not take the graves as mosques. I forbid you that."[203]

He further said:

"Allah has cursed women visiting graves frequently and those who take them as mosques and light lamp on them."[204]

In another version he said:

"Allah's anger is very severe about the people who take the graves of their prophets as mosques."[205]

---

[201] Bukhari (435), Muslim (529)
[202] Bukhari as 'Ta'liq' (13: 14) It is reported by Ahmad (1: 435), Ibn Khuzaymah (789), Ibn Hibban (340)
[203] Muslim (532)

[205] Abd al-Razzaq (1587), Ibn Abi Shaybah (3: 345), Malik (414), Ahmad (2: 246)

He also said:

"When a righteous man from among the people before you died, they built a mosque on his grave and painted the images. They will be the worst people to Allah on the Day of resurrection."[206]

This is the case of the one who bows down in prostration to Allah on a grave in a mosque. What will be the case of the person who bows down for the grave itself?

The Prophet, Allah's blessing and peace be upon him, prayed:

"O Allah, do not make my grave idol to be worshipped."[207]

Allah, the Exalted has protected the side of Tawhid very well to the extent that performing supererogatory prayer for Allah at the sunrise and sunset was forbidden because it is the time the worshippers of the sun bow down for it. For this reason prayer after *'Asr* and dawn prayers was forbidden because at this time the disbelievers prostrate for the sun.

Bowing down in prostration to other than Allah has been forbidden. The Prophet, Allah's blessing and peace be upon him, said:

"It is not appropriate for a person to prostrate to anyone besides Allah."[208]

The expression "not appropriate" is used in the statements of Allah and His Messenger to indicate that the act is religiously very bad. It is attested by the words of Allah:

"It is not appropriate for the Most Merciful that He should have an offspring." (19:92)

"We did not teach him poetry and it was not appropriate for him." (36:69)

"The Devils have not brought it down, it is not appropriate for them." (26:210-211)

---

[206] Bukhari (434), Muslim (528)
[207] Bukhari (435), Muslim (529)
[208] Tirmidhi (1159), Ibn Hibban (4162), Hakim (4: 171)

Almighty said about the angels that they would say:

**"It was not appropriate for us to take any allies besides You."
(25:18)**

5.6 Association in talk

One type of association of others with Allah is to associate someone with Him in talking like taking oath by other than Him. The Prophet, Allah's blessing and peace be upon him, said:

"Whoever swears by other than Allah has committed shirk."[209]

It includes saying that 'what Allah willed and you willed.' It is reported that a man said to the Prophet, Allah's blessing and peace be upon him: 'What Allah willed and you willed'. The Prophet, Allah's blessing and peace be upon him, said to him:

"Did you make me rival to Allah? Say, What Allah alone willed."[210]

The Prophet disproved it though Allah has established will of the slave. He said:

"Whoever among you wills to take the right course." (81:28)

Now compare what the man said: 'What Allah willed and you willed' and saying of someone: 'I put my trust in Allah and in you. Allah is sufficient for me and you.' 'There is no one for me except Allah and you.' 'This one is from Allah and from you.' This is of Allah's blessings and yours.' Allah is for me in the heavens and you on the earth.' Or saying of someone: 'By Allah and by the life of so and so.' Or saying: This is vow for Allah and for so and so.' I am turning in repentance to Allah and to so and so, 'I hope Allah and so and so', and similar statements.

Then decide which one was more horrible. You will find that the people who said those words deserve more the reply of the Prophet, Allah's blessing and peace be upon him, that they made him a rival to Allah. These people make someone who cannot reach the Messenger of Allah, blessing and peace be upon him, in anything but may be among his enemies, a rival to the Lord of the worlds.

---

[209] Ahmad (2: 34, 86) Abu Dawud (3251)Tirmidhi (1535), Ib Hibban (1177), Hakim (1: 18; 4: 297)

[210] Ahmad (1: 214, 224, 283, 347), Bukhari in al-Adab al-mufrad (783), Ibn Majah (2117)

Bowing down in prostration, worship, putting trust, to return in repentance, consciousness, fear, sufficiency, repentance, making vow, taking oath, glorification, exaltation, praise, seeking forgiveness, shaving the head in devotion, circling round any other house besides the Sacred House, and calling upon – all these are the right of Allah. It is not appropriate for anyone else whether a favourite angel or sent prophet.

It is reported that a man who had committed a sin was brought to the Prophet, Allah's blessing and peace be upon him. When he stood before him, he said: "O Allah, I turn to You in repentance and not to Muhammad." The Prophet said:

"He recognised the right for its owner."[211]

As for the association in intentions and objectives is concerned, it is very wide like an ocean which has no shore. Very few people are safe from it. Anyone who intends by his deed other than the pleasure of Allah, or intends to come close to others expecting reward from them, he has associated with Allah in his intention and volition.

Sincerity requires that a person should be sincere to Allah in his words, deeds, intentions and objectives. This is Hanifiyyah (inclination to Allah in truth), the way of Abraham which Allah has commanded all his servants to adhere to. He will not accept anything else from anyone. It is the real essence of Islam. Allah said:

"If anyone seeks a religion other than Islam (complete devotion to Allah), it will not be accepted from him; and he will be one of the losers in the Hereafter." (3:85)

This is the religion of Abraham and anyone who forsakes it is the greatest fool.

5.7   The true nature of the shirk

If you have understood this preamble, the answer to the above mentioned query will have been clear to you. Now we explain it further by the help of Allah, and from Him we draw the right answer.

The true nature of the *shirk*, association of partners with Allah, is to claim similarity with the Creator and compare the creature with Him. This is the real comparison not establishing the Attributes of perfectness which

---

[211] Ahmad (3: 435), Hakim ($; 255), Tabarani in Kabir (839)

Allah has stated for Him, and His Messenger described Him with them. But the one whose heart was made upside down, his eyes are made blind and was afflicted with the confusion reversed everything and made Tawhid comparison and considered it exaltation and obedience. A person involved in association claims similarity of the Creator with the created in the qualities of the Lord.

The special qualities of the Lord Almighty are that He alone controls harm and benefit, giving and withholding. It requires that the people must turn to Him in supplication and fear, have hope and put their trust in Him alone. Anyone who turns to a created person in this has put that person as a rival to the Creator. He has made someone who has no power to cause harm or benefit for himself let alone others, nor has he control over death or life or resurrection similar to the One who has full command in His hand. Everything goes to Him, what He wills is done and what He does not will is not found. There is no one to withhold what He gives and no one to give what He withholds. When He opens the door of His mercy for His slave nobody can withhold it, and if He withholds it from him nobody can release it. It is absurd to compare this naturally incapable and destitute with the One Who is essentially Powerful and Free from need. Another quality of the Lord is full perfectness from every side; there is no defect in Him at all. It requires that all the worship should be for Him. Exaltation, glorification, fear, supplication, hope, turning in repentance, putting trust and seeking help belong to Him alone, and He is to be loved with utmost humility. All these qualities belong to Him alone by the evidence of reason, religion and natural disposition, and there is no share for anyone else in them. Anyone who assigns any of these to someone else he has compared him with the One who has no one similar, resembling or rival with Him. This comparison is the most horrid and terrible act. Because of its gravity and being the greatest injustice Almighty has told His servants that He was not going to forgive it though He has decreed mercy upon Himself.

Another special Divine attribute of the Lord is to show humble veneration to Him, which has two fundamental bases namely utmost love and extreme submission. This is perfect humble veneration; the different levels of the people are expressing veneration in accordance with their difference in these two attitudes. Anyone who gives his love, humility and veneration to someone else, he has put him as a rival to the Creator in His essential right. It is something which no religion can allow at all. Its absurdity is deeply rooted in every instinct and reason. The devils, however, changed the natural dispositions and reasons of many people, spoiled them and turned them from its natural form. Only such people who Allah has decreed His blessing remained on the original instinct. Allah sent to His Messengers and revealed His Books which agree with their instincts and reasons. This increased their light upon light.

"And Allah guides to His light whoever He wishes." (24:35)

When these matters have been understood then we repeat the special Divine attributes:

One of them is to bow down in prostration to Him; anyone who bows down before another he has compared the Creator with the created.
Another special attribute is to put trust in Him; anyone who relied on others has assigned a rival for Him.
Another exclusive duty of the people is to turn to Him in repentance; anyone turns to someone else he has assigned a partner with Him.
It is also His exclusive right that His name be mentioned at swearing as a sign of glorification and veneration; anyone who takes an oath in the name of others has compared Him with them.

As regards similarity with Him, anyone who shows arrogance and haughtiness and calls people to praise him, glorify him, submit to him and show humility to him and attach his heart to him in fear and hope, expecting help and support from him, he is claiming to be similar to Allah and has challenged Him in His Lordship and being object of worship. Such a person deserves to be humiliated by Allah and completely disgraced by Him and be subjected to authority of His creature.
It is reported in an authentic Divine Hadith that the Prophet, Allah's blessing and peace be upon him, said:

"Greatness is my wrap and majesty is my robe; anyone who contends with Me in any of these, I will punish him."[212]

When the person who makes pictures by his hand will be given severest punishment on the Day of Resurrection merely because of claiming similarity in creation, what will be the case of someone who tries to contend His Lordship and being object of worship? The Prophet, Allah's blessing and peace be upon him, said:

---

[212] Muslim (2620)

"The people subjected to the severest punishment are those who make pictures. It will be said to them: 'Put life in what you have created.'"[213]

In another Divine Hadith Allah said:

"Who is more unfair than a person who tried to create something like My creation. Let him then create an atom or create a grain or create a grain of barley."[214]

The aim is to tell that this is the case of someone who tried to match Allah in making an image, then what will be the fate of the one who tries to claim similarity with Him in the special feature of His Lordship and being object of worship? The same is the case of a person who attempts to acquire the name which is purely for Him like 'the king of the kings, the judge of the judges' and so on.
The Prophet, Allah's blessing and peace be upon him, said:

"The most ignoble name to Allah almighty is '*shahanshah*' that is the king of the kings. There is no King but Allah."[215]

In another version it is:

"The most hateful person to Allah is a man who is called the king of the kings."[216]

Allah's wrath and anger are for the person who tries to take the name which is only appropriate to Allah. He, the Glorious, is the King of the kings alone; He is the greatest Judge of all the judges. He is the One who rules over all the judges, and decides for them no one else does it.

5.8 To have evil thought about Allah is one of the grave sins

After this has been clear there is an important principle which will reveal the secret of the issue. It is to have evil thought about Allah; it is the greatest sin with Allah Almighty. The person who has poor opinion about

---

[213] Bukhari (5950), Muslim (2108)
[214] Bukhari (7559), Muslim (2111)
[215] Bukhari (6205), Muslim (2143)
[216] Muslim (2143)

Allah has embarked on challenging His sacred perfectness, and presumed something which is in contradiction with His Names and Attributes. This explains why Allah, the Exalted threatened the people who had poor opinion about Him in a way He did not threaten anyone else. He said:

"(Allah will) torment the hypocritical and idolatrous men and women who harbour evil thoughts about Allah – it is they who will be encircled by evil. Allah is angry with them, has rejected them and He has prepared for them Hell, an evil destination." (48:6)

Almighty said about those who denied an Attribute of Him:

"It was your thought which you entertained about your Lord that led to your ruin, and you became losers." (41:23)

Allah related about Abraham that he said to his people:

"What are you worshipping? How can you choose false gods instead of the true God? So what is your opinion about the Lord of all the worlds?" (37:85-87)

That is what do you think Allah will do to you when you meet with Him when you have worshipped other than Him? What did you think about Him that you worshipped with Him others? What fault did you notice in His Names and Attributes and the quality of Lordship that you went to worship someone else? If you had thought about Him what He was worthy of - that He was aware of everything, has power over everything, is not in need of anyone else and everyone is in need of Him; He maintains the creation with justice, He alone controls the affairs of His creation no one has any part in it, you should have been careful. He knows the details of all the matters, nothing is hidden from Him. He alone is sufficient for all His creation without being in need of anyone. He is Merciful by Himself and does not need anyone to show mercy to Him unlike the kings and rulers of the world who are in need of some people to inform them about their subjects and their needs. They need helpers to carry out the duty of fulfilling of their subjects' need, and to someone who can plead for mercy and make intercession. In this way they need intermediaries to fulfil their duties because of their weakness, incapability and lack of knowledge.

This is the condition of the kings and rulers of the world but Allah has power over everything, free from need of anyone, is aware of everything. He is the Merciful, Compassionate, His mercy encompasses everything.

To put intermediaries between Him and His creation is to violate the right of His Lordship and being the sole object of worship. Those who do it have poor opinion about Him. It is impossible that He assigns or allows intermediary for His worshippers. It is inconceivable in the reasons and instincts and most absurd in accordance to sound reason.

It is illustrated by the fact that a worshipper respects his deity, honours him surrenders in humility to him; and it is only the Lord, the Glorious, who deserves full respect, complete honour, submission and surrendering to Him. It is His exclusive right, and it is ignominious injustice to give His right to anyone else or make someone a partner in it especially when the one who is made the partner is His slave and bondsman. Allah, the Most High, has spoken about it in the following verse:

"He gives you this example, drawn from your own lives: do you make your slaves full partners with an equal share in what We have given you? Do you fear them as you fear each other? This is how We make Our messages clear to those who use their reason." (30:28)

It means that if one of you disdains that his owned slave be his partner in his possessions, how then you make from My slaves partners in what belongs exclusively to Me and that is being object of worship, which is not suitable for anyone else and is not appropriate for anyone other than Me? Anyone who claims this has not appreciated Me as it is due, nor glorified Me the way it should be done and he did not single Me out for what is My right alone. Anyone who worshipped another object besides Allah has not appraised Him right appraisal. Allah said:

"People, here is an illustration, so listen to it carefully: those who call on others besides Allah could not, even if they combined all their forces, to create a fly, and if a fly should take something away from them, they would not be able to retrieve it. How feeble are the pursuer and pursued! They did not appraise Allah with true appraisal. Allah is truly Most Strong and Mighty." (22:73-74)

He who worshipped besides Allah, who was unable to create the feeblest and most despicable creature, did not appraise Him with true appraisal. If the tiny fly takes away something from him, he is not able to retrieve it. Allah also said:

"They have not appraised Allah with true appraisal, while the earth entirely will be within His grip on the Day of Resurrection, and the

heavens will be folded in His right hand. Exalted is He and High above what they associate with Him."(39:67)

Those who assigned partner with Allah in worship did not appraise Almighty who is so great and magnificent. The ones who are considered to be partners have no power over anything, but they are the weakest and most incapable. Anyone who associated with the Strongest and Mighty the weak and feeble one, did not make the right appraisal of Him.

Also those who claimed that Allah did not send any messenger to His creation nor did He send down a book have not appraised Him as it is due. They ascribed to Him what is not appropriate right for Him by saying that He neglected His creation, left them without guidance and created them in vain and for no purpose.

Those who rejected the realities of His beautiful Names and sublime Attributes are also guilty of not appraising Allah with right appraisal. They denied His hearing, seeing, willing choosing and being above His creatures. They also denied His speaking and addressing whoever He wished from among His creation. They also denied His comprehensive Power and its connection with the actions of the people as regards their obedience and evil deeds. They took all these from His power and will and made the people create for themselves what they wished without the will of the Lord, which means that what He does not want takes place in His kingdom and what He wants does not happen. Allah is Exalted and High above the statements of the like of the Magians!

He also did not appraise the Lord with right appraisal who said that He punishes the servant for what he has not done, because the servant has no power for doing anything. All his actions are the work of the Lord, so the servant is punished for actions which he did under compulsion of the Lord. His forcing the slave on action is more serious than coercion of a man of another man.

It is established in the reasons and instincts that if a master forces his slave on doing something or compels him on it and then punishes him for doing it, it is ignominious. How can the most Just of all the just and the Fairest of all the judges and the Most Merciful of merciful force the servant to do something which he has no power or will of doing then punish him with eternal torment? Allah, the Exalted and High above this. Their statement is more abominable than the statement of the like of the Magians. Both groups did not appraise Allah with true appraisal.

The same is the case of those who did not keep Him away from filth, lavatory and places where He should not be mentioned, but claimed that

He was in every place, and kept Him away from being established on His Throne while He said:

"Good words rise up to Him and He lifts up the righteous deed." (35:10)

The angels and Spirit ascend to Him and descend.

"He runs everything from the heavens to the earth, and everything will ascend to Him in the end, on a Day that will measure a thousand years in your reckoning." (32:5)

Nevertheless, these people kept Him away from the Throne of the king and put Him in every place which a human being and even an animal does not like to be in.

Those who denied the reality of His love, mercy, kindness, pleasure and His wrath and anger are also lacking the appraisal of Allah Almighty. It also includes those who denied the reality of His wisdom which are the intended objectives of His act, and denied His actions, and did not assign any action for Him to do by His will. They made all His acts separate from Him, so they denied His real coming, establishing Himself on His Throne, speaking to Moses from the side of the mountain, and His coming on the Day of Resurrection to judge between His servants by Himself. They denied other actions related to His perfection and claimed that by denying them they have appraised the Lord with true appraisal.

In the same way he who made spouse and son for Him has not grasped the true measure of Him. The same is true of those who claim that He incarnates in His creatures or those who claimed to have found Him in everything. The same is true about those who claim that He raised the enemies of the Messenger of Allah, blessing and peace be upon him, and their families to high ranks and raised their prestige and gave them power, caliphate and honour, and degraded the allies and the members of the family of the Messenger, Allah's blessing and peace be upon him, disgraced them and put them under humiliation whenever they are found. This is extreme vilification of the Lord. He is exalted and far above the statement of the Rafidah.

This statement is taken from the saying of the Jews and the Christians about the Lord of the Worlds that He sent a tyrant king who claimed to be prophet and told lie about Allah. He remained for a long period telling lie about Him and saying: 'Allah said this and that, He ordered this and that, and forbade this and that.' He cancelled the religious rules of the prophets and messengers before him, and regarded shedding blood of their followers and appropriating their properties and women as lawful. He justified it by saying that 'Allah has given me permission for it.' Allah gave him support and power and honour, granted his supplication and gave him power over his opponents. Almighty provided evidences on his truth. No one stood against him but he was able to overcome him and make him to believe in his words and deeds. He was supported by evidences one after the other.

It is clear that it is greatest vilification and accusation of Allah, the Exalted and defaming the Lord in His knowledge, wisdom, mercy and Lordship. Almighty is exalted and far above the claim of these rejecters.

Compare the statement of these people and the statement of the Rafidah, you will notice great resemblance in them.

They also did not recognise the greatness of Allah who said that He may punish His allies and those who have not committed any evil deed at all, and put them in Hellfire. He may honour His enemies and those who never believed in Him at any time, and admit them into the abode of pleasure. Both matters are equal to Him. However, the information is contrary to this statement. He, the Exalted, has denied vehemently in His Book, and declared this statement a very absurd judgement. He said:

"It was not without purpose that We created the heavens and the earth and everything in between. That is what the disbelievers assume. Woe to those who disbelieve from the Fire. Would We treat those who believe and do good deeds and those who spread corruption on earth as equal? Would We treat those who take heed of Allah and those who are wicked in the same way?" (38:27-28)

"Do those who commit evil deeds really think that We will deal with them in the same way as those who believe and do righteous deeds, that they will be alike in their living an their dying? How badly they judge! Allah created the heavens an earth for a true purpose: to reward each soul according to its deeds. They will not be wronged." (45:21-22)

"Will We treat those who submit to Us as We treat those are criminals? What is the matter with you? How do you judge?" (68:35-36)

Those who claim that Allah will not bring the dead back to life, will not raise those in the graves and will not gather His creatures on a Day to reward the righteous for his good deeds and the wrong doer for his evil deeds; and that He will not take the right of the wronged from the one who wronged him. They also claim that He will not honour those who undertake hardship in this world for the sake of Him and to seek His pleasure with the prestigious honour, and make clear what they had been disputing among themselves and to make the disbelievers realise that they were liars.

He also did not recognise the authority of Allah, who took His command lightly and did not comply with it, and considered His prohibition simple and committed it. He did not acknowledge His right and neglected it, did not take care of His remembrance and ignored it and his heart was neglectful of it. His desire was more preferable to him than the desire of seeking the pleasure of Allah. The submission to the creature was more important for him than the submission to Allah. For Allah is residue in his heart and word and deed, others are placed ahead of Him because they are more important. He looked down upon the look of Allah, while he is in His grip and his forelock is in His hand. He values the look of the creature to him and inclines with all his heart and organs towards him. He is ashamed of the people and does not feel shame from Allah; fears people and does not fear Him. He treats the creature in the best way he can and if he comes to deal with Allah, he uses the cheapest and the lowest way. When he stands in the service of a human whom he loves, he shows enthusiasm and makes effort to please him. He puts him before many of his interests and devotes his heart and organs to him. On the other hand if he wants to pay the due to his Lord, if the decree helps him, he does it in a way which no creature will accept from another, and spends from his wealth what he will feel ashamed of spending for a creature like him. Has this man with this behaviour fulfilled the respect of Allah as it is due?

Did such a person fully appreciate the sublimity of Almighty, who combined Him and His enemy in His pure right of respect, greatness, obedience, submission fear and hope? If he has set a close person as partner in this, it would have been pouncing upon His exclusive right, showing disregard to Him and making someone a partner in what was not appropriate and suitable but for Him alone. Then what will be the case when he joins Him with the most hateful, disgraceful and detestable creature who is His real enemy? Anyone who worships any object besides Allah in reality worships Satan. Allah, the Exalted, said:

"Children of Adam, did I not command you not to worship Satan, for he was your sworn enemy, and to worship Me? This is the straight path." (36:60)

When the disbelievers worshipped the angels in their opinion, their worship in reality went to the Devils while they thought that they were worshipping the angels. It has been attested by Allah, the Exalted, in the following verse:

"On the Day He will gather them all together, He will say to the angels, 'Was it you these people worshipped?' They will reply, 'May You be Exalted! You are our supporters against them! Really they worshipped the Jinn, most of them believed in them.'" (34:40-41)

Satan prompts the disbeliever to worship him putting in his mind that he is an angel. The same is true of the worshippers of the sun, the moon and stars, they assume that they are worshipping the spirits of these stars, and they are the ones who address them and fulfil their needs. That is why when the sun rises, Satan comes before it and the disbelievers prostrate to it. Their prostration goes to him and the same happens at the sunset. It also applies to those who worship the Christ and his mother. Their worship goes to Satan not to them. They believe that they worship the one who has ordered them to worship the Christ and his mother. It is the accursed Satan, not the slave and the Messenger of Allah. All these acts fall under the words of Allah:

"Did I not command you, children of Adam, not to worship Satan; he is a clear enemy of you, and to worship Me. This is a straight path." (36:60)

No one from the children of Adam worshipped anyone besides Allah, no matter who he was, but his worship goes to Satan. The worshipper gets benefit from the worshipped in achieving his objective and the worshipped enjoys from the worshipper his veneration of him and putting him as the partner of Allah. This is the aim of Satan, which makes him pleased. Allah has spoken about it:

"On the Day He will gather everyone together (and say), 'Company of Jinn! You have seduced a great many humans.' Their adherents among mankind will say, 'Our Lord, we have benefitted from one another, but now we reached the appointed You decreed for us.' He will say: 'Your home is the Fire, and there you shall remain forever unless Allah wills otherwise. Your Lord is All-Wise, All-Knowing." (6:128)

This is unique indication of the secret for which the *shirk*, i. e. association of partner with Allah, is the gravest of the major sins with Allah. He will not forgive it without repentance, and it will make the person remain in the Fire for ever. It was not forbidden and considered the most abominable act but because it is impossible for Allah, the Exalted, to ordain the worship of any other deity for His servants as it is unthinkable that He does something that contradicts His perfect Attributes and majesty. How can one think that the One who deserves alone the qualities of Lordship, being sole deity, greatness and sublimity, will allow anyone to share with Him in this? Allah is exalted and far above it.

5.8 Association and arrogance are contrary to the obedience of Allah alone

Since association is in direct contradiction with the purpose for which He has created the creation and ordered it, it is the gravest of the major crimes to Allah. The same is true of arrogance and its supplements. Allah, the Exalted, created the creation and revealed the Books in order to make obedience for Him alone, and the association of partner and arrogance are contrary to it. For this reason Allah has forbidden Paradise for the people of shirk and arrogance, even if anyone who has an atom's weight of arrogance.

5.9 Speaking about the Names and Attributes and Actions of Allah with knowledge

Next to it in gravity is speaking about Allah concerning His Names, Attributes and actions and describing Him with the opposites of what He had described Himself or His Messenger, Allah's blessing and peace be upon him, had said. It is directly against the wisdom of the One to whom belong the perfect creation and command, and is depreciation of His Lordship and qualities of being the deity. If it was done with knowledge, it is obstinacy which is more serious and greater sin than association. A disbeliever who acknowledges the Attributes of the Lord Almighty is better than the one who denies the perfect Attributes of Him. He is like a man who acknowledges the sovereignty of the king, does not reject his power or the qualities by which he deserved to be king but he puts someone as partner to him in some of the affairs to come closer to him through this partner. He is better than the one who denied the feature of the king and the qualities which put him in that position. This is a matter which is well established in the instincts and reasons. Where is belittlement of the perfect Attributes and denial of them from the worship of an intermediary between the deity and the worshipper, who tries to come closer to him by the worship of that intermediary as showing respect and honour to him? The disease of denial of the Attributes is an incurable one which has no cure.

Allah related about the leader of the deniers, Pharaoh that he rejected what Moses told him that his Lord is above the heavens. He said to his minister:

"Haman, build me a tall tower so that I may reach the ways that lead to the heavens to look for this God of Moses. I am convinced that he is lying." (40:36-37)

Shaykh Abu al-Hasan al-Ash'ari quoted this verse in argument against those who denied the Divine Attributes. We have cited his argument in another place.[217]

Talking about Allah without knowledge and association of partner with Him are inseparable.

The misguiding innovations are based on ignorance of the Attributes of Allah and rejection of what He had said about Himself and His Messenger, because of obstinacy and ignorance; these innovations are among the gravest sins. They are below disbelief but more liked by the Devil than major sins. Some early man said:
'Innovation is dearer to Iblis than evil deeds. It is because there is a chance of repentance from the evil deeds but for innovation there is no chance of it.'

Iblis said: 'I destroyed the children of Adam by evil deeds and they destroyed me by seeking forgiveness and declaration that 'there is no deity but Allah.' When I noticed this I consolidated desires in their hearts, so they commit sins and do not repent because they think that they are doing good work.'

It is well known that the harm of a sinner is on himself, but the harm of an innovator is for all the people. The corruption of the innovator is in the basis of the religion while the corruption of the sinner lies in desire. The innovator sits on the straight path to misguide the people while the sinner is not like that. The innovator finds fault in the Attributes of the Lord and His perfectness while the sinner is not like that. The innovator opposes

---

[217] He mentioned it in his book 'ijtima' al-juyush al-Islamiyyah'.

what the Messenger has brought, but the sinner does not do that. The innovator blocks the path of the Hereafter for the people, while the sinner walks slowly to it because of his shortcomings.

5.10 Injustice is one of the most offensive acts to Allah

Since the injustice and aggression were in contradiction with justice by which the heavens and the earth are established, and Allah, the Glorious, sent His Messengers, peace be upon them, and revealed His Books so that people may maintain their affairs with justice, injustice was among the most serious offences to Allah, and its degree is according to its damage. Allah, the Exalted, has created the hearts on the love and affection and kindness towards children and He especially gave the parents the big share of it. After that if a man kills his young child who has no fault with the fear that he will join him in his food and drink and property, it is the most ignoble and most despicable crime. The same is true about the child killing his parents who were the cause of his coming to this world; and killing of any blood relative. The level of the crime will be different in line of its severity and deservedly of the person who was killed for the purpose of his survival.

For this reason the person to be punished most severely on the Day of Resurrection will be the one who killed a prophet or killed by him. Next in line is a man who killed a ruler or a learned man who used to command people to uphold justice and call them to Allah and give them good advice about their religion. Allah, the Exalted, prepared the recompense of the person who kills deliberately a believing soul permanent punishment in Hellfire; in addition to the anger of Almighty, His curse and severe torment. This is the result of killing a believer deliberately unless there is some impediment. There is no dispute among the scholars that embracing Islam by the killer of his own will after killing is a barrier to the implementation of that punishment.

Whether the repentance of the Muslim after this incident is going to stop the punishment? There are two views for the learned people in this regard. They are reported from Imam Ahmad.
Those who say that repentance will not stop the punishment argue that it is the right of a human which he did not get in this world and left it with his wrongdoing. He must be recompensed for it in the Home of Justice.
They added that what the heir has received in the form of blood money was his right which Allah gave him choice between taking in full or forgiving. The killed person is not going to benefit from receiving the full

compensation by his heir. Injustice done to him is not removed by his heir's taking money.

It is the more correct statement of the two. The right of the killed person is not written off by taking the blood money by his heir.

The other group who hold that the right of the killed is dropped by repentance and taking money by the heir, say that repentance wipes out any crime committed before it, and the prescribed punishment of the crime he committed was administered.

They added that if repentance can erase the effect of disbelief and sorcery, which are more serious crime than murder, how will it fail to erase the effect of murder? Allah has accepted the repentance of those disbelievers who killed His allies, and made them among the best of His slaves. He called those who burnt His allies and seduced them from their religion to turn to Him in repentance. He said:

"Say: 'My servants who have wronged against themselves by their own excess, do not despair of Allah's mercy. Allah forgives all sins." (39:53)

This is as far as the right of the repentant is concerned, which includes repentance from disbelief and lower sin.

They further argued that how can a person repent from the sins and be punished as well for them after making repentance? This is well known that it will not happen in the rules of Allah concerning His recompense.

They also said that the repentance of the criminal was to surrender himself to the killed and since it was not possible for him to surrender himself to the killed, the Shari'ah put his guardian in his place and made him surrender himself to him. It also made the receiving of the money by his heir as surrendering himself to the killed.

Strictly speaking on the issue is that murder has three rights connected with it:

a) The right of Allah,
b) The right of the murdered person and
c) The right of his guardian.

If the killer surrendered himself voluntarily to the guardian to express his regret of his doing, and for fear of Allah and sincerely repented, the right of Allah will go away. The right of guardian will be fulfilled by taking the compensation or by reconciliation or pardoning. Only the right of the victim remains which Allah will compensate on the Day of Resurrection for his sincere repentance and good deeds. Almighty will make settlement between him and his victim and as such neither party's right will be wasted.

The case of money is disputed: A group says that when the due amount was paid to the heir then the man is free from his responsibility in the Hereafter as he was free from it in the world.

But another group said: the demand of the wronged remains on the Day of Resurrection. The victim did not receive the compensation by his heir's taking it. The killer prevented him from benefitting from it for his whole life; he died and could not use it. This was an iniquity which he was unable to redress; the others took benefit of it. They deduced from it that if the money moved from one person to another and there were many heirs, each one of them has right to demand. It was a right to be given to each of them. It is the view of the followers of Malik and Ahmad.

Our Shaykh (i.e. Ibn Taymiyyah) set the case in detail between the two groups saying: If the inherited person was able to take the money but he did not take it and did not demand it, the right of it will remain for the heir in the Hereafter, as it is in the world. However, if he was unable to take the money and he was stopped from it unfairly and unjustly then the demand will be in the Hereafter.

This is the best solution. For if the money was consumed by the testator and it became difficult for the heir to take it, it became like his slave who was killed, or his house which was burnt down by someone or his food and drink which was taken by another person. In all these cases the responsibility is on the testator not on the heir. The right of demand, therefore, is for the one who lost his possession.

Now remains an issue that if the possession is a building or plot of land or something which is remaining after the death, it will be owned by the heir if a person has seized it illegally, he has to return it at any time. If he did not return the same property, he will be demanded with Allah as he is to be demanded here in the world.

It is a strong point and there is no solution for it except by saying that the usurper will bear the responsibility in both worlds. It is like money owned by a group together every share holder has right to demand his share. Or if a person takes possession of an endowment which was meant for the members of the family, and he took it, each of them will have right to demand his due on the Day of Resurrection. Allah knows better.

5.11 The evil impact of murder and the sin of the murderer

Since the act of killing was very serious Allah, the Exalted, said:

"Because of that We decreed upon the Children of Israel that whoever kills a soul unless for the retribution for a soul or spreading corruption in the land – it is as if he had killed mankind entirely, and whoever saves one it is as if he had saved mankind entirely." (5:32)

This verse has posed a problem for many people. They said; It is well known that the crime of killing hundred people is more serious to Allah than killing one person. They were victim of thinking that the comparison was in the scale of sin and punishment while the words do not indicate this. Comparison of one thing with another does mean to be similar in every aspect. Allah said:

"On the Day they see it, it will seem they have not remained (in this life) except for an evening or its morning." (79:46)

"On the Day they see what they had been warned about, it will seem to them that they lingered no more than an hour of a day." (46:35)

It does not mean that stay in the world was this much.

The Prophet, Allah's blessing and peace be upon him, said:

"Whoever performs the night prayer (i.e. 'Isha') in congregation as though he has kept vigil half the night, and the one who performed dawn prayer in congregation as if he had passed the whole night awake (in worship)."[218]

It is about a person who performed dawn and night prayers in congregation, as it is stated in another version.[219]

Clearer than this is the saying of the Prophet:

---

[218] Muslim (656)
[219] Ahmad (1: 58), Tirmidhi (221) Ibn Hibban (2058)

"Whoever fasted Ramadan and the followed six days from Shawwal as though he had fasted the whole year."[220]

Or his saying:

"Anyone who reads, 'Say Allah is one' (chapter 112) as if he has read the whole Qur'an."[221]

It is well known that the reward of these acts do not reach the reward of those acts with which they are compared, and they are the same. If the amount of reward had been the same, there would have not been for the person who performed the night and dawn prayers in congregation any benefit except the exhaustion and tiredness. No one has been given –after belief – more precious thing than understanding the message of Allah and His Messenger, peace be upon him. It is Allah's favour He grants it to whoever He wishes.

If it is said: in which way the comparison is made between the killer of one person and the killer of all the people?
The answer is that it is in many ways:

1. Both of them disobeyed Allah and His Messenger, Allah's blessing and peace be upon him, and exposed himself to the punishment of Allah. Each one of them incurred the wrath and curse of Allah, deserved to be put in Hellfire for ever and suffer from the severe torment. The difference will be in degree; so the crime of the one who killed a prophet or a just ruler or a learned person engaged in enjoining people to deal with justice, is not similar to the crime of someone who killed an ordinary person.
2. Both are equally guilty of taking life.
3. They are similar in embarking on shedding the sacred blood. Anyone who kills with just cause, but only to spread corruption in the land or for taking the money, he can kill anyone one he gets hold of him and gets an opportunity for killing. He is enemy of the human race.
4. He is called a killer, defiant, wrongdoer, and disobedient for killing one person and for killing of all the people.
5. Allah Almighty has made the believers in their mutual affection, mercy and good relation like one body, when one part of it feels pain the rest of the body feel it by fever and sleeplessness.[222] When the

---

[220] Muslim (204)
[221] Tirmidhi (2898), Ahmad (5: 141) See also Bukhari (5015), Muslim (812)
[222] This is the statement of the Prophet in a Hadith. See Bukhari (6011), Muslim (2586)

killer destroyed one part of this body, he as though had destroyed the whole of it and caused pain to every part of it. Anyone who had caused pain to one believer, as though he had caused pain to all believers. Hurting the believers is hurting all mankind. This is because Allah protects the mankind through the existence of believers among them. The Prophet, Allah's blessing and peace be upon him, said:

"No soul is killed unjustly but some of the responsibility of his blood will be on the first son of Adam because he was the first one to start killing."[223]

This threat was not given in the case of the first adulterer or the first thief or the first drinker of wine. The first person to start association of partner with Allah deserved it more than the first murderer. For this reason the Prophet, Allah's blessing and peace be upon him, saw 'Amr ibn Luhayy al-Khuza'i being punished with severe torment in the Hellfire, because he was the first person to change the religion of Abraham.[224]
Allah, the Exalted, said:

"Do not be the first to reject it." (2:41)

It means that do not be the first one to reject it so the people follow you and their sins come on you. It is the case of anyone who started a bad way and was followed by others.
Ibn Abbas reported that the Prophet, Allah's blessing and peace be upon him, said:

"The murdered will bring the murderer on the Day of Judgement his forehead and head will be in his hand and his veins gushing forth with blood; he will say: My Lord, ask him, for what reason he killed me?"[225]

They mentioned repentance to Ibn Abbas, and he recited the verse:

"Whoever kills a believer deliberately his retribution is Hell fire where he will remain forever." (4:93)

He said: This verse has not been abrogated or changed, then how he will repent?

---

[223] Bukhari (3335), Muslim (1677)
[224] See Bukhari (4623), Muslim (2856)
[225] Tirmidhi (3029), Ibn Majah (2621), Nisa'i (8: 63)

Nafi' related that Abdullah ibn 'Umar looked one day at the Ka'bah and said:

'How great you are! And how great is your sacredness! However, a believer is more sacred than you to Allah.'[226]

Jundub reported the Prophet, Allah's blessing and peace be upon him, saying:

"The first thing of the human being to decay is his stomach. Whoever is able to eat only pure things, he should do it. Whoever is able not to have a handful blood he shed be a barrier between him and Paradise should do it."[227]

Ibn 'Umar reported that the Messenger of Allah, blessing and peace be upon him, said:

"A believer remains in ample opportunities from his religion as long as he does not shed a sacred blood."[228]

Ibn 'Umar said:

'Among the difficult situations from which there is no escape is shedding the sacred blood for no justification.'[229]

The Prophet, Allah's blessing and peace be upon him, said:

"Engaging in abusing a Muslim is an evil act and fighting him is disbelief."[230]

He, peace be upon him, said:

"Do not turn after me disbeliever killing each other."[231]

He also said:

"Anyone who killed a man who was given protection will not get the smell of Paradise while its smell is experienced from the distance of forty years."[232]

---

[226] [226] Tirmidhi (2032)
[227] Bukhari (7152),
[228] Bukhari (6862)
[229] Bukhari (6867)
[230] Bukhari (48), Muslim (64)
[231] Bukhari (70), Muslim (65)

This is the punishment of the enemy of Allah if he is given protection by Him, then what will be the punishment of a person who murdered a believer?

If a woman was cast in the Fire because she tied a cat till it died out of hunger and thirst, the Prophet, Allah's blessing and peace be upon him, saw her in the Fire being scratched by it in her face and chest,[233] what will be the torment of a man who put a believer in prison without any crime till he died?

The Prophet, Allah's blessing and peace be upon him, said:

"The destruction of the world is easier to Allah than killing a believer unjustly."[234]

5.12 The crime of adultery is one of the greatest evils

Since the evil act of adultery was one of the most serious crimes, it was placed after murder among the major sins. Adultery was considered very serious because it is in contradiction with the system of the world in protection of the families, guarding of the private parts, safeguarding the sacred matters and keeping away from what creates greatest enmity and hatred between the people. It also leads to spoiling of the spouse of a person, his daughter, sister and mother, in which lies the destruction of the world. For that reason Allah, the Exalted, joined it with murder in His Book, and His Messenger put it together with murder in his Sunnah.

Imam Ahmad said: 'I do not know any crime after killing a soul more ignominious than adultery.'

Allah, the Exalted, has confirmed its prohibition by saying:

"Those who never invoke any other deity beside Allah, nor take a life, which Allah has made sacred, except for the cause of justice, nor commit adultery. Whoever does these things will face the punishment, their torment will be doubled on the Day of Resurrection, and he will remain in it, disgraced, except those who repent." (25:68-70)

---

[232] Bukhari (3160)
[233] Muslim (2242)
[234] Tirmidhi (13450, Nisa'i (7: 83)

Here Almighty joined adultery with association of partners with Allah and killing of a soul, and decreed the recompense of them eternal remaining in doubled torment, unless the culprit removes the cause of these sins by repentance, belief and good deeds.

Allah also said:

"Do not go anywhere near adultery; it is an outrage and an evil path." (17:32)

Almighty told us about its loathsome in itself. It is extremely abominable and its horribleness is settled in the reason of many animals. Bukhari related 'Amr ibn Maymun al-Awdi saying:

'I saw in pre-Islamic days a monkey who committed adultery with a female monkey, so the group of monkeys gathered and stoned them to death.[235]

Almighty said that it was an evil path because it was the path of destruction, ruin and disgrace in the world, and the path of torment, humiliation and an example in the Hereafter.

As the intercourse with the spouses of the fathers was most horrendous, He condemned it by saying:

"It was indeed a shameful thing to do, loathsome and leading to an evil." (4:22)

The Lord Almighty attached the success of a person to the protecting of his private parts, and asserted that success cannot be gained without it. He said:

"The faithful have succeeded: those who pray humbly, who shun frivolity, who pay the prescribed alms, who guard their chastity except with their spouses or their slaves – with these they are not to blame, but those who seek to go beyond this are exceeding the limits." (23:1-7)

The above verses include three matters: Anyone who did not guard his chastity, would not be among the successors. He is to blame and is transgressor. He missed the success and committed transgression and was

---

[235] Bukhari (3849)

to be blamed. Enduring the pain of lust and controlling it is easier than some of these.

Similar to this is the condemnation of human being by Allah that he has been created anxious unable to exercise patience in happiness and adversity. When he gets wealth, he becomes stingy and withholds, and when he is afflicted by harm, he is fretful except those whom Allah took out and saved them. He mentioned among them:

"Who guard their chastity from all but their spouses or their slave-girls; they are not to blame, but those whose desires exceed this limit are truly transgressors." (70:29-31)

Allah, the Exalted, ordered His Prophet, Allah's blessing and peace be upon him, to teach the believers to lower their gaze and guard their chastity, and tell them that He was watching their acts and was aware of them.

"He is aware of the most furtive of glances, and all that hearts conceal." (40:19)

Since the starting point of this crime is from eyes, He ordered lowering of glances before guarding the chastity. The incidents start from gazing as the big fire starts from the sparks. First comes glance, then imagination then initiation of step and finally the sin. It is said that anyone who guards these four things has saved his religion: glances, imagination, words and steps.
A slave is required to be gatekeeper of these four gates, taking position on their fronts. It is from these that the enemy enters and then ravages the homes and destroys completely what comes under his power.

5.13 How does a believer fall in sinful acts?

The evil deeds enter the life of a believer from above four gates. We are going to discuss each of them in a separate section.
The first one is the glances. They are the vanguard and messenger of the desire; its guarding is basis of guarding chastity. Anyone who left his eyes loose has brought himself to places of ruin.
The Prophet, Allah's blessing and peace be upon him, said:

"Do not follow a glance with another; you are allowed the first one but not the second one."[236]

He also said:

"Glance is a poisoned arrow of Iblis. Anyone who lowers his gaze from a woman for the sake of Allah, Allah will put in his heart sweetness to the Day he will meet with Him."[237]

He advised his followers:
"Lower your gaze and guard your chastity."[238]

He also said to them:
"Avoid sitting on the roads."

They said: 'These are our meeting places, Messenger of Allah. We cannot help it.'

He said:

"If you insist on doing it, then give the road its due."

They asked what its due was. He replied:

"It is lowering the gaze, preventing the harm and answering the greeting."[239]

Gazing is in fact the root of the troubles which a man faces. A glance produces thought and it produces an idea, which develops into desire, which becomes intention and then it becomes strong to be a resolve or decision and leads incvitably to commit the act unless there is some impediment. It is said:
'Patience on keeping the gaze low is easier than patience on the pain which will follow.'
A poet has said:

'All the troubles start from gazing, and big fire is caused by small spark.

---

[236] Abu Dawud (2149), Tirmidhi (2777), Ahmad (5: 353, 357)
[237] Hakim (4: 313), Ahmad (5: 264), Tabarani in Kabir (7843) See Majma' al-zawa'id (4: 63)
[238] Ahmad (5: 323), Ibn Hibban (2547), Hakim (4: 358) See Majma' (4: 145)
[239] Bukhari (2465), Muslim (2121)

How many a glaze affected the heart of its person like the effect of arrow
between the bow and string.
A person who turns his eye to others is standing on danger.
His eye is pleased with what will harm his soul. No welcome for a delight
that turns into harm.'

Among the destructive features of gazing is that it produces regrets, moaning and agony. The person sees what he is not able to get or to be patient from it. It is the most painful torment to look at what you cannot control yourself from it and you have no power to get it.
A poet said:

'If you leave your eye as vanguard for your heart, the views will make
you tired.
You will see something which you have no power to achieve all of it
neither you are able to be patient from some of it.'

How many people sent his gazes loose and the result was that he was murdered between them, as it is said in a line of poetry:

'O gazer whose gazes did not stop till he was murdered between them.'

I said the following lines:

'He was fed up of peace, so he fixed his gazes on ruin which was
considered beautiful.
He remained gazing at it until he fell dead among them.'

It is strange that the gaze of the spectator is an arrow which does not reach the object of gazing but makes a place in the heart of the spectator.
I said in a poem:

'O the one shooting with the arrows of gazing, you are the target of your
shooting, so do not hit it.
The motive of the gazing looks for cure of it. Control your envoy, it
should not cause your perish.'

More strange is that the look causes a wound in the heart and follows wound after wound, but the pain of wound does not make him refrain from wishing more of it.
I said to express this meaning:

'You continued gaze after gaze at every charming boy and girl.

You think that it is the medicine of your wound while in fact it is injury after injury. You killed your eye by gazing and by crying; as a result your heart is completely slaughtered.'

It is said that 'controlling the gazes is easier than permanent moaning.'

5.14 The next cause of the sin is imagination

The matter of imagination is more difficult, as they are the starting point of good and evil. From them are produced intentions, resolutions and determinations. If a person controls his imaginations, he will be in control of his soul and suppress his desire; but anyone whose thoughts dominated him, his desire and soul will not be in control. Anyone who underrates his imaginations they will drag him to the ruins. The thoughts continue coming to the heart till they turn into false desires as explained in Qur'an:

"Like a mirage in a desert: the thirsty person thinks there will be water but, when he gets there, he finds it nothing. There he finds Allah, who pays him his account in full. Allah is swift in reckoning." (24:39)

The lowest person in resolution and the least capable is the one who is pleased with false desires instead of realities. He brought them to himself and adored himself with them while they, by Allah, are the capitals of the destitute people and commodities of untrue traders. They are the nourishment of the empty soul which is content with the visit of the phantom in place of real union, and with false desires instead of realities. A poet says:

'The desires of Su'da are pleasing appearance on thirst. Su'da supplied it as cool water on thirst.
If these desires are true they are excellent desires, otherwise we have lived with them for a long time.'

They are the most harmful for a person and are produced by incapability and laziness. They produce negligence, regret and sorrow. The person who failed to get the real physical union with his beloved painted her image in his heart, hugged her and embraced her and in this way he was satisfied with the union of imaginary picture made by his thought. It is not to bring him any comfort and his likeness is like the hungry and thirsty person who paints in his imagination the picture of food and drink while he is not able to eat and drink. Satisfaction with this and bringing it to the mind is a sign of the lowliness and meanness of the soul; while the nobility, purity, sublimity and greatness of the soul depend on expelling any though that is not real. One should not allow the false thoughts to take place in his heart and dismiss them immediately.

The imaginations are divided into four categories:

a) Imaginations that bring about the benefits of the world;
b) Imaginations that repel the harms of the world;
c) Imagination that bring about the benefits of the Hereafter; and
d) Imaginations that are used to repel the harms of the Hereafter.

Now the slave should encircle his imaginations and thoughts in these four categories. When he is able to do it then whichever is possible for him he should not leave it for others. But when the imaginations are crowded together because of the crowd of their objects, he should put the most important one ahead and delay what is not important to the end.

There are two more categories:

i.   An important aim which is not to be missed;
ii. And an unimportant one which may be missed.

Each one of them has something urging to put it first. Here the hesitation and confusion appear. If he puts the important one ahead, he will fear the loss of the lesser one; and if he puts the lesser one first, he will be engaged with it from the important one. This will be in the case that he is confronted by two matters the combination of which is not possible, and one of them cannot be achieved except by losing the other.

This is the situation in which reason, understanding and knowledge are used. This is the place where he who went high, went high, and he who was successful became successful, and failed the one who failed here. You will see most of those who give importance to his reason and knowledge prefers the unimportant one in order not to miss the important one. Hardly do you find a person who is safe from this; some of them have many and others have a few.

The judgement in this regard is based on the big principle on which the Shari'ah and decree depend, and to it the creation and command return. That is to prefer the bigger and higher of the two interests, even if the lesser interest is missed. It is better to undertake the lesser evil to repel what is bigger. An interest is lost in order to achieve bigger than that, and an evil is committed to repel what is bigger than that.

The imaginations of the reasonable person and his ideas do not go beyond that. This is what the religions have brought and on it the interests of the world and the Hereafter are based. The highest and the most useful idea is the one which is for Allah and the Hereafter. What is for Allah has different categories:

1. One is to contemplate over His revealed verses, to ponder and to try to understand their objects. Allah has revealed them for this purpose not for mere recitation. Recitation is only a means. Some early scholars said: 'Allah sent down the Qur'an to be put in action but the people took its recitation as an action'.

2. The second is to understand its verses and learn lessons from them, and use them to know His Names, Attributes, His wisdom, kindness, benevolence, and His generosity. Allah, the Exalted, has urged His servants to give thought to His verses, to contemplate and to understand them. He has condemned those who are heedless of it.

3. The third is to speculate about His favours, bounties and His grace on His creatures, and His vast mercy, forgiveness and pardon. These three categories produce in the heart the knowledge of Allah, His love, and fear and hope. Continuous thinking about it fully colours the heart with the knowledge and love of Almighty.

4. The fourth is to think about the defects of the souls and their calamities, and to realise the faults of acts. This thought is very useful and is the gate of every good, and it works in breaking the power of the commanding soul for evil. When its rage is subdued, the peaceful soul comes back to life and is animated and the judgement becomes to it. This result in the life of the heart and its order come in force in its kingdom, and it spreads its workers and soldiers to work for its interests.

5. To take care of time and its duty, and to focus all the thoughts on it. The clever person is the son of his time; if he wasted it, he wasted all his interests. All the interests start from time, if it was wasted, it could not be redressed.

Imam al-Shafi'i said:

'I lived in the company of the Sufis and learnt only two things from them:

i.   One their saying, 'Time is sword, if you do not cut it, it will cut you.'

ii.   The second that, 'If you do not engage yourself with truth, it will engage you in falsehood.'

The time of a person is in fact his life, and it is the source of his eternal life in permanent pleasure, and it is also the source of the hard life in painful torment. It runs faster than the cloud; so the time he passes for Allah and by Allah is his life and duration of his living; anything else is not counted in his life. If he lived like animals and passed his time in heedlessness, lust and false desires, and the best thing he did was sleeping and idleness, then his death was better for him than his life. When a person performing prayer does not benefit from it except what he understood of it, in the same way no time of his life is beneficial for him except what he passed for Allah and by Allah. Other imaginations and thoughts are either whispers of Satan or false desires and deceiving thoughts like the imaginations of those affected in their reasoning from among the drunks, users of hashish or obsessed with delusions. When the realities are exposed they will say:

'If my position on the Day of Gathering is what I face, then I wasted my life. It was a desire my soul enjoyed for a time and today I think that it was confusing dreams.'

Know that coming of the thought in one's mind is not harmful; the harmful is to retain and harbour it. Thought is like a person passing on the way; if you do not invite him and left him go, he would go ahead and turn away from you. However, if you call him, he will fascinate you with his talk and deception, which is the lightest thing on empty and useless soul, and the hardest on the noble and peaceful soul and heavenly heart.

Allah, the Exalted, has put two souls in human being: a evil commanding soul and a peaceful soul. They are enemy of one another. What is easy for one is hard for the other, what is delightful for one is painful for the other. There is nothing more difficult for the evil commanding soul than working for Allah and preferring His pleasure over its desire while this is the best course for it. On the other hand there is nothing harder for the peaceful soul than working for other than Allah and responding to the motive of the desire. It is the most harmful thing for it. On the right side is the angel and on the left is Satan; and between them the war is continuous and will not come to an end till it completes its life of the world. The wicked forces stand with Satan and the evil commanding soul, and the truth joins the angel and the peaceful soul. The war has alternate result, and the victory rests on patience. So whoever exercises patience, keeps firm and has fear of Allah, will have best outcome in the world and the Hereafter.

Allah has decreed - and His decree can never change - that best outcome is for being conscious of Allah and the people who are conscious of Him will have the best result. Heart is an empty tablet and thoughts are painting engraved on it. How can a sensible person agree to have his tablet painted with lies, deception, delusional false desire and unrealistic mirage? Which wisdom, knowledge and guidance will be painted with these false images? If he is interested getting on his heart the painting of knowledge and wisdom, it will be difficult because his heart is full of painting of what is useless. Unless he clears his heart from these rubbish thoughts the useful thoughts will not settle in it. The useful thoughts settle in a place which is empty as it is said (in a line):

'Her love approached me before I could know what the love was; it found an empty heart and settled in it.'

In this way many followers of mysticism built their behaviour on the protection from the thoughts and tried not to let any thought enter their heart so that the hearts are free, capable of illumination and appearance of higher realities in them. These people remember something and missed many others. They saved their hearts from the entrance of any thought, and the result was that the hearts remained free. Satan found them empty and sowed the seeds of falsehood in them giving them the impression that they were the highest and noblest things. He substituted them for the thoughts, which were the source of knowledge and guidance. When Satan found the hearts free he filled them with abandoning the orders of Allah and forsaking the world completely. He put in their minds that their perfectness lies in this emptiness and freedom. How far it is! The perfectness of the heart lies in its being full of the thoughts, intentions and ideas to receive the pleasures of Allah and the people, to think about their ways to acquire them. The most perfect person is the one who has many thoughts, intentions and ideas in this regard while the most imperfect person is the one whose heart is full of thoughts and ideas for his desires. Allah's support is to be sought.

Look at 'Umar ibn al-Khattab the thoughts for the pleasures of Allah swarmed his heart, and sometimes he faced them while performing prayer. He set his military expedition while in prayer; and in this way he combined the prayer and jihad together. It is the case of assimilation of many acts of worship in one. This is a very noble and honourable aspect available only to those who have sharp heart, high resolution and great knowledge to be able to start an act of worship and succeed to enter in various good deeds. This is the favour of Allah, He gives it to whoever He wishes.

5.15 Another source for evil acts is utterances

Utterances are the next step of falling in a sin, and a righteous person has to protect his tongue from speaking foolish words. He should utter only what is going to be beneficial and useful for him in his religion. Before talking he should check whether what he is going to say carries any benefit or not. If there is no benefit in it, he should keep his tongue closed; if there is a benefit in it then he has to see whether by uttering it he is going to lose some more beneficial talks. He should not let the more useful be lost for this less useful one. If you are interested in checking what is in the heart, use your tongue to find out; it will tell you what is in the heart whether you like it or not.

Yahya ibn Mu'adh said:
'Hearts are like cooking pots boiling with what is in them, and tongues are their scoops. Look at the person when he speaks, his tongue will take out what is in his heart, sweet or savour, fresh or bitter and so on. The portion coming from his tongue will tell you the taste of his heart.'[240]

The meaning is that as you taste by your tongue the flavour of the food in the pots and learn its real taste, you taste what is in the heart of the man from his tongue. You taste what is in his heart from his tongue, as you taste the food of the pot by tongue.

Anas reported the Prophet, Allah's blessing and peace be upon him, saying:

"The faith of a person will not be right unless his heart is straight, and his heart will not be right unless his tongue is straight."[241]

The Prophet, Allah's blessing and peace be upon him, was asked:
'What is the most common cause of going to Hell?' He replied:

"The mouth i.e. tongue and the private part."[242]

---

[240] Abu Nu'aym in al-Hilyah (10: 63)
[241] Ahmad (3: 198), see Majma' (1: 53)

Mu'adh enquired the Prophet, Allah's blessing and peace be upon him, about the act that will take him to Paradise and keep him away from Hell. The Prophet told him about the head of Islam, its pillar and the peak of its hump, then said:

"Should I not tell you about the foundation of all that?"

He said: 'Yes, indeed, Messenger of Allah.'
The Prophet held his tongue and said:

"Control this."

Mu'adh asked: 'Are we going to give account of what we speak?'
He replied:

"May your mother be bereaved of you, Mu'adh! What else brings people on their faces in Hell but the yields of their tongues?"[243]

It is strange that a person finds it easy to keep away and avoid eating prohibited materials, wrongdoing, adultery, stealing and drinking wine, gazing at prohibited images and other such things, but finds it difficult to control his tongue. You may see a man to be pointed with piety and worship utters words which anger Allah Almighty, but he does not pay attention to it while one word of his talk will bring him farther than the distance between the east and west. How many people you see being very careful from immoral acts and injustice, but his tongue invents lies about the honour of living and dead people without caring about what he says!
If you want to learn more about it look at the report in Sahih of Muslim reported by Jundub ibn Abdullah that the Messenger of Allah, blessing and peace of Allah be upon him, said:

"By Allah, Allah will not forgive so and so.' Allah, the Exalted said: 'Who is that to claim that I will not forgive so and so? I forgave him and destroyed all your deeds."[244]

---

[242] Tirmidhi (2004), Bukhari in al-Adab al-mufrad (294), Ibn Majah (4246), Ibn Hibban (1923), Hakim (4: 324)
[243] Tirmidhi (2616), Ibn Majah (3973), Abd al-Razzaq ((11: 194), Hakim (4: 286)
[244] Muslim (2621)
2. Ahmad (8275), Abu Dawud (4901)
3. Bukhari (6478)
4. Muslim (2319) see also Bukhari (6477), Ahmad (3: 469), Ibn Majah (3969), Ibn Hibban (280)
5 Tirmidhi (2319)

This man engaged in the worship of Allah as much as Allah willed for him, and one word destroyed all his deeds.
This report has come from Abu Hurayrah as well which has the following wording:

"He spoke a word which destroyed his world and the Hereafter."[245]

Abu Hurayrah reported that the Prophet, Allah's blessing and peace be upon him, said:

"A man utters a word pleasing Allah but does not pay attention to it, and Allah raises him in grades because of it; and a person speaks a word causing anger of Allah and does not pay attention to it but he falls because of it in the Hellfire."[246]

In another version:

"A person speaks a word without realising its seriousness falls because of it in the Hellfire the distance between the east and the west."[247]

Bilal ibn al-Harith al-Muzani reported that the Prophet, Allah's blessing and peace be upon him, said:

"One of you speaks a word pleasing Allah and he does not think it will have much effect, but Allah writes because of it His pleasure till the Day he will meet Him. And one of you speaks a word causing anger of Allah and he does not think that it will be so serious, but Allah writes for him because of it His wrath to the Day he will meet Him."[248]

'Alqamah, a reporter of the Hadith said:
'Many things I controlled from speaking because of the report of Bilal ibn al-Harith.'
Anas reported:
'A man from among the Companions died, so someone said:
'Rejoice the good news of Paradise.'
The Messenger of Allah, blessing and peace of Allah be upon him, said:

"How would you know, he may have uttered something about a matter which did not concern him, or kept and did not spend what he did not need?"[249]

In another report it is said:
'A boy was martyred in the battle of Uhud, and a stone was found tied on his stomach because of hunger. His mother wiped the dust from his face and said:
'I hope you enjoy Paradise!'
The Prophet, Allah's blessing and peace be upon him, said:

"How would you know? It maybe that he was talking about matters which did not concern him, and keep what was not needed from giving others."[250]

Abu Hurayrah reported that Allah's Messenger, blessing and peace be upon him, said:

"Whoever has faith in Allah and the Last Day should utter a good word or keep quiet."[251]

In another version:

"Whoever has faith in Allah and the Last day, when he witnesses a matter, should speak good words or keep quiet."[252]

The Prophet, Allah's blessing and peace be upon him, said:

"The beauty of Islam of a person is not to be concerned with what does not concern him."[253]

Sufyan ibn Abdullah al-Thaqafi reported:
'I said, 'Messenger of Allah, tell me something after which I do not need to ask anyone.'
He replied:

"Say: 'I believe in Allah,' and stand firm on it."

---

[249] Tirmidhi (2316), Abu Ya'la (4017) See majma' (10: 302)
[250] Abu Ya'la (6646)
[251] Bukhari (6475), Muslim (48)
[252] Muslim (1468)
[253] Tirmidhi (2317)

'I said: 'Messenger of Allah, what is the most dangerous thing you fear from me?'
He held his tongue and said:

"This one."[254]

Umm Habibah, the wife of the Prophet, Allah's blessing and peace be upon him, reported that the Messenger of Allah, blessing and peace be upon him, said:

"Every word of the son of Adam goes against him except enjoining what is good, forbidding what is bad or remembering Allah, The Most High."[255]

The Prophet, Allah's blessing and peace be upon him, said:

"When a person enters the morning, all his organs warn the tongue saying: 'Fear Allah concerning us, we are by you. If you are right, we will be right, and if you are crooked, we will be crooked as well."[256]

The early people used to be careful even in saying 'a hot day, a cold day'.

An important person was seen in dream and was asked about his condition and he said:
'I am halted for a word I uttered. I said: 'How much people are in need of rain! I was told: 'How would you know? I am aware of My slaves' interest.'
Some Companion said one day to his slave girl: 'Bring the dining table we play with it.'
Then he said: 'I did not speak a word but tried to restrain it except this word which came out from me without checking and restraining.'
The easiest movement of the parts of the body is the movement of the tongue, and it is the most dangerous one.

The scholars of the past and present are in disagreement whether all that a man speaks are recorded or only good or bad words?
There are two opinions; the clear one is the first one.
Some early people said that every word of the son of Adam goes against him and not in favour except remembrance of Allah and similar words.

---

[254] Muslim (38)
[255] Tirmidhi (2412), Ibn Majah (3974), Hakim (2; 512)
[256] Tirmidhi (2407), Ahmad (3: 95), Abu Ya'la (1185)

Abu Bakr al-Siddiq used to hold his tongue and say:
'This brought me to the places of destruction.'[257]

Words are your captive, but when they come out of your mouth, you become their captive. Allah is with the tongue of every speaker.

"He does not utter a single word without an ever-present watcher." (50:18)

There are two great evils with the tongue, if a person gets rid of one of them, he will not be able to get rid of the other. They are: the evil of speaking, and the evil of keeping silent. Sometimes each of them may be more serious than the other. The one who keeps silent from truth is a dumb Satan, disobedient of Allah, showing off and irresponsible; and the one who speaks false is a speaking Satan disobedient of Allah. Most of the people are deviating in their speech and silence, so they are between the above two categories.

The people who are in the middle and are followers of the straight path control their tongues from vain talks and use them for speaking about matters which will bring them benefit in the Hereafter. You will not find anyone of them uttering a useless word which cannot produce good result, let alone to cause him harm in the Hereafter. A man will come on the Day of Judgement with righteous deeds like the mountains and discover that his tongue had destroyed them all, while a man will come with evil deeds like mountains and find that his tongue has wiped them all because of engagement in the remembrance of Allah and similar things.

5.16 A serious cause of the evil acts is steps

A serious person is required to safeguard his steps and not to proceed but towards things which will bring him reward. If there is no additional reward in his steps, sitting is better for him. It is possible for him to extract from every step he takes to a permissible matter a good deed by which he can come closer to Allah by making it for the sake of Almighty. Since the stumbling is of two types: stumbling of the feet and that of the tongue, they were put together in the following words of Allah:

---

[257] Abu Ya'la (5), Ibn al-Sunni (7)

"The servants of the Lord of Mercy are those who walk humbly on the earth, and who when aggressive people address them, reply with words of peace." (25:63)

Almighty described them to be straight in their speech and their steps, as He joined the gazing and imagination in the following:

"He is aware of the stealthiest of glances and all of that hearts conceal." (40:19)

5.17 The prohibition of immoral acts and obligation of the guarding of chastity

All that we have said above is an introduction to prohibition of the immoral acts and obligation of guarding the chastity.
The Prophet, Allah's blessing and peace be upon him, said:

"The most of what takes people to the Hellfire is the mouth (i.e. tongue) and the private part."[258]

He also said:

"Taking the life of a Muslim is not allowed except for one of three reasons: a married adulterer, killing as revenge for killing, and the one who deserts his religion and leaves the community."[259]

This Hadith in putting the adultery together with disbelief and killing a soul is like what is said in the verse of Qur'anic chapter 25, The Differentiator (Al-Furqan).

It started with what is more often committed then followed by the next. Adultery is more often committed than killing a soul, and killing a soul is more common than apostasy. It is also moving from the more serious crime to the one which is much more serious. The evil of adultery is in contradiction with the interests of the world. When a woman commits this crime, she brings shame to her family, her husband and her relatives. She makes them lower their heads among the people if she conceives. If she kills her child, she combined the adultery with murder, and if she ascribed

---

[258] Tirmidhi (2004), Ibn Hibban (1923), Ibn Majah (4246) Hakim (4: 324)
[259] Bukhari (6878), Muslim (1676)

him to the husband, she admitted to his family and her family a stranger not belonging to them. He will inherit while he is not one of them, and will be alone with her and relate himself to them while he is not one of them and many other bad consequences of her adultery. The crime of the man is also bad and leads to mixing of the blood relation and ruining the life of an innocent woman and exposing her to perish. This major sin leads to ruin of the world and the Hereafter. It will cause the torment of the Fire in *Barzakh* and the Hereafter. How many evils are committed through adultery from trespassing the scared limits, to violating the rights and committing injustice? Its special characteristic is that it causes poverty, reduces the life span, covers the face of the person with black and produces hatred of the people. Its other features are that it shatters the heart, makes it ill if it does not kill, brings worry, grief and fear, and takes the person away from the angel and brings him closer to Satan. There is no crime more ignoble after the crime of murder than it. This explains why the culprit is punished by killing in the most horrible and horrid way. If a person gets the news that his wife or a member of his family has been killed, it will be easier for him to endure than the news that she has committed adultery.

Sa'd ibn 'Ubadah said:

'If I see a man with my wife, I will kill him with my naked sword.' The Messenger of Allah, blessing and peace be upon him, heard of it and said:

"Are you astonished by the sense of shame of Sa'd? By Allah, I have more sense of shame than him, and Allah has more sense of shame than me. Because of that sense Allah has forbidden immoral acts open and hidden."[260]

The Prophet, Allah's blessing and peace be upon him, also said:

"Allah has sense of shame and the believer also has the sense of shame, and Allah's sense of shame requires that the servant should not commit what He has prohibited for him."[261]

In another Hadith the Prophet, Allah's blessing and peace be upon him, said:

"No one has stronger sense of shame than Allah. Because of that sense He has forbidden the immoral acts open and hidden. No one loves excuse more than Allah and for that reason He sent messengers

---

[260] Bukhari (7416), Muslim (2760)
[261] Bukhari (5223), Muslim (2761)

giving good tidings and warning. No one loves praise more than Allah, for that reason He has praised Himself."[262]

The Prophet said in his sermon at the time of eclipse:

"Community of Muhammad, by Allah, no one has more sense of shame than Allah from His slave or maiden committing illegal sexual act. Community of Muhammad, by Allah, if you were to know what I know you would laugh little and cry much."

Then he raised his both hands and said:

"O Allah, have I conveyed the message?"[263]

In citing this major sin especially after the eclipse prayer there is a wonderful secret for those who pay attention. Spread of adultery is one of the signs of the ruin of the world and the indication of the Hour as Anas related saying:
'I will narrate a Hadith, no one else will narrate something like it after me I heard it from the Messenger of Allah, blessing and peace of Allah be upon him, say:

"Among the signs of the Hour is that the knowledge will be taken away, ignorance will prevail, wine will be drunk, adultery will spread, the number of men will be reduced and the women will be plenty to the extent that there will be one caretaker for fifty women."[264]

Allah's way in His creatures has gone ahead that when adultery spreads His wrath becomes intense, and it is necessary that His wrath creates punishment on the earth.
Abdullah ibn Mas'ud said:
'Adultery and usury do not prevail in a town but Allah decides its destruction'.[265]

One of the rabbis of the Children of Israel noticed his son blinking a woman, and he said: 'Easy, my son'. Then the father fell down from his bed and his spinal cord was broken, and his wife has miscarriage. He was

---

[262] Bukhari (4358), Muslim (2760)
[263] Bukhari (997), Muslim (901)
[264] Bukhari (81), Muslim 2671)
[265] Abu Ya'la (4981)

told: 'This is how your anger is for Me? There will be no good person in your line.'

Allah Almighty put three particular features in the punishment of the adultery:

1. One is to kill the culprit in most horrible way. When there is light punishment He joined the punishment by lashes on the body and moral punishment by sending him in exile from his home land for a year.

2. Second, He ordered His servants not to show leniency towards the adulterers, which may make them cancel the execution of the punishment. It was for the mercy and kindness of Allah that He prescribed that punishment for them. He is more merciful to them than you, and His mercy did not stop Him from prescribing this punishment. The leniency in your hearts, therefore, should not prevent you from carrying out His order. Although it is common in all the prescribed punishments, but was mentioned mainly in the case of the punishment of adultery due to the crucial need to mention it. People do not feel in their hearts harshness and bitterness towards an adulterer which they find against the thief, accuser and drinker of wine. Their hearts are inclined in mercy towards the adulterer more than they are inclined towards the criminals of other offences. It is proved by the experience. For that they were forbidden to show sympathy to the adulterer and abandon the implementation of the punishment of Allah. The reason for this mercy comes from the fact that this crimes occurs from noble, middle class and lower people, and the souls have big motives for that and it is committed by many. The main cause of it is love, and the hearts are created to show kindness to the lovers. Many people consider their help an act of obedience and good deed though the loved image is forbidden on him. Do not regard it strange because it is rooted in the souls of those whom Allah wills among the people like the animals. A great deal of the stories has been related to us mostly about those who have less understanding like women and servants. It is a crime which takes place with the consent of two parties, so there is no aggression; injustice and offence which make the soul hate it. It is the result of dominant desire and a person images this in himself and feels sympathy, which prevents him to apply the punishment. All this is the result of the weakness of faith. The power of faith is that he has strength to implement the command of Allah, and has also mercy towards the culprit. In this way he will be in line with Almighty in His command and His mercy.

3. Thirdly, Allah Almighty ordered that the punishment of adultery be implemented in the presence of the believers. It should not be done

privately where nobody can witness. Doing it in public will be more effective and wise in teaching a lesson. The punishment of the adulterer is taken from the punishment of Allah, the Most High, for the people of Lot, who were destroyed by stones dropped over them from the sky. This is because the adultery and sodomy are similar in immorality. Each of them contains corruption which is in contradiction with the wisdom of Allah about His creation and command. The sodomy has unlimited evil effects. Killing the object of the act is better than leaving him alive because he will spoil the society beyond the reform and destroy all its good aspects. The earth sucks the source of life from his face, so he will never feel shame after that neither from Allah nor from His creature. The sperm of the doer will work in his heart and soul what the poison does in the body.

The people are in disagreement concerning the fate of the object of sodomy: will he go to Paradise?
There are two views in this regard I heard Shaykh al-Islam describing them.
Those who said that he would not be admitted into Paradise argued by the following points:

One of them is that the Prophet, Allah's blessing and peace be upon him, said:

"The child born as a result of adultery will not go the Paradise."[266]

If this is the situation of the child born by adultery though it was not his fault, but there is doubt of him being the source of every evil and corruption, then what will be the result of the one who was involved in the heinous crime? The child born of adultery is not supported to produce any good ever because he is the product of a filthy drop of sperm. When a body brought up by the unlawful materials deserves to be cast in the Fire, then what will happen to a body created by the illegal drop of sperm?

They further argued that the object of sodomy is worse than the illegitimate child. He is very disgraceful, filthy and shameless; it is very unlikely that he does anything good. Anytime he does something right Allah decrees something which spoils his good deeds as a punishment for him. Rarely do you see a person who was in that habit in his young age,

---

[266] Darimi (2: 112), Ahmad (2: 203), Nisa'i (8: 318), Ibn Hibban (3383)

but he becomes more evil when he grows up. He is not helped for any useful knowledge, righteous deed or sincere repentance.

The right view in this matter is that if the affected person repents and turns to Allah with regret and helped in making sincere repentance and doing righteous deeds, he will be better in his later age than he was in his young age. Allah Almighty will change his evil deeds to good ones, and will wash away the shame of it by variety of righteous deeds and good acts. Almighty will make him lower his gaze and guard his private parts from prohibited matters. If he is sincere with Allah in his dealing, he will be forgiven and will be among the people of Paradise. Allah forgives all the sins. If repentance can forgive every sin even association of partner with Allah, murdering His prophets and messengers, sorcery, disbelief and other major crimes, it will not fall short of wiping this sin. Allah's wisdom has gone in justice and favour to the point where "A man repenting from a sin is like the one who never committed a sin."

Allah has guaranteed for those who abandon association of partners, killing a person and committing adultery and repent to change their evil deeds to good ones. It is a general rule for every person who repents from any sin.

Allah has announced:

"Say: O My servants Who have transgressed against themselves, do not despair of the mercy of Allah. Indeed, Allah forgives all sins. Surely, He is the Most forgiving, the Most Merciful." (39:53)

No sin is excluded from this general statement; however it applies to those who turn to Allah in repentance.

If the object of sodomy happens to be worse in his later age than he was in his young age, was not helped for the sincere repentance and good deeds, and did nothing to redress the evil he did and did not change his bad deeds to good ones, he is far from being helped at the time of his death with righteous deeds to deserve to enter Paradise. He will have to suffer for his actions. Allah punishes an evil deed by another evil deed, and the punishment of evil deeds multiply as He rewards a good deed by another.

When you look at the conditions of many those who approach their death, you will notice that a barrier was made between them and the good ending as a punishment for their wicked deeds.

Hafiz Abu Muhammad Abd al-Haq al-Ishbili said:[267]

---

[267] In his book Al-'Aqibah' (178-180)

225

'Know that for the evil ending - may Allah protect us from it! – there are causes and doors, the greatest to which is to bend on the world and turn away from the Hereafter, and advance and embark with carelessness on the evil deeds. Sometimes a man is overwhelmed by an evil and act of disobedience, and shows disinterest in the life to come and goes ahead daringly and without fear; the thing has full controls over his heart, has enchained his reason, extinguished its light and covered it by curtains: for such a person no admonition or reminder works, death may come to him and he is in that condition. He hears a call from far and does not understand what it says though the caller repeated his call.

He (Abd al-Haq Al-Ishbili) narrated an incident:
'It is reported that death approached some men of al-Nasir and his son said to him: say, 'There is no god but Allah', he said, 'Al-Nasir is my master!' The son repeated his request but he said the same in answer. Then he was unconscious and when he regained his consciousness, he said' 'Al-Nasir is my master!' This was how he behaved, anytime he was told to say, 'there is no god but Allah', he said' Al-Nasir is my master!' Then he said to his son: 'Al-Nasir knows you by your sword, and murder, murder' then he passed away.

Abd al-Haqq said:
'It was said to a person I knew, 'say there is no god but Allah', he started saying, 'such and such house, repair in it such and such, such and such garden do in it such and such.'

He further said:
'Death approached a man and he was asked to say, 'there is no god but Allah,' he started saying in Persian: ten for eleven.'

Another person was asked to say, 'there is no god but Allah,' and he said: 'Where is the way to the bath of Minjab?'
This saying has a story: A man was standing in front of his house, the door of which resembled the door of the bath of Minjab. A beautiful young woman passed by him and asked: 'Which is the way to the bath of Minjab?'
He replied: 'This is the bath of Minjab. She entered the house followed by him. When she found herself inside the house, she realised that she was deceived. She showed him happiness and delights for being with him, and said to him: 'Look it is better to have something to make our meeting pleasant and delightful.'
He told her: 'I will bring you now all that you desire and wish.'

He went out of the house and left her there without locking the door. He took all that he thought good and returned, but found that the lady had gone without taking anything of his property. The man became crazy and mentioned her very often. He walked in the streets and alleys saying:
'Oh a girl who said after being exhausted, 'which is the road to Minjab?'
While he was saying this one day, a girl answered to him from a window:
'When you got hold of her why did you not quickly put a safety on the house or a lock on the door?' After that his craziness increased and his affection went beyond control. He remained repeating that line until he departed from the world.

Sufyan al-Thawir cried one night till morning. In the morning he was asked, 'was that for the fear of the sins?'
He took a straw from the ground and said:
'Sins are easier than this, I cry for the fear of the evil end.'

It is the great understanding that a man should fear from being deserted by his sins which may become barrier between him and good end.

When Abu al-Darda' was about to die, he used to faint and recover and read:

"And We would make their hearts and their eyes turn away, just as they refused to believe in it the first time, and leave them to flounder in their obstinacy." (6:110)

That is the reason the early Muslims were scared of sins being a barrier between them and the good end.

He (Abd al-Haq) further said:
'Know that the bad end – May Allah protect us from it – does not happen to those whose outer is straight and inner is right. It has not been heard or known for such people, thanks to Allah. This happens to those whose belief is corrupt or those who insist on committing the major sins. Sometimes it takes hold of him till death descends on him before repentance. He dies before putting his inner-self right, and redressing the faults. Satan succeeds to get hold of him at this shocking moment and sweeping away at that horrible point. May Allah protect us!'

He also wrote:
'It is reported that there was a man in Egypt regularly attending the mosque for adhan, iqamah and prayer. On him were the brilliance of obedience and the lights of worship. One day he climbed up to the

minaret as usual for calling adhan, there was under the minaret the house of a Christian. He looked down at it and saw the daughter of the owner of the house and was enchanted by her. He left his duty of calling for prayer, came down and entered the house and faced her. She asked: 'What is the matter with you and what do you want?'

He replied: 'I want you.'

She asked: 'what for?'

He said: 'You have taken away my reason and overwhelmed my heart.'

She said: 'I will never surrender to you for immoral act.'

He said: 'I want to marry you.'

She said: 'You are Muslim and I am a Christian and my father will never agree with my marriage with you.'

He offered to be Christian.

She said: 'If you do that, I will marry you.'

The man converted to Christianity for the purpose of marrying her, and stayed with them in their house. During his stay he climbed one day to the roof of the house, fell down and died. He did not get her and lost his religion.'

He mentioned another story as follows:

'A man loved a person and his affection became intense, and his passion took hold on his heart till his pain made him lie on bed. Still his beloved refused to yield and his aversion became unbearable. The intermediaries frequented between the two until he promised to visit him. The desperate man was informed and he felt extremely happy, and his sorrow was removed. He started waiting for the time he fixed, but when the time approached the envoy came and said to him: 'He came with me to some distance then returned. I spoke to him and pleaded but he said: 'He remembered me and felt happy, and I am not going to enter a place of suspicion and expose myself for accusations. I pleaded but he refused and went back.'

When the desperate man heard this, he was bewildered and returned to worse situation than before, and the sings of death appeared on him. He started saying (the following lines):

'O Salm, O comfort of the ill, and the cure of the slim seriously ill person, Your pleasure is more delicious to my heart than the mercy of the Great Creator.'

I said to him: 'So and so, have fear of Allah!'

He said: 'It was'.

I stood up to go, and did not cross the door of his house, that I heard the screaming of death.'

Allah's refuge is sought from evil end and unfortunate consequence.

5.18 The damaging consequence of sodomy is one of the biggest

As the evil of sodomy is one of the biggest crimes, its punishment was the severest in the world and in the Hereafter. The scholars dispute whether its punishment is harsher than adultery, or adultery is more disastrous than sodomy, or both are equal?

There are three opinions in this regard:

1. Abu Bakr al-Siddiq, Ali ibn Abi Talib, Khalid ibn al-Walid, Abdullah ibn al-Zubayr, Abdullah ibn Abbas, Jabir ibn Zayd, Abdullah ibn Ma'mar, al-Zuhri, Rabi'ah ibn Abd al-Rahman, Malik, Ishaq ibn Rahwayh, Imam Ahmad, - in one of his two statements – and al-Shafi'i in one of his two statements, are of the opinion that the punishment of sodomy is more severe than that of adultery. Its punishment is killing of the culprit whether he is married or unmarried.
2. 'Ata' ibn Abi Rabah, al-Hasan al-Basri, Sa'id ibn al-Musayyib, Ibrahim al-Nakh'i, Qatadah, al-Awza'i, al-Shafi'i, Ahmad in the second opinion, Abu Yusuf and Muhammad said that the punishment of sodomy and adultery was equal.
3. Al-Hakam and Abu Hanifah hold that its punishment is lighter than the adultery, and it is *Ta'zir* (chastisement).

They argued that it is an evil act of disobedience for which Allah and His Messenger have not prescribed a fixed punishment. It should be, therefore, put under ta'zir, like eating carrion, blood and pork.

They also argued that it is intercourse in a place which is abhorred by nature. Allah, the Exalted, has created in the nature of even animals to consider it abominable. Therefore there is no prescribed punishment for it like having intercourse with the donkey and other beast.

They also said that the person committing it is not called adulterer in language or religion or custom; as such it cannot be included in the texts speaking about the punishment of the adulterers.

They further said that we have noted in the principles of the Shari'ah that when the deterrent of a sinful act is natural, it would be enough as the punishment. If the nature is inclined to it, then a punishment is prescribed in line with the interest of the people. For that reason the punishment of adultery, stealing and drinking wine is made higher than eating carrion, blood and pork.

They said that it is known that having intercourse with an animal or a dead person has no prescribed punishment. Allah, the Exalted, has put in the nature of the people to loath the intercourse with a man, as He made it abhorrent for calling a man to have intercourse with him, unlike the adultery because the motive in it comes from both sides.

They further said that if one species enjoys with its kind, there is no punishment, as when two lesbian women engage and enjoy with one another.

The people who hold the first view – that the punishment of sodomy is harsher than that of adultery – they are majority of the Muslims and many people say that it was a consensus among the Companions. They said that there is no crime more dangerous than the sodomy. It is next to disbelief, and it may be more serious than killing of a person, as we will explain, if Allah will.

They said that Allah, the Glorious, did not afflict anyone of the people before the people of Lot, and He meted out a punishment to them which no other community was made to suffer. Almighty combined on them variety of punishments from destroying them, turning their towns over them, making them be swallowed by the earth and raining stones on them from the heaven. He made them an example which no other community was made. All this because of the severity of this crime, which almost made the earth to shake when it is committed on it. When the angels witness it from all corners of the heavens and the earth, they run away for the fear that punishment is going to come to those people, and they as well may be affected by it. The earth cries out to its Lord Almighty and the mountains almost move from their places.

Killing of the object of sodomy is better than having intercourse with him because if a person has intercourse with him, he has killed him beyond any hope of his survival, but if he is killed, he is wronged martyr and may benefit from it in the Hereafter.

They said that the proof of it is that Allah, the Exalted, made the punishment of the murderer to the choice of the guardian; if he wishes, he will kill, and if he wants, he can forgive. But He decreed the punishment of the sodomite killing him. This is an agreed opinion of the Companions of the Messenger of Allah, blessing and peace be upon him, and it is established in the Sunnah of the Prophet, Allah's blessing and peace be upon him. His Companions and the rightly guided Caliphs followed it.

It is reported that Khalid ibn al-Walid found in some areas of the Arabs a man being used for intercourse like a woman. He wrote to Abu Bakr al-

Siddiq, who consulted the Companions and Ali ibn Abi Talib's opinion was very harsh in this respect, he said:

'This crime was committed by only one nation and you are aware of what Allah did with them. My decision is that he should be burnt in fire.'

Abu Bakr wrote to Khalid and he burnt the man.[268]

Abdullah ibn Abbas said:

'The sodomite should be thrown from the highest building on his face, and then followed by stones.'[269]

Abdullah ibn Abbas took this punishment from what Allah did with the people of Lot. It is Abdullah ibn Abbas who reported the Prophet, Allah's blessing and peace be upon him, as saying:

"If you find someone committing the crime of the people of Lot, kill the doer and the object."[270]

They also said that the Prophet, Allah's blessing and peace be upon him, said:

"May Allah curse the person who does the act of the people of Lot!"
"May Allah curse the person who does the act of the people of Lot!"
"May Allah curse the person who does the act of the people of Lot!"[271]

The Prophet, Allah's blessing and peace be upon him, cursed the sodomite three time and there is no report in which he cursed the adulterer three times. He cursed a number of people who committed major sins but he condemned them only once. He condemned the sodomite three times.

The Companions of the Prophet, Allah's blessing and peace be upon him, are unanimous that a sodomite must be killed, there is no dispute among them on this issue. They differed in the way of his killing and it was taken by some people to be difference of opinion about his killing, and they cited as a matter of dispute among them while it is an agreed matter without any dispute.

They further said:

'Anyone who pays attention to the words of Allah:

---

[268] Al-Bayhaqi in Sunan (8: 232)
[269] Al-Bayhaqi (8: 232), Ibn Abi Shaybah (9: 529)
[270] Abu Dawud (4462), Tirmidhi (1456), Ibn Majah (2561), Ahmad (1: 300), Hakim (4: 355)
[271] Ahmad (1: 309), Abu Ya'la (2539), Ibn Hibban (4417), Hakim (4: 356), al-Bayhaqi (8: 231)

"Do not go anywhere near adultery: it is an outrage, and an evil path." (17:32)

And His words about sodomy:

"How can you practise this outrage? No other people have done so before." (7:80)

Anyone who pays attention to the above statements will realise the difference between them. Allah, the Almighty, put the word *fahishah* in indefinite form in the case of adultery to indicate that it was an outrageous act, and put it in definite form in the case of sodomy to indicate that this outrageous act is comprehensive of all the evil acts.
It is like saying:
'How can you commit an act, the immorality of which is established with every one? Because of its outrageous characteristic it does not need to be named. It is like the saying of Pharaoh to Moses:

"And you committed that crime of yours." (26:19)

It means that you committed that outrageous crime known to every body. After that Almighty stressed its abhorrence by saying that no one did it before. He also described it in a way which will make the hearts hate it and the nature feel disgusted saying that you approach men in lust in place of women. Then He pointed out that their reason for doing it is nothing more than satisfying their desire not those matters for which a male inclines to a female, which are satisfying the desire and enjoying the copulation. Other objectives of the meeting of male and female are the mercy and affection, which makes the woman forget her parents and remain with her spouse, and the procreation to protect the race of the noblest creatures. They also include security of the woman and fulfilling of her desire and the establishment of the relation by marriage. One of the main objectives is that it leads to produce the most beloved people to Allah like the prophets, allies of Allah and the believers and many other good objectives of the marriage. Sodomy demolishes all that and produces unlimited evil effects known only to Allah.

Allah, the Most High, stressed the severity of the crime by saying that the sodomites reversed the natural disposition which Allah created men with. They reverted the nature which Almighty placed in the male species, which is desire of women and not of men. These people reversed the matter and upset the nature and character, and used men for sexual purpose in place of women. For this reason Allah turned their towns upside down over them; this is how their hearts had become and they would be thrown on their faces in torment.

Allah Almighty affirmed the ugly face of the crime by judging it as transgression, which is crossing the boundary. Lot said to his people:

"You are transgressors of all limits." (7:81)

Is there any statement similar to it in the case of adultery?
Allah indicated their evil acts by saving His prophet from their town:

"We saved him from the town which was engrossed in filthy acts." (21:74)

Almighty condemned them by two abominable qualities, He said:

"They were shameless people who defied Allah's rules." (21:74)

He called them corrupt in the words of their Prophet:

"My Lord, help me against these people who spread corruption." (29:30)

He called them wrongdoers in the words of the angels to Abraham:

"We are to destroy the people of that town. They are wrongdoers."(29:31)

Consider the people who were punished with such measures, and condemned. When Abraham, the friend of Allah, pleaded with the angels about them when they informed him about their destruction, it was said to him:

"Abraham, cease your pleading, what your Lord has ordained has come about. Punishment is coming to them, which cannot be turned back. (11:76)

Look at the vulgarity of the sodomites and their defiance of Allah when they learnt that some most handsome guests had come to their Prophet, they rushed to his house. He said:

"My people, these are my daughters, they are purer for you." (11:78)

He tried to ransom his guests by his daughters and offered them in marriage to them with fear of shame for himself and his guests and said:

"My people, here are my daughters, they are purer for you. Fear Allah, and do not disgrace me concerning my guests. Is there not a single man of reason among you?" (11:78)

They answered him with arrogance:
"You know very well that we have no claim whatever to your daughters. You know very well what we want." (11:79)

The Prophet of Allah emitted the painful sound from a wounded heart and said:

"If only I had strength to stop you or could rely on strong support!" (11:80)

The messengers of Allah (angels) relieved him and revealed the real situation, and told him that they were not to be reached by any means. So, there is no need to be sacred or worried. Take it easy. They said:

"Lot, we are your Lord's messengers. They will not reach you." (11:81)

They informed him about the mission they had come for to fulfil Allah's promise for him and the torment for his people. They said:

"Leave with your household in the dead of night, and let none of you turn back except your wife who will suffer the fate that will befall the others. Their appointed time is the morning: is the morning not near?" (11:81)

By Allah, there was no time between the destruction of the enemies of Allah and the rescue of His messenger and his followers more than dawn and sunrise. Their towns were pulled out from the foundation and raised towards the sky till the angels heard the barking of the dogs and braying of the donkeys. The order of the Mighty Lord was given to Gabriel to turn their dwellings upside down as He told us in His Book:

"When what We had ordained came about, We turned their town upside down and rained stones of baked clay on it." (1:82)

Almighty made them a sign for the people of the world and a lesson for the righteous ones, and a warning for those criminals who participated with them in their crimes. He made their towns on the road of the travellers.

"There are truly signs in this for those who can learn. It is still there on highway. There is truly a sign for those who believe." (15:75-77)

The punishment took them unawares when they were asleep, and His punishment suddenly came to them while they were in their intoxication wandering blindly. Nothing of what they earned could save them, and those joys turned to pains and they were punished by them. The enjoyments were gone, and regrets followed; lust disappeared and misfortune remained. They enjoyed little and suffered much; they feasted dangerous pasture which resulted in painful torment. The wine of that lust intoxicated them and they did not regain their consciousness but in the towns of the punished people. The heedlessness made them sleep and they did not wake up but in the dwellings of destroyed men. They regretted when regret did not avail anything, and cried on their behaviour with blood instead of tears. If you are able to see the higher and lower of them in the Hellfire while the fire is coming out from the holes of their faces and bodies, and they drink the cups of boiling water instead of delicious drink! It will be said to them while they are dragged on their faces: Taste what you used to earn.

"Burn in it, it makes no difference whether you bear it patiently or not. You are only repaid for what you have done." (52:16)

Allah has made the distance of torment between this community and their partners in act, and He said:

"It is not far from the wrongdoers." (11:83)

A poet has said:
'O the people involved in intercourse with males receive good news, on the Day of Resurrection you are going to get reward!
Eat and drink, commit adultery and sodomise and learn that you will be taken to red garden.
Your brothers before you have prepared the home for you and they are saying, 'come quickly, you have good news.
We are your predecessors waiting for you. The Compeller will bring us together in His big Fire.'

Do not think that those whom you used for sex will be away from you, you will see them openly.

Every one of you will curse the other and the grieved will be left in pain in the Hereafter.

Everyone will be punished with his partner as they shared the joy that produced the burden of the sin.'

5.19 Refutation of the view of those who made the punishment of sodomy less than the punishment of adultery

Now let us argue against those who claimed that the punishment of sodomy was less than the punishment of adultery.

They said that it was a crime for which Allah has not prescribed a fixed punishment.

Its answer is that the person who was appointed as messenger of Allah fixed the punishment of the person doing it as killing. What the Messenger of Allah, Allah's blessing and peace be upon him, has enacted comes from Allah. If you want to say that its limit is not known, it is false. If you want to claim that it is not established by the text of the Book, it does not necessarily mean that there is no punishment because it has been established by the Sunnah.

This goes against you because the stoning to death in the case of adultery is also established by the Sunnah.

If you claim that it was established by the Qur'an but its words were abrogated and the ruling remained.

We will say that your argument is demolished by the punishment of the drinker of wine.

Again the absence of particular evidence does not necessarily mean the absence of general evidence. We have said that your argument for the absence of the evidence was not valid.

Your claim that it is intercourse in a place which is not desired by nature, it is something which Allah has put in the nature of people to be disgusting, so it is like having sex with a dead or an animal; its refutation is from following different aspects:

1. It is a wrong analogy rejected by the Sunnah of the Prophet, Allah's blessing and peace be upon him, and the consensus of the Companions, as has been explained.

2. The comparison of sex with a handsome young man, which is an evil above all other evil, with having sex with donkey or dead woman is the most erroneous comparison. Had anyone said poetry for the love of a donkey or a cow or a dead woman? Had this enchanted the reason of a lover, arrested his heart or dominated his thought? This is the most erroneous analogy.

3. This argument is invalid in the case of having sex with one's mother, daughter or sister. The natural hatred is available in it, yet the punishment of it is the severest one and that is killing of the culprit whether he is married or not. This is one of the statements of Ahmad, and it is the view of Isahq ibn Rahwayh and a group of the scholars of Hadith.

Al-Bara' ibn 'Azib reported:
'I met my uncle holding the banner; I asked him where he was heading to? He replied: 'The Messenger of Allah, blessing and peace of Allah be upon him, has sent me to a man who had married the wife of his father after him, to kill him and take his property.'[272]

Ibn Abbas reported that the Allah's Messenger, Allah's blessing and peace be upon him, said:

"Anyone who has sex with a forbidden relative kill him."[273]

The case of a man who forced his sister to have sex with him was brought to al-Hajjaj. He ordered him to be imprisoned and said, 'Ask anyone of the Companions of the Prophet, Allah's blessing and peace be upon him, about this. They asked Abdullah ibn Abi Mutarrif who said:
'I heard the Messenger of Allah, blessing and peace be upon him, saying:

"Whoever crosses the sacred boundaries of the believers cut him from the middle with sword."[274]

This proves that he should be killed from the waist. The above report proves that anyone who has intercourse with someone which is prohibited should be punished by killing like the sodomite.

The Muslims are agreed that anyone who has sex with a forbidden relative must be punished. They disagreed concerning the way of

---

[272] Abu Dawud (4291), Tirmidhi (1373), Nisa'i (6: 109), Ahmad (4: 295)
[273] Tirmidhi (1487, 2564), Ibn Majah (2564), Hakim (4: 356) Bayhaqi (8: 234)
[274] Tabarani in Kabir, see Majma' (6: 269), Bayhaqi in Shu'ab (5473)

punishment whether it is killing in any case or it is the punishment of adultery.

Imam al-Shafi'i, Malik, Ahmad hold that his punishment is that of adultery. Ahmad in one report and Ishaq and a group of the scholars of Hadith say that his punishment is killing in any case.

They are also agreed that if he had sex with her in the name of marriage knowing that it was forbidden, he will be punished except Abu Hanifah who sees in it a doubt which will do away with the punishment.

His opponents argue that if he approached her in the name of marriage his crime becomes more serious because he committed two offences: the prohibition of contract and the prohibition of intercourse. How then the punishment will be waived while he committed two prohibitions?

As for having sex with dead there are two opinions: One that the culprit will be punished. This is the opinion of al-Awza'i because his act is greater crime and more serious sin as he combined the immoral act with violating the respect of dead.

5.20 Ruling about the man who had sex with animal

In the case of having sex with animal the Jurists have three opinions:

One that the culprit will be chastised and there is no punishment for him. This is the opinion of Malik, Abu Hanifah, al-Shafi'i in one of his statements as well of Ishaq.

The second is that he will be given the punishment of adultery; if he is unmarried, he will be lashed, and will be stoned to death if he is married. This is the opinion of al-Hasan.

The third is that he will be dealt like a sodomite. Ahmad stated it. In his opinion it is either killing or the punishment of adulterer. Those who say his punishment is killing argue with the report of Ibn Abbas that the Prophet, Allah's blessing and peace be upon him, said:

"Anyone who has sex with an animal kill him and kill the animal as well."[275]

They argued that it is an act which is not permitted at any rate, so its punishment will be killing like the sodomite.

---

[275] AbuDawud (4464), Ahmad (1: 269), Tirmidhi (1454), Hakim (4: 355)

Those who said there was no punishment contested that the quoted Hadith was not authentic. If it were authentic, we would have followed it. There is no doubt that the natural deterrent from having sex with an animal is stronger than that of sodomy, and the two matters are not equal, so putting them together is the worst deduction.

5.21 Comparison of a man's sex with two women's rubbing with one another is a wrong deduction

Your deduction of a man having sex with another man with two women's rubbing with one another is wrong inference. There is no penetration here and it is like copulation of a man with another without penetration. There is a Hadith that
"when a woman has sex with another, both of them are adulterers."
However, there is no punishment in this case because there is no penetration though it is called adultery like the adultery of the eye, hand, feet and mouth.
When this is established then there is consensus among the Muslims that the ruling concerning having sex with his slave is as the ruling about sex with others. Anyone who thinks that sodomy with one's slave is permitted and argues by the words of Allah:

"Except with their spouses and slave, for which they are not to be blamed." (23:6; 70:30)

Who deduces it for his owned slave girl, he is a disbeliever. He will be asked to repent, if he refuses, he will be killed.
The sin and ruling of sodomy of a person with his slave is like his sodomy with the salve of another person.

CHAPTER 6 - TREATMENTS OF PERVERSIONS AND SINFUL ACTS

6.1 Treatment of sodomy

If it is asked: Despite all this, is there a remedy for this serious malady? Is there any incantation for this killing magic? Is there any trick to get rid of this mental disorder? Is there any way to get help? Is it possible for the drunkard of the wine of the passion to recover? Will the lover get control over his heart when the love has penetrated to its bottom? Can a physician use a method to remedy him from his evil disease? He has reached a stage where if a person blames him, he enjoys his blame because it reminds him of his beloved; if a person censures him, it provokes him and makes him go ahead in the way of his desire. His condition speaks on his tongue:

'The love has taken me where you are; I cannot retreat or proceed from this situation.
You disgraced me so I disgraced myself. Is there anyone who is humble from those who are honoured?
You resembled my enemies so I started loving them because my share from you is like my share from them.
I find the blame in your love delicious out of affection for you. Let the blamers blame me.'

May be this was the aim of the first query for which the religious opinion was sought, and this is the disease for which medication is required.

6.2 The medication of this disease is of two ways

It will be said that: 'Yes, there is a remedy for it. Allah has not send down a disease but He has fixed a medication for it; the one who knew it, knew it; and the one who did not know it was unaware of it.

The discussion of the medication of this disease is of two ways:
One to terminate its source before it affects.
Second to uproot it after it has affected.
Both of these two are easy for those Allah made easy for them, and hard for those who are not helped. All the control of matters is in His Hand.
There are two ways to prevent this disease to happen:

One to keep the gaze low, as it has been said earlier. Glance is a poisoned arrow of Iblis. Whoever lets his glance loose, his regrets will continue.

There are many advantages in lowering the eyes; and it is an important ingredient of the useful medication:

i.   One advantage is that it is following the command of Allah which is the utmost happiness for the slave in his life and the Hereafter. There is nothing more beneficial for a person than abiding by the orders of Allah, the Exalted and Blessed. Anyone who was fortunate in the world and the Hereafter was so for carrying out the orders of Allah, and whoever was unfortunate in the world and the Hereafter was so because of neglecting His commands.

ii.   The second advantage is that it prevents the effect of the poisoned arrow, which may cause his ruin, from reaching his heart.

iii. The third is that it produces familiarity and friendliness with Allah Almighty. Leaving the eye loose crushes and shatters the heart and makes it far from Allah. There is nothing more harmful for the heart than leaving the eye loose; it creates estrangement between the salve and his Lord.

iv.   The fourth is that it provides the heart with strength and happiness; on the other hand leaving it loose causes grief and weakness for it.

v.   The fifth is that it produces light in the heart and becoming victim of lustful gaze causes darkness. This is why Allah, the Glorious, arranged the verse of light after the command of lowering the eye. He said:

"Tell the believers to lower their eyes, and guard their chastity." (24:30)

He said after that:

"Allah is the light of the heavens and the earth. His light is like this: there is a niche, and in it a lamp, the lamp inside a glass" (24:35)

When the heart retains the light, the delegates of good come to it from every side. When it is dark, the clouds of afflictions and evil approach it from every place. All the innovations, misdeeds, following the lust and keeping away from guidance and turning away from the sources of happiness, and engaging in the sources of misfortune – all these are removed by the light of the heart. When this light disappears, the person remains like a blind man who wanders in the deep darkness.

vi.   The sixth advantage is that it produces the real discernment which helps the person to distinguish between the truth and falsehood and right and wrong. A learned man said: 'Anyone who enriches his outer by following the Sunnah and his inner by regular surveillance, and lowers his eye, guards his soul against the doubtful matters and eats lawful things will not miss discernment.' Allah, the Exalted, recompenses a person with a similar thing to his act.

"Whoever leaves a thing for the sake of Allah, He will compensate him something better than that."[276]

When a person lowers his eye from what Allah has prohibited, Allah will compensate him by widening the light of his vision in recompense of controlling his eye for the sake of Allah. He will open for him the door of knowledge and faith, awareness and true discernment which is achieved by the perception of the heart. Opposite of it is the wandering with which Allah described the sodomites, He said:

"By your life, they wandered on in their wild intoxication." (15:72)

Almighty described them with intoxication which is the corruption of the reason, and with wandering which is the corruption of insight. Attachment with images leads to the corruption of reason, loss of insight and intoxication of the heart. A poet says: *'I am intoxicated by two things, the intoxication of passion and the intoxication of wine, and how can a man with two intoxications recover* Another poet said: *'They said that you become crazy by the one you love. I said to them, 'Passion is greater than what is with crazy people. The man affected by passion never comes to sense while the crazy man gets his fit for a time.'*

vii.   The seventh is that it produces in the heart firmness, courage and power. Allah puts for him the power of help and argument and the strength of control and power as it is said: 'Whoever goes against his desire Satan is scared of his shadow.'

You will notice in a person who follows his desire that Allah has assigned humiliation, lowliness, disgrace, shame and abasement for him.

---

[276] Said by the Prophet, peace be upon him, reported by Ahmad (5: 363)

Hasan said:

'Although the mule clatter and the horses amble with them, the disgrace of disobedience is in their necks. Allah does not agree but to humiliate the one who disobeys Him.

Allah, the Glorious, has linked honour with His obedience, and humiliation with disobedience. He said:

"Honour belongs to Allah, His Messenger and the believers." (73:8)

Almighty also said:

"Do not lose heart and do not despair, you will be superior if you are (true) believers." (3:139)

Faith consists of words and action, inner and outer. Allah, the Exalted, said:

"If anyone desires honour, all honour belongs to Allah; good words rise up to Him, and He lifts up righteous deed." (35:10)

This means that anyone who desires honour should look for it in the obedience of Allah, His remembrance by pure words and righteous deed.
In the supplication of *Qanut* the Prophet, Allah's blessing and peace be upon him, taught to say:

"The one whom You befriend does not face humiliation, and the one You hate cannot get honour."[277]

Anyone who obeys Allah becomes an ally of Allah in what he does, and he achieves honour according to his righteous deed; anyone who disobeys Allah, he has become His enemy in what he disobeyed Him and receives disgrace according to his disobedience.

viii.   The eighth is that it blocks for Satan entrance to the person's heart. Satan enters with the glance. He penetrates the heart faster than the wind in an empty place; he depicts the image of the person who is the object of glance, beautifies him and makes him an idol on which the heart bends. Then he promises him, raises desire and kindles the fire of lust in the heart and throws the woods of evil deeds to which the

---

[277] Abu Dawud (1425)

man was not able to reach without that image. As a result the heart burns in the flame. From that flame come those breaths in which he finds the heat of the fire, moaning and burning. The heart becomes surrounded by fire from every side and it falls in the middle like a goat in the middle of the oven. For this reason the punishment of the people who are enchanted by forbidden images was made that an oven of fire is lit for them and their souls are deposited in it till the Day their bodies will be resurrected. This was shown by Allah to His Prophet, Allah's blessing and peace be upon him, in dream.[278]

ix.   The ninth advantage is that it makes the heart free to think about its interests and engage in them, while letting the eye loose makes him to forget them and blocks the thought of them. As a result his affairs are scattered and he falls in following his desire and becomes unmindful of his Lord's remembrance. Allah Almighty said:

"Do not obey those whose heart We have made heedless of Our remembrance and who follow their own low desires and whose ways are unbridled." (18:28)

Letting the eye loose produces all these three results according to its impact.

x.   The tenth is that there is a passage and outlet between the eye and the heart requiring the separation of the one from the other. Each of them becomes right when the other is right and becomes corrupt when it is corrupt. When the heart is corrupt, the gaze is corrupt; and when the gaze is corrupt the heart is corrupt. It is the same as far as the rightness is concerned. When the eye is spoiled, the heart is spoiled and becomes corrupt. It becomes like a dunghill which is the place of filth, dirt and rubbish. It remains no more a right place for the knowledge of Allah and His love and return to Him or familiarity and happiness with His closeness. It becomes the place of the opposite of those matters.

These are indications of the benefits of keeping the gaze low.

The second way of preventing the disease of the attachment of the heart is to keep the heart busy in what will take it away from it and be a barrier between it and being a victim of it. That will be available by a disturbing fear or agonising love. When the heart is free from the fear of losing something the loss of which is more harmful to it than the achieving of the desired goal, or is free from the fear of that the achievement of which is more harmful than losing, that desired goal or the love of what is more

---

[278] Bukhari (6640), Muslim (2275)

beneficial and better than this desired one and its loss is more painful than the loss of this desired goal, he will not escape the love of the images.

It is explained in the following way: the soul does not abandon a desired object but for something more lovable than it or because of a harmful matter the achievement of which is more painful than the loss of this desired one. The person in this situation is in need of two matters if he misses both or one of them, he will not get benefit for himself. These matters are:

First, a right perception which guides him to distinguish between the degrees of the loved and hated matter. By this perception he will prefer the higher desired matter over the less desired one, and will tolerate the lower hateful thing to get rid of the higher one. This is the work of reason and anyone who is not at this stage is not a sensible person, but the animals may be better than him.

Second, power of will and endurance which makes him able to accept or abandon. It happens very often that a person is aware of the degree of difference but the weakness of his soul and his resolution prevents him from choosing what is more advantageous for him. This is caused by his greed, avidity, meanness of his soul and lowliness of his willpower. This type of person cannot benefit himself or give benefit to others. Allah, the Exalted, has forbidden the leadership of His religion from the people who lack patience and certainty. He said:

"We raised leaders among them guiding by Our command when they were patient and were certain of Our message." (32:24)

This is the person who will benefit from his knowledge and pass the benefit to others; the one who does not have these qualities cannot get benefit by his knowledge and will not be able to benefit others. However, there are people who get benefit by their knowledge but do not pass it to others. The first one is a person who walks in his light and people walk with him in his light, while the second one's light has departed, so he walks in darkness and his followers walk in darkness as well. The third one walks in his light alone.

CHAPTER 7 - CATEGORIES AND DYNAMICS OF LOVE

7.1   True love requires devoting to the highest beloved

When you have learnt this preamble then know that it is impossible that the love of the highest beloved and passion of the images come together in the heart of a person. They are two opposites which can never be found together; one of them must expel the other. So the one whose love's power is all for the highest beloved, the love of others beside Him is vain and a torment for him, he will be turned away from the love of any other person beside Him. If he loves him, he will love him for the sake of his Supreme beloved, or because it is a means to reach His love or removing what may be contrary or contradictory to His love.

True love requires to single out the beloved and not to associate with him anyone in this love. The lover should hate anyone else, keep him away and should not give him a chance of coming close to him and consider his claim of love a lie. When a beloved creature disdains and rejects that anyone else be a partner in love, what will be the case with the highest beloved who deserves love for Himself alone. Any love for others is a torment and has evil consequence for the lover. This is the reason that Allah, the Glorious, will not forgive that another person be associated in this love, and He will forgive anything else for whoever He wills.

The love of images makes the slave to lose the love of the One who is more valuable for him. It makes him to lose what there is no favour no blessing or favourable life without his love alone. The slave has option of choosing one of the loves, for they cannot come together in the heart neither can they go out of the heart. Anyone who turns away from the love of Allah and forsakes His remembrance and the desire of meeting with Him, Allah will afflict him with the love of others and punish him by it in the world, the *Barzakh* and the Hereafter. He may try him with the love of idols or crosses or beardless young men or women or money or companions or friends or anything less than them in despicability and ignominy. A human being is the slave of his beloved no matter who he is. A poet has said:

'You are slain by anyone you love; so choose for yourself whosoever you like for love.'

Anyone whose deity is not his master and helper, his deity will be his desire. Allah, the Exalted, said:

"Have you seen the one who has taken his own desire as a god, whom Allah has sent stray due to knowledge, and has set a seal upon his ears and his heart and put covering on his eyes; who can guide such a person after Allah? Will you not take heed?" (45:23)

7.2 Worship is love with humility and submission to the beloved

The characteristic of the devotion is to love with submission and humbleness for the beloved. Anyone who loves something or surrenders to it, his heart has been devoted to it. Devotion is the last stage of love; it is also called enslavement.

The first stage of love is **attachment**; it is so called because of the attachment of the heart of the lover with the beloved. A poet said:

'I was attached to Lyala when she was wearing amulets and no size for her breast appeared for her friends.'

Then comes **fervent longing**; it is so called because of the longing of the heart to the beloved. A poet said:

'The lovers complain the fervent longing. I wish I would bear alone what they are suffering from.
In that case all the joy of love would have been for my heart, which no one experienced before or after me.'

Then is the stage of **infatuation** which means settlement of the love in the heart permanently without getting out. Allah said:

"Its torment goes on and on." (25:65)

Then comes **passionate love**, which indicates extreme love. For this reason Allah is not described by it and it is not used concerning Him.

It is followed by **yearning** which means the quick journey of the heart to the beloved. It has been used concerning Allah Almighty as reported by Ammar ibn Yasir who performed a prayer and finished it quickly. The people spoke to him about it and he said:

'I supplicated in it what the Messenger of Allah, blessing and peace of Allah be upon him, used to say, and that is:

"O Allah, by Your knowledge of unseen and Your power of creation, keep me alive as long as life is good for me, and cause me to die when

death is better for me. O Allah, I ask You to grant me Your fear in private and public, and ask for speaking truth in anger and pleasure, I ask You for moderation in poverty and wealth. I ask You for a favour which does not end and I ask You for the coolness of eye which does not finish, I ask You for the joy of life after death and I ask You for the delight of looking at Your face. I ask You for the yearning of meeting with You without any harm or misleading trial. O Allah, decorate us with the decoration of faith and make us guides and guided."[279]

In another Divine words Allah said:

'The yearning of the righteous ones has been long, I am more yearning to meeting with them.'

This sense was expressed by the Prophet, Allah's blessing and peace be upon him, in his words:

"Whoever loves meeting with Allah, Allah loves meeting with him."[280]

Some scholars of understanding said concerning the words of Allah:

"Whoever hopes meeting with Allah, the appointed time of Allah is coming." (29:5)

When Allah, the Exalted, knew the yearning of His friends to meet Him, and that their hearts will not get rest without meeting Him, He set a time for His meeting to make their souls be comfortable.
The most pleasant and blissful life is the life of those who love, yearn and find peace with Allah. Their life is the real pleasant life. There is no life more blissful and more enjoyable for the heart than this. This is the pleasant life which Allah mentioned in His Book:

"Whoever does righteous deed, whether male or female, while he is a believer, We will surely cause him to live a pleasant life." (16:97)

It is not meant the life shared by the believers and disbelievers, righteous and wicked, which they enjoy of good food, drink, dress and spouse; it

---

[279] Ahmad (18351), Nisa'i (3:54), Ibn Hibban (1971) Hakim (1:524)
[280] Bukhari (6507), Muslim (2683)

may be that the enemies of Allah have far more of them than His allies. Allah, the Glorious, has guaranteed for every one who does righteous deeds a pleasant life. He is truthful and never fails in His promise. Which life is more enjoyable than the life of a person whose entire worries have become one worry for achieving the pleasure of Allah! His heart is not disrupted but focused on Allah, and his intentions and thoughts which were divided to many directions become devoted to the remembrance of his Highest Beloved, meeting with Him and acquiring peace in meeting with Him. All his worries, intentions and thoughts even the vibrancy of his heart revolves around Him. If he is quiet, he is quiet for the pleasure of Allah; if he speaks, he speaks in obedience of Allah; if he listens, he listens for Allah and if he looks, looks for Allah. He catches by Allah, walks by Him, moves by Him, rests by Him; lives by Him and dies by Him and by Him he will be raised. It is as said by the Messenger of Allah, Allah's blessing and peace be upon him, in a Divine Hadith:

"None of My servants approaches Me with more acceptable duty than what I Have prescribed for him. My servant continuously tries to come close to Me by supererogatory acts of worship till I love him. When I love him I become his ear by which he hears, his eye by which he sees, his hand by which he holds and his legs by which he walks. If he asks Me for anything, I will grant him, if he seeks refuge with Me, I will provide him with refuge. I never hesitated in anything I was going to do as much as I hesitate taking the life of My servant. He dislikes death and I do not like to do what he does not like; he, however, is to die."[281]

This noble Divine Hadith, which the people of hard and thick heart find understanding difficult, has limited the sources of the love of Almighty in two things: Carrying out the obligatory duties and trying to come close to Him by supercrogatory acts.

Almighty stated that the performance of obligatory duties assigned by Him is the most lovable of the acts of all that those who seek coming closer to Him, then come supererogatory. The lover performs supererogatory acts frequently till he is loved by Allah. When he becomes beloved of Allah, his love of Allah produces another love for Allah above this love. This later love engages his heart from the thought of anyone else because it has overwhelmed his soul and has not left any space for anyone else. The remembrance of his beloved, his love and his high

---

[281] Bukhari (6503)

position has dominated his heart and has taken possession of his soul like the possession of the beloved over the true lover whose powers of love overwhelm him.

No doubt such a lover if hears, hears by his beloved; if sees, sees by him; if holds, holds by him, and if walks, walks by him. He is in his heart and with him, his companion and friend. The preposition "ba'" in the Hadith is for closely association which has no match for it. This cannot be understood by mere information because the issue is conditional and not pure scientific.

When a creature feels like that in the love of another creature for which he has not been created, then what will be the situation with the love of the Highest Beloved.

Some of the lovers said:

'Your image is in my eye and you name on my mouth and your place is in my heart, so where can you hide?'

Another poet said:

'It is amazing that I long for them and ask anyone I meet about them while they are with me.

My eye looks for them while they are in my eyeball; and my heart yearns for them while they are within me.'

Another poet said:

'If I say that you are away, my heart does not believe me because you are in the secret place of it, not being away.

If I say you are not away my eye says this is a lie. Now I am puzzled between truth and lie.'

There is nothing closer to a lover than his beloved. Sometimes the loves overwhelms him till it becomes closer to him than his soul to the extent that he forgets himself but does not forget him.

It is said:

'I wish to forget her memory and as though Layla appears to me in every way.'

In the Hadith mainly ear, eye, hand and feet are mentioned because they are the tools of feeling and acting. The ear and eye bring liking and disliking to the heart and produce love and hatred, then the person uses his hand and foot. When the hearing and seeing of the servant are by Allah, he will be safe in the tools of his understanding and be protected in his love and hatred and be guided in his holding and walking.

Consider how only ear, eye hand and foot were mentioned and the tongue was left out because the hearing and seeing can happen with the will of the person and sometimes without his intention, but the movement of the tongue is by the will of the servant, and a person can withhold it except in the situation he is commanded to use it.

Also the excitement of the tongue from the heart is more perfect than the excitement of other organs, as the tongue is the messenger and interpreter of the heart.

Consider also how Almighty said: "He then listens by Me, looks by Me and hold by Me." He did not say: 'He hears for Me, sees for Me and holds for Me.'

Someone may think that preposition '*lam*' was more appropriate in this place because it denotes the aim and objective of these matters taking place for Allah. This is wrong. The preposition '*ba''* here is not for mere getting help as the movements of the righteous and wicked people are by the help of Allah. '*Ba''* here is for giving the sense of companionship meaning that the servant hears, looks, hold, and walks while I am his companion and with him. It is like the words of Allah in another Hadith:

"I am with My servant when he remembers Me and his lips move for Me."[282]

This companionship is a special one as shown in His statement:

"Do not grieve, certainly Allah is with us." (9:40)

And the saying of the Prophet, Allah's blessing and peace be upon him:

"What do you think about two people, Allah is third of them?"[283]

It is also shown in the statements of Allah, the Exalted:

"Surely Allah is with the righteous ones." (29:69)

"Certainly Allah is with those who are mindful of Him and those who do righteous deeds." (16:128)

"Be patient, Allah is with those who are patient." (8:46)

---

[282] Bukhari as ta'liq (9: 187), Ahmad (2: 540), Ibn Majah (3792), Ibn Hibban (2316) Bayhaqi in Shu'ab (1: 315)
[283] Bukhari (3453), Muslim 92381)

"No! With me is my Lord who will guide me." (26:62)

He said to Moses and Aaron:

"Surely, I am with you both, hearing and seeing everything." (20:46)

The letter *'Ba'* is illustrating the sense of this companionship, which *Lam* does not do. A person cannot gain patience, sincerity and trust and he cannot reach the stages of devotion except with this *'Ba'* and this companionship.

When a slave is with Allah, all the troubles become easy for him, and all fears turn into safety for him. With Allah every difficult matter becomes easy, every hardship turns to simple and every far comes nearer. With Allah the worries, sadness and sorrows are dispersed. There is no worry with Allah and not any sadness and sorrow except where the sense of this *'Ba'* is missing. In that condition the heart of the slave becomes like the whale when it is out of the water; it jumps and turns upside down until it returns to it.

When this agreement is achieved from the slave for his Lord, He agrees to fulfil all his needs and requirements. He said:

"If he asks Me for anything, I will surely give him, if he seeks refuge in Me, I will surely give him refuge."[284]

It means that as the servant agreed what I want from him by carrying out My orders and approaching Me with what I love, I will fulfil his desire and fear in what he asks Me to do for him and to protect him. This agreement becomes strong between two sides to the extent that the Lord Almighty hesitates to cause death to His slave because he dislikes death. The Lord dislikes what His slave does not like and He does not like to displease him. This requires that He should not cause him to die, but his interest is in his death. He does not cause him to die but in order to bring back to life. In the same way He does not cause him to be ill but to cure him and give him health. He does not make him poor but to give him plenty, and does not withhold but to give him more. He did not bring him out of Paradise in the loins of his father but to return him to it. He is the beloved in reality and no one else. If every root of the hair of the slave

---

[284] Bukhari 6503

contained full love for Allah, it would be only some of what He deserved from His slave.

'Move your heart in love wherever you wish, the love belongs to the first beloved.

How many places a man halts on the earth, but his longing always are for the first station?'

7.3   Infatuation is the last stage of love

The last stage of love is infatuation which means devotion of the lover to his beloved. The servant in this stage submits and surrenders to his beloved. For this reason the noblest station of the slave is devotion, there is nothing more honourable than it. Allah mentioned the noblest of His creation and most beloved to Him, His Messenger Muhammad, Allah's blessing and peace be upon him, in his most illustrious condition i.e. the position of calling to Him, challenging by prophethood and the honour of being taken to the heavens by saying:

"When Allah's servant stood up to pray to Him, they almost swarmed over him." (72:19)

"If you have doubts about the revelation We have sent down to Our servant, then produce a single surah (chapter) like it." (2:23)

"Glory is to Him who made His servant travel by night from the sacred mosque to the farthest mosque, whose surroundings We have blessed." (17:1)

In the Hadith of intercession the people will be told:

"Go to Muhammad, a servant whom Allah has forgiven his past and future sins."[285]

Allah, the Exalted, created the people for His worship alone without joining anyone with Him. This is the highest kind of love which is done with perfect submission and humility. It is the real Islam and the religion of Abraham, anyone who turns away from it makes fool of himself.

"Who but a fool would forsake the religion of Abraham? We have chosen him in this world and he will rank among the righteous in

---

[285] Bukhari (7410), Muslim !93)

the Hereafter. His Lord said to him: 'Devote yourself to Me.' He replied: 'I devote myself to the Lord of the Universe.' Abraham commanded his sons to the same, as did Jacob: 'My sons, Allah has chosen this religion for you, so make sure that you do not die except while you are Muslims.' Were you there to see when death came upon Jacob? When he said to his sons: 'What will you worship after I have gone?' They replied: 'We will worship your God and the God of your fathers, Abraham and Ishmael and Isaac – one God. We submit to Him." (2:130-133)

For this reason association of partners with Allah was the most heinous crime. Allah will not forgive association with Him. The root of the association of others with Allah is to join them in love as He has said:

"There are some who choose to worship others besides Allah as rivals to Him. They love them as it is due to Allah, but those who believe have greater love for Allah." (2:165)

Here Allah says that there are some people who commit association with Him and take rival whom they love as Allah should be loved. Almighty also said that those who believe have greater love for Allah than the followers of rivals have for their rivals.

It is said that the meaning is that the believers' love for Allah is greater than the love of those people who have set rivals to Him. Although these people love Allah, but since they joined Him with their rivals in love, their love for Allah became weak. On the other hand since the sincere believers' love was exclusively for Allah, it was greater than their love.

Allah wished from His creation to make His love purely for Him, He, therefore, rejected completely those who took friend and intercessor besides Him. Almighty sometimes put the two together and sometimes mentioned only one. He said:

"Your Lord is Allah who created the heavens and earth in six days, then established Himself on the Throne, governing everything; there is no one that can intercede with Him, unless He has given permission: this is Allah your Lord so worship Him. How can you not take heed?" (10:3)

"Allah is the one who created the heavens and the earth and everything between them in six days. Then He established Himself on the Throne. You have no one but Him to protect you and no one to intercede for you, so why do you not take heed?" (32:4)

"Use it (the Qur'an) to warn those who fear being gathered before their Lord, they will have no one but Him to protect them and no one to intercede, so that they might become conscious of Him." **(6:51)**

Almighty said about Himself:

"Have they taken intercessors besides Allah? Say, 'Even though these have no power or understanding? 'All intercessions belong to Allah alone." **(39:43-44)**

"Hell is behind them and their gains will not benefit them, nor will the beings they took as protectors beside Allah, a tremendous torment awaits them." **(45:10)**

When a slave befriends his Lord alone, He brings for him intercessors and forms friendship between him and other believers who become his allies in Allah's cause, unlike that who takes a creature an ally beside Allah. So this is one thing and that is another thing.

The false intercession is one thing, and the true and firm intercession which can be gained by declaring oneness of Allah is another. This is the point of separation between the people of Tawhid and the followers of shirk. Allah guides whoever He wishes to the straight path.

The point is that the reality of devotion cannot be achieved with association in love with Allah. Love for Allah alone is the prerequisite of devotion. Also the love of the Messenger, putting him before oneself and the fathers and the sons is a necessary condition for the faith. It is because the love of the Prophet is from the love of Allah, and so is every love which is in Allah and for Allah.

The Messenger, Allah's blessing and peace be upon him, said:

"No one can get the sweetness of faith unless three things are found in him: Allah and His Messenger are more beloved to him than anything else; he loves a person only for the sake of Allah; and he hates to return to disbelief after Allah has saved him from it as he hates to be thrown in the fire."[286]

---

[286] Bukhari (16, 6041), Muslim (43)

He also said:

"Whoever loves for the sake of Allah, hates for His sake, gives for Him and withholds for Him has completed the faith."[287]

The Prophet, Allah's blessing and peace be upon him, also said:

"No two persons love one another but the best of them will be the one who has greater love for his friend."[288]

This love is the outcome of the love of Allah, and the stronger it is, its basis also will be like that.

7.4   The categories of love

There are four categories of love which are to be distinguished from one another. Failing it causes many people to go astray.

1. The first category is love of Allah; it alone is not enough to save from the torment of Allah and gain His reward. The polytheists, the Jews and worshippers of the cross and other objects also love Allah.
2. The second is love of what Allah loves. It is the quality which admits a person into Islam and takes him out of disbelief. The most loved person to Allah is the one who is holding fast this love and clings to it.
3. The third one is love for Allah and in Him[289]. It is the ultimate result of the love of what He loves. The love of what Allah loves will not be right without the love for Him and in Him.
4. The fourth is love with Allah; it is the joined love. Anyone who loves something with Allah and not for Allah, not for the sake of Him or in Him, he has taken that thing as rival beside Allah. It is the love of the polytheists.

There is a fifth category which we are not concerned with and that is natural love. It is the inclination of a person to what suits his nature like the love of the thirsty for water, hungry for food, and love of sleep, spouse and child. These are not bad unless they distract a man from the remembrance of Allah and keep him busy from the love of Allah.
Allah, the Exalted said:

---

[287] Abu Dawud (4681), Tabarani in Kabir (7613, 7737)
[288] Bukhari in al-Adab (544), Abu Ya'la (3419), Ibn Hibban (566) Hakim (4: 171)
[289] This is a spiritual terminology and refers to the love for the sake of Allah.

"You who believe, do not let your wealth and your children distract you from remembering Allah." (63:9)

"Men who are not distracted, either by commerce or sale, from remembering Allah." (24:37)

7.5 Intimate Friendship includes full love

Then comes the intimate friendship which means full and whole love, so there is no place left in the heart for any other person. It is a position where there is no possibility of sharing it with anyone else. This position was limited for the two friends of Allah, Abraham and Muhammad, Allah's blessing and peace be upon them, as our Prophet, Allah's blessing and peace be upon him, said:

"Allah took me a friend as He took Abraham as a friend."[290]

He also said:

"If I were to take a person from the people of the earth as friend, I would have taken Abu Bakr as friend, but your companion is the friend of Allah."[291]

In another Hadith he said:

"I am free towards every friend from his friendship."[292]

When Abraham asked Allah to give him a son, he was given. The love of the son stuck to his heart and settled in one corner of his heart, the beloved felt jealous of His friend to see in his heart a place for anyone else. He ordered to sacrifice him, and the order was given in dream to make the implement more difficult and big trial. The aim was not to sacrifice the child, it was rather to kill him from his heart so that it becomes purely for the Lord. When the friend went ahead in carrying out the order and put the love of his Lord over the love of his son, the aim was achieved, the order of sacrifice was lifted and the son was ransomed by a big sheep. The Lord Almighty does not order something then cancels it altogether but He likes to retain some of it as He retained the rule of

---

[290] Muslim (532)
[291] Bukhari (3456), Muslim (2383)
[292] Muslim (2383)

ransom. He reserved desirability of the charity before supplication, and kept five prayers after instead of fifty and retained their reward and said:

"My word will not be changed and I am not unjust My servants. They are five in deed and fifty in reward."[293]

7.6 Love is general and intimate friendship is special

Some mistaken people think that love is higher than friendship. Abraham is the friend of Allah and Muhammad is beloved of Allah. It is based on ignorance because love is general and friendship is special, and friendship is the highest position in love. The Prophet, Allah's blessing and peace be upon him, said that Allah has taken him as a friend as He has taken Abraham as a friend. The Prophet denied that there was any friend of him except his Lord while he expressed his love for 'A'ishah and her father as well as for 'Umar ibn al-Khattab and others.

Allah, the Glorious, said:

"Surely, Allah loves those who turn to Him in repentance and He loves those who keep themselves clean." (2:222)

"He loves patients." (3:146)

"He loves those who do good." (3:148)

"He loves just people." (5:42)

The young man who turns to Allah is the beloved of Allah; His friendship is especially for the two of His chosen servants. The claim that love is higher than friendship was the result of lack of knowledge and understanding the words of Allah and His Messenger, Allah's blessing and peace be upon him.

The slave leaves what he loves and is fond of for the sake of whom he loves and adores.

It has already been said that the slave does not leave what he loves and likes but for the sake of the one whom he adores and loves. He abandons what is less liked by him for that which he likes more. He does what he

---

[293] Bukhari (349), Muslim (162)

dislikes to gain the love of the one whose love is stronger than the disliking of what he does. His disliking is stronger than the disliking of what he does.

It has also been mentioned that the characteristic of the reason is to prefer the higher beloved over the lower one and the easier hateful thing over the more hated one. It is based on the power of love and hatred. This is not possible but by two things: power of perception and courage of the heart. Doing opposite of it will be either because of the weakness of perception as he did not realise the degrees of loved and hated as they are, or because of the weakness of the soul and incapability of the heart as it does not conform to him in preferring the better to raise his knowledge of it being better. When his perception is correct and his soul is strong, his heart will be encouraged to prefer the higher loved and the lowest hateful. This person has been helped for the causes of happiness.
There are people whose desire's power is more powerful than the power of his reason and his faith, and as a result the powerful dominates the weaker. On the other hand there are those whose faith and reason are stronger than his desires.

The doctors tell many people to avoid what is harmful for them, but their desire forces them to take it; they put their desire before their reason. This type of people is called by the physicians as insensitive. Most affected people in their hearts prefer what increases their illness; they are unable to control it.

The root of the evil is lack of perception and weakness and meanness of the soul while the basis of the good is maturity of perception and power, nobility and courage. Love and intention are the cause and beginning of everything, and the disliking and hatred are the source of every abandoning. These two powers of the heart are the cause of the happiness and wretchedness of every person. Any deed of free will is found by its cause of love and intention. Not doing any deed sometimes is because of the lack of its cause and sometimes due to disliking and hatred which prevent it. It is the subject of command and prohibition, which is known as abandoning, on which the reward and punishment depend. This removes the confusion concerning whether it is positive or negative. The fact is that it is of two kinds: abandoning due to the lack of cause is negative, and abandoning because of the preventive cause is positive.

7.7 A living person prefers optional doing and avoiding

The living person likes to do or to avoid optional matter because it has benefit in it or it removes the pain and brings cure for him. That is why it is said, 'his chest was cured, and his heart was cured'.

This is something which every sensible person, but even the animal prefers. However, many people make big blunder in it and they run after the joy which results in the great pain for them. They cause pain for themselves from where they think they are gaining the joy, and cure their hearts with what causes them greater pain. It is the character of the one who has restricted his eye on what is available and did not look at the consequences. The intrinsic nature of the reason is to look at the consequences. The most sensible person is the one who puts his coming joy and comfort before the immediate and ending enjoyment. The most stupid person is the one who sold the lasting pleasure, permanent good life and great enjoyment, which has no problem or trouble at all, for the vanishing joy mixed with pains and fears and which is going quickly to end and terminate.

One of the learned men said:

'I considered what the sensible people are struggling to acquire, and found out that all their efforts are centred around one object though their means to get it are different. I noticed that all of them are striving for removing the worries and sorrow from themselves. Some of them take resort in eating and drinking, others in commerce and earning, some in sexual joy, some in listening to songs and amusing sounds and some in play and amusement. I said that this object was the target of the sensible people, but all the means are not leading to it, rather many of them may lead to its opposite. I did not see in all these ways any which can take them to their quest except devotion to Allah, dealing with Him alone and preferring His pleasure over everything else. If the person following this way misses his share of the world, he succeeds in getting the higher share without loss. If he gets it, he gets all things; and if he misses it, he misses everything. If he gains his share of the world, he receives it in the most pleasant manner. So, there in now way for a person more useful than this, and no other way can take him to his joys, delight and happiness. Allah alone is the source of help.

7.8 The categories of the loved

The loved object is of two kinds:

1. One which is desired for itself, and
2. The other which is desired for other reasons

This last one must end in the one which is desired for itself. Everything beside the true loved one is loved for other causes. There is nothing which is loved for itself except Allah alone. All other matters which are desired, their desire follows the love of the Lord, the Glorious and Exalted, like the love of His angels, His prophets and His allies. It is the result of His love as the love of the beloved makes the love of that which He loves necessary. This is a subject which must be considered properly because it is the criterion between the love which is useful and the love which is not going to be useful but may be harmful.

Know that no one is loved unless his perfection is the requirement of His essence. His being the deity, and His lordship and independence are all part of His essence. Anything else is disliked and hated because it does not agree with His loved materials and is opposed to it. His hatred and disliking are in line with the degree of this opposition. What is the most contradictory to His loved matters is the most hateful among the substances, qualities, deeds and intentions and other things. This is a just balance to assess the approval and disapproval of the Lord Almighty, and His friendship and hatred. When we see someone who loves what the Lord Almighty hates, and hates what He loves, we will know that he has His hatred according to it. When we notice a person who loves what the Lord loves and hates what He hates, and anything which is liked by the Lord, it is loved and preferred by him, and anything that is hateful to Him, is hateful to him and he keeps away from it, we learn that this person has achieved the friendship of Allah according to the degree of his feeling.
Hold on to this principle for yourself and regarding others. Friendship means to be in conformity with the Praiseworthy Ally in matters of His pleasure and displeasure. Friendship is not acquired by plenty of fasting, praying, getting torn to pieces or exercise.

The object which is loved for others is also of two kinds:

a) One which the lover enjoys by receiving and acquiring it

b) The second which causes him pain, but he endures it because it takes him to the loved just like taking bitter medicine. Allah, the Exalted, said:

"Fighting has been ordained for you, though it is hard for you. You may dislike something although it is good for you, or like something although it is bad for you. Allah knows and you do not." (2:216)

Allah Almighty told us that fighting is hateful though it is good for the people as it takes them to the greatest and most beneficial loved one. The souls like rest, relaxation and comfort, which are bad for them as they lead to missing that loved object. The sensible person does not look at the delight of immediate dear thing and prefers it, and the pain of immediate hateful object and turns away from it because it may be bad for him. It may cause him utmost pain and make him miss the greatest joy. The intelligent people of the world undertake hard matters because they take them to enjoy the delight after that.

So, the matters are four:

i.   A hateful thing that leads to hateful result,
ii.   A hateful matter that leads to loved result,
iii. A loved matter that takes to the loved result, and
iv.   A loved matter that produces a hateful result,

The loved matter leading to the loved aim has two incentives for it, and the hateful matter leading to hateful has two causes for leaving it. The remaining two categories have both types of incentives, which try to pull the person to their side, and this is the field of test and trial. The soul prefers the nearest one which is immediate, while reason and faith tend to like the most advantageous and lasting one. The heart is hanging between the two incentives, and moves to this one at one time and to that one at other time.

This is the place of religious and decreed trial. The incentive of reason and faith is always calling 'come to the success', because in the morning the traveller praises night marching, and after death the slave is pleased with the result. If the darkness of the night of love becomes intense and the power of desire and intention dominates he says:

'O soul, be patient! It is only for a while then it will go and all this will come to an end and pass away.'

7.9 Love is the basis of every deed whether good or bad

Since the love is the basis of every deed whether right or wrong, the basis of the religious deeds is the love of Allah and His Messenger, and the basis of religious statement is the confirmation of Allah and His Messenger. Any thought that creates obstacle in the perfection of the love of Allah and His Messenger and blocks it or any doubt that creates problem in the way of the confirmation, is obstructive to the basis of faith or at least the cause of weakening it. If it gets strong and opposes the basis of the love and confirmation, it turns to the disbelief or blatant polytheism. If it is not strong to oppose it, it will create defect in its perfectness and produce weakness and slackness in the willpower and struggle. It is a cause of preventing the endeavouring person, halting the seeker and turning away the desirous. The friendship cannot be complete without showing enmity, as Allah has cited the leader of the devoted and loving people that he said to his people:

"Do you see what you have been worshipping, you and your ancient forefathers? They are my enemies, except the Lord of the worlds." (26:75-77)

The friendship of the Friend of Allah was not perfect without confirming this enmity. Certainly, there is no friendship but for Allah, and that cannot be complete without declaring the freedom from every deity beside Him.

Allah, the Exalted, said:

"You have a good example in Abraham and his companions, when they said to their people: 'We are dissociated from you and what you worship besides Allah. We have denied you, and until you believe in Allah alone the animosity and hatred will remain for ever between us.'" (60:4)

"(Remember) when Abraham said to his father and his people, 'I am dissociated from what you worship, except for Him who created me, and it is He who will guide me'. He bequeathed these to his descendants so that they might return (to Allah)." (43:26-28)

He made this friendship for Allah and animosity for any deity besides Him a word which remained in his descendants inherited by the prophets and their followers from one another. This word is, 'There is no god except Allah.' It is the one which the leader of the devoted bequeathed to his followers until the Day of Resurrection. It is the word by which the heavens and the earth are established, and Allah created the entire creation on it. The religion was set up on it and the Qiblah was decided and the swords of the jihad were raised for it. This is the pure right of Allah on the entire people, and by this word their blood and that of their descendants was spared in this world, and it will save them from the torment of the grave and the Fire. It is the ordinance without which no one can enter Paradise. It is the word of Islam and the key to home of peace (i.e. Paradise). It is the dividing factor between the lucky and wretched, amiable and rejected. By it the home of disbelief was separated from the home of faith, and abode of pleasure was distinguished from the abode of disgrace and humility. It is the pillar which holds the obligatory and Sunnah duties.

"Any one whose last word was 'there is no god but Allah' will be admitted to Paradise."[294]

The spirit and secret of this word is to single out the Lord – great is His praise, pure are His names, exalted is His name, sublime is His favour and there is no god besides Him – to single out Him with love, honour, glory, hope and fear and what follows them like trust, turning to Him, desire and awe. The devoted slave does not love anything beside Him; anything he loves it is offshoot of His love and a source of increasing His love. He fears only Him, puts his hope only in Him, trusts Him only, is inclined to Him alone, has no fear but of Him. He takes oath only in His name, makes vow for Him, turns to Him, expects reward only from Him, and seeks no help at the time of troubles but from Him. He turns to Him for refuge, bows down only before Him, and sacrifices only for Him and His name. All these actions are included in one word that is: All the acts of worship belong to Him alone. This is the confirmation of the testifying that there is no god but Allah.

For this reason Allah has forbidden the Fire on those who attest that there is no god but Allah in real sense. It is impossible that a person who performed this testimony perfectly and fulfilled its requirements goes to the Fire. Allah, the Most High, has said:

"Those who are upright in their testimony." (70:33)

---

[294] Ahmad (5: 233), Abu Dawud (3116), Hakim (1: 351)

He holds his testimony faithfully outwardly and inwardly in his heart. There are people whose testimony is dead, and those whose testimony is sleeping, when it is roused it awakes. Some other's testimony is lying down; some others have it closer to the standing posture. However, it is in the heart like the spirit for the body. So there is a dead spirit, a sick spirit close to death, another which is close to life and the right spirit which takes care of the body

The Prophet, Allah's blessing and peace be upon him, said:

"I know a word no slave says it at the time of his death but his soul finds its spirit."[295]

The life of the soul is by the life of this word in it, as the life of the body is by the soul in it. Anyone who died on this word he would be in Paradise, and anyone held to it and fulfilled its requirement, he would enjoy in Garden of Refuge and his life would be the most pleasant one. Allah, the Most High, said:

"For anyone who feared the meeting with his Lord and restrained himself from base desires, Paradise will be his home." (79:40-41)

Paradise will be his refuge on the Day of Meeting. The garden of knowledge, love and intimacy with Allah, desire of meeting with Him and satisfaction with Him is the refuge of his soul in this world. And anyone who has this Paradise for him here, the Paradise of Eternity will be his refuge on the Day of Return. Anyone who has been deprived this garden here he will be more deprived of that Garden there. The righteous people are in bliss though the life is hard and they suffer in the world, the wicked are in the Hellfire even if the world is plentiful for them.
Allah, the Exalted, said

"Whoever, male or female, does good deeds and has faith, We shall give him a good life." (16:97)

Good life is the Paradise of the world.

Almighty also said:

---

[295] Ahmad (1: 63), Ibn Hibban (204), Hakim (1: 72)

"When Allah wishes to guide someone, He opens his breast to Islam; when He wishes to lead him astray, He closes and constricts his breast as if he is climbing up to the skies." (6:125)

What is more pleasant than the expansion of the breast? What is more painful than constriction of the breast?

Allah also said:

"For the allies of Allah there is no fear, nor shall they grieve. Those who believe and are conscious of Allah, for them there is good news in this life and in the Hereafter. There is no changing the word of Allah; that is the supreme triumph." (10:62-64)

The sincere believer in Allah lives pleasant life, has delightful mind, expanded breast and happy heart. This is the immediate Paradise before the coming one.

The Prophet, Allah's blessing and peace be upon him, said:

"When you pass by the meadows of Paradise, graze in them."

They asked: 'What are the meadows of Paradise?'
He replied:

"They are the circles of remembrance of Allah."[296]

It is like his saying:

"Between my house and my pulpit is a meadow of Paradise."[297]

His reply to his Companions when they asked him about his continuous fasting:

"I am not like you; I am with my Lord who provides me with food and drink."[298]

He told them that the provision he receives from his Lord substitutes for material food and drink, and this is something special for him, no one

---

[296] Tirmidhi (3510), Ahmad (3: 150), Abu Ya'la (3432)
[297] Bukhari (1195), Muslim (1390)
[298] Bukhari (1964), Muslim (1105)

shares it with him. If he abstains from food and drink, he gets something, as a replacement.

A poet says:

'She has talks from your remembrance, which keep her busy from drink and provision. She finds light from your face which she walks in and from your talk she has a leader.
When she complains from the tiredness of walking, the spirit of meeting raises her spirit and she is stimulated.'

When the existence of a thing which, he needs badly, is useful for a person, its loss is more painful for him. When its absence is more useful for him, its existence is very disastrous for him. Nothing is more advantageous for the salve than his devotion to Allah, keeping busy in His remembrance, rejoicing His pleasure and putting it above everything for gaining His pleasure, then the absence of it is the most painful and distressing for him. The soul does not feel this pain and distress because of its engagement in other matters. It does not realise the pain of losing the most loved and useful to it. This is the stage of the drunkard who is completely absorbed in his intoxication to the extent that his house is burnt ad his belonging and family are destroyed, but he does not feel the pain of his loss. When he recovers and the veil of intoxication is removed and he awakes from the slumber of the wine, he knows his situation better.

This is the situation when the veil is removed and first indications of the Hereafter appear and departure from the world becomes clear, and moving to Allah becomes certain. The feeling of distress, pain and regret will be many times more painful than the pain of the world. A person afflicted by a mishap in the world may get some compensation but his suffering there has no substitute and the whole world cannot compensate for it. If Allah had decreed death for him due to his pain and regret, the slave deserved it; death becomes his biggest wish. This if the pain is only due to the loss, but what will be case when there is torment for the soul and body for other matters, which cannot be measured?
Exalted is He who empowered this weak creature to endure these two great pains which the big mountains are unable to carry.

Now present to yourself the thing which is dearest to you in the world, and you are not living happily without it, and then it was taken away from you and you were barred from getting it, what will your condition be? This is where there is a substitute for everything, what will be the case with something which has no substitute? Some one has said in a line of poetry:

'For anything you lose there is a substitute, but if you lose Allah, there is no substitute.'

It is said in a Divine report:

'Son of Adam, I created you to worship Me, so do not play; I have undertaken to provide you, so do not tire yourself. Son of Adam, obey Me you will find Me, and when you find Me, you will find everything; and if I escaped you, you will miss everything. I am the most beloved to you than everything.'

7.10 Love is a category under which there are various kinds

Love is a general category including various kinds in grade and quality. Most of its kinds that is mentioned concerning the right of Allah Almighty are the ones which are suitable and exclusively for Him and those which are not appropriate for Him alone like worship, devotion to Him and similar things. Worship is exclusively for Him and so is devotion.

Sometime love is mentioned by its general name like Allah's saying:

"Allah will bring other people whom He will love and they will love Him." (5:54)

"There are some who choose to worship others besides Allah as rivals to Him, loving them with the love due to Allah, but the believers have greater love for Allah." (2:165)

The greatest reprehensible love is the one in which the lover makes Allah's love and the love of the rival he has taken as equal. The most praiseworthy love is the one which is exclusively for Allah, and the love of what He loves. This love is the root of happiness without which no one can be saved from the punishment. On the other side the reprehensible love is the one where someone is joined with Allah. It is the root and basis of the misfortune the people of which will suffer from the punishment forever. Someone who was subjected for committing some sins will not remain in it.

The Qur'an's main instructions are concerning the command of the first love and its requirement and prohibition of the other love and its consequences. The Holy Book sets example for both kinds, cites the stories of both groups and details of the deeds of both types and the objects of their worship. Almighty also informed about what He will do with these two categories and their situations in three abodes: the world, the abode of the *Barzakh* and the abode of peaceful rest. The Qur'an deals with the conditions of the two.

The basic call of all the messengers, from the beginning to the end, was to worship Allah alone, Who has no partner. That worship was to be based on full love of Him, complete submission and surrendering to Him and to express His honour and majesty. The fundamental consequence of all that is obedience of Allah and being conscious of Him.

Anas reported that the Prophet, Allah's blessing and peace be upon him, said:

"By the One in whose hand is my soul, no one of you will be believer till I become more beloved to him than his children, his parents and all the people."[299]

In another report 'Umar ibn al-Khattab said to the Prophet, Allah's blessing and peace be upon him:
'Messenger of Allah, By Allah, you are most beloved to me except myself.'
The Prophet said to him:

"No, O 'Umar, until I become dearer to you than yourself."
'Umar the said;
'By the One who sent you with truth, You are the dearer to me than myself.'
He said:

"Now, O 'Umar."[300]

If this is the case of the love of Allah's Messenger and slave, Allah's blessing and peace be upon him, which requires putting it above the love of the person, his children and his parents and all the people, what do you

---

[299] Bukhari (14, 15), Muslim (44)
[300] Bukhari (6632)

think of the love of the One who sent him, glory and exaltedness be to Him? His love must be placed above all others.

The Lord Almighty's love is distinguished from any other love in its quality and extent and being totally for Him alone. It is required that He should be dearer to the slave than his children and his parents, as well as his ear, eye and the soul inside him. His true God and Divine Being should be dearer to him than all these things. A thing sometimes is loved in some ways and is loved for other reasons, but the object which is to be loved in the way through is Allah alone; divinity belongs to Him.

He said:

"If there had been in the heavens and earth any gods but Him, both would have been ruined." (21:22)

7.11 Love is the cause of every movement in upper and lower worlds

Every movement in the upper or lower world emanates from love; it is its cause and objective. This is because the movements are three types:

i.   An intentional and optional move,
ii. Natural move and
iii. Move by force

The basis of the natural move is stillness. When a body gets out of its natural position and centre, it moves to return to it. Its movement from its centre and station is due to a force which moves it. So, it has a move by force of an object and natural move to return to its centre. Both movements are the result of forceful mover; it is the cause of both moves. The optional and intentional move, which is the basis of the two moves, emerges from intention and love. It shows that all three movements are the result of intention and love.

The proof of the movements limited to three is as follows:

If the moving object has sense of movement, its move is intentional, if it has no sense of its move, it is either according to its nature or not in line with it. The first one is natural and the second one is forced.

When this is proved then all the movements in the heavens and earth and between them such as the sun, moon, stars, winds, cloud, rain, plants and the foetus in their wombs of the mothers – all these are managed by the angels who arrange the matter and distribute the ordinance as the texts of the Qur'an and the Sunnah have described in many places. To have faith in it is part of the faith in angels. Allah, the Exalted, has assigned angels to the wombs, angels for rain, angels for plants, angels for winds, angels for the skies, the sun, the moon and the stars. He has appointed four angels to every human, two recorders on his right and left side, two guards in front and behind him. He has assigned angels to take his soul and take it to its place in Paradise or Hell. He set angles to question and test him in his grave and to arrange for his torment or bliss there. Other angels are given the duty of driving him to the place of gathering when he rises from his grave, others to arrange his punishment in the Hellfire or comfort in Paradise. Almighty has assigned angels to the mountains, and to the clouds, they take them where they have been ordered, and other to drop the rain by His command and in the amount decided by Him. He appointed angels to prepare the utilities of Paradise: its bedding, furniture, dresses, etc. He has appointed angels for Hell as well.

The greatest forces of Allah are angels who are to carry out the orders of Allah. They have no authority, all authorities are in the hand of Allah, the angles are to manage the affairs, and operate by the order and permission of Allah. Almighty said on their tongue:

"We only descend at your Lord's command, everything before us and everything behind us, and everything in between, all belong to Him. Your Lord is never forgetful." (19:64)

He also said:

"There are many angels in heaven whose intercession will be of no use except after Allah has permitted to whom He wills and approves." (53:26)

Almighty swore by a group of angels, who carry out His orders in the world, saying:

"By those (angels) ranged in rows, who rebuke reproachfully, and recite Allah's word." (37:1-3)

"By those sent forth in swift succession, violently storming, scattering far and wide, separating forcefully, delivering a reminder, as a proof or warning." (77:1-6)

"By those who extract with violence, who remove with ease, who glide as if swimming, those who race each other in a race and those who sort each matter out." (79:1-5)

We have explained the meaning and the secret of the oath by certain objects in our book *"The oaths of the Qur'an."*

When you understand it, then remember all these loves, movements, intentions and acts are the worship of the Lord of the heavens and earth by the angels. All forced and optional movements are subject to them. If there had been no love, the heavens would not have moved, the bright stars would have not rotated, the subjugated wind would not have been blown, the clouds carrying the rain would not have passed, the foetus would not have moved in the wombs of the mothers, and the variety of plants would not have sprouted from the grain, and the waves of the overflowing seas would not have got in commotion. Those angels who arrange the matters and distribute the provision would not have moved, the heavens and the earths and various creatures in them would not have glorified their Creator.

"The seven heavens and the earth and everyone in them glorify Him. There is not a single thing that does not celebrate His praise, though you do not understand their praise. He is Most Forbearing, Most Forgiving." (17: 44)

7.12 Every living thing has intention and love

When this is understood, then it should be noted that every living creature has intention and love and deeds in accordance with it. Every moving object moves because of its intention and love. The creatures will not be right except by making their movements and love for their Creator and Inventor alone. He is the one who brought them into existence. For this reason Allah Almighty said:

"If there were in them (the heavens and the earth) other gods besides Allah, they would have been ruined." (21:22)

Almighty did not say that they would have not been found or they would have been annihilated, because He has power to retain them with their corruption. It will not have been possible for them to remain in right order unless their God and the God of all that is in them was One. If there were two Gods for the world, its system would have fallen to ruin. This is simple to understand because in that condition every god would like to overwhelm the other and take the position of being god for him alone. Partnership is a defect in the perfect godhead, and a god would not accept to be an imperfect god. Now if one of them dominates the other, he will be god alone, the defeated being is not a god. If no one was able to defeat the other, it would mean that both of them are incapable and defective in their godhead. There will be a need for another god above them who can dominate them and rule over them, otherwise each of them will take what he has created and will seek supremacy over the other. This will destroy the system of the heavens and the earth and all those who are in them. It is well-known that if there are two matching kings in a country, it would end up in ruin. The same will happen in the case a woman has two husbands and a she camel when she has two male camels.

The main cause of the viciousness of the world is the disagreement of the kings and the rulers. Never did the enemies of Islam try to invade Islam but in the time of multiplicity of the kings of the Muslims and their fighting among them and the attempt of some to hold power alone and dominate over others.

The proper standing of the heavens and the earth and their stability and the arrangement of the affairs of the creation in the best way are clear evidence that there is no god but Allah alone without any partner. To Him belongs the sovereignty and the praise, He gives life and causes death, and He has power over everything. All other objects of worship from His Throne to the bottom of His earth are false. He declared:

"Allah has never had a child. Nor there is any god beside Him. If there were, each god would have taken his creation aside and tried to overcome the others. May Allah be exalted above what they describe! He knows what is not seen as well as what is seen, He is above any partner they claim for Him." (23:91-92)

"Have they chosen any gods from the earth who can give life to the dead? If there had been in the heavens or earth any god but Him, both (the heavens and the earth) would be in ruin. Allah, the Lord of the Throne, is far above the things they say. He cannot be called to account for anything He does, whereas they will be called to account." (21:21-23)

"Say, 'If there were other gods along with Him, as they say there are, then they would have tried to find a way to the Lord of the Throne.' (17:42)

It was said that the meaning of the last verse was that they would have tried to find a way of contesting and dominating as the kings do with one another. It is supported by His saying:

"Some of them tried to overcome others." (23:91)

Our Shaykh (Ibn Taymiyyah) said: The correct meaning is that they would have tried to find a way to be close to Him and obey Him; how then you worship them beside Him? If they were gods as they claim, they would have been His worshippers. He said this meaning was supported by many ways:

First, Allah said:

"Those they pray to, are themselves seeking a way to their Lord, even those who are closest to Him. They hope for His mercy and fear His torment." (17:57)

The meaning is that those beings you worship beside Me are My slaves as you are My slaves; you hope for My mercy and fear My torment. Then why do you worship them?

Secondly, Almighty did not say, 'They would have tried to find a way over Him', but said:

"They would have tried to find a way to the Lord of the Throne". (17:42)

This expression is used to seek closeness as Allah has said:

"You who believe, be mindful of Allah and seek ways to come closer to Him." (5:35)

Where competition is intended the preposition *'ala'* is used, as in the following sentence:

"If they obey you, you have no right to act against them." (4:34)

Thirdly, they did not say that their gods seek to overcome and dominate Him; they said their gods seek to come close to Him. Allah said: 'If the matter was as you say, these gods would have been slaves to Him. Why then you worship them beside Him?

7.13 The effects of love and its supplements, requirements and rules

Love has its outcomes and there are supplements and requirements as well as rules whether it is praiseworthy or blameworthy, useful or harmful. It produces passion, taste, sweetness, yearning, intimacy, desire to be close to the beloved and fear of getting away from him. Other effects of it are: Turning away and desertion, happiness and joy, crying and grief and so on.

The praiseworthy love is the one which is useful and brings what is helpful to the person in his world and the Hereafter. This love is the sign of happiness; opposite it is that which brings to the person what is harmful for him in his world and the Hereafter.

It is obvious that a living intelligent person will not choose what is going to cause him harm and distress. It could be the result of ignorance and wrongdoing. The soul may like something which is harmful and not useful for it. It is injustice of the human for his soul, which is either unaware of the condition of its lover, and loves and desires something without realizing its bad effect in its love. This is the situation of a person who follows his desire without knowledge. Or it knows the bad effect of it in its love, still chooses its desire above its knowledge. Its love may be composed of two matters:

i.   False belief and
ii. Reprehensible desire

It is the situation of the one who follows guesswork and the whim of his soul. The corrupt love is the result of ignorance or false belief, or overwhelming of false desire or a combination of all. It becomes doubt and desire, doubt which confuses the truth with the falsehood and beautifies the object of the beloved; and the desire which calls to gaining it. The army of doubt and desire combine their forces against the army of reason and faith; and the victory will be for the more powerful one.

When it is noted then the subsidiaries of every type of love is ruled by the original. So, the useful praiseworthy love, which is the sign of happiness of the slave, all its subsidiaries are useful for him. If he cries, it helps him, if he is grieved, it is helpful for him, if he is pleased, it brings him benefit, and if he is depressed, it is beneficial for him and if he is delighted, it is good for him. As a result he rolls in the stages of the love and its rulings in additional profit and closeness.

On the other hand the harmful blameworthy love and all its subsidiaries are harmful for its person and takes him away from his Lord. He is always in loss and far away from Him

This is how the result of every righteous or evil deed is. What is produced by righteous deeds gives additional reward and brings the person close to the Lord; and what is the result of disobedience is source of loss and takes the person far away from Him.

Allah, the Exalted, said:

"If ever they suffer any thirst, weariness, or hunger in Allah's cause, or take any step that angers the disbelievers, or gain any advantage over an enemy, a good deed is recorded in their favour on account of it. Allah never wastes the reward of those who do good deed. If they spend a little or a lot for Allah's cause, if they traverse a mountain pass, all this is recorded to their credits so that Allah can reward them with the best of their deeds." (9:120-121)

Allah, the Exalted, said in the first verse that for any act produced by their obedience and movements, a good deed is recorded for them. He said in the second one that their good deeds which they carried out are also recorded in their favour. The difference between the two is that the first one was not done by them, it was result of their obedience, which was recorded for them; and the second one was done by them.

The man killed by love should pay full attention to this section in order to know what is in his favour and what is against him.

7.14 Love and intention are the basis of every religion

As the love and intention are the basis of every action, as said earlier, they are the basis of every religion as well whether true or false. Religion comes from open and secret deeds, which emerge from love and intention. Religion means submission, worship and behaviour. It is based on permanent obedience which turns into manner and habit. For this reason the character is explained as religion in the following verse:

"Truly, you have a great moral character." (68:4)

Ibn Abbas explained it as 'great religion.'

'A'ishah was asked about the character of the Messenger of Allah, blessing and peace of Allah be upon him, and she said:

'His character was the Qur'an.'[301]

Religion has the sense of submission and surrender; it also has the sense of humility, servility and obedience. It may come from the top to the bottom and from the bottom to the top. The secret religion must have love and submission just like worship; the open religion does not necessarily have love though it has outside humility and obedience.

Allah, the Exalted, named the Day of Resurrection as the Day of Judgement, because the people will be judged on it by their deeds, if good, then good reward; but if bad, then bad recompense. It means that they will be judged and recompensed.

Allah, the Glorious, said:

"Why, do you not, if you are not to be recompensed, bring it back, if what you say is true? (56:86-87)

The meaning is that if you are not to be subdued, be recompensed and under control, restore the soul to its place. This verse is in need of explanation. The disbelievers by rejecting the resurrection and recompense have denied the power, Lordship and wisdom of their Lord. So, either they declare that they have a powerful lord who deals with them as he wishes, gives them life when he wishes and causes them to die when he wants, he gives them orders and prohibitions and gives good reward to the one who does good and punishes the one who commits evil; or they do not affirm the existence of such a lord. If they affirm the existence of him, they have believed in resurrection and return and the command and recompense. If the reject and deny, it means that they claim that they are not under the power of a lord and not going to be judged, and they have no lord who can deal with them as he wishes. Then why do they not have power to repel the death when it comes to them, and to restore the soul to its place when it reaches the throat?

It is said to the people who are present with a man who is going to die and they witness his death. Allah asks them: why then do you not return the soul to its place if you have power and you are not under the authority

---

[301] Muslim (746)

of a powerful and prevailing lord whose rules operate upon you and his commands work in you? It is the utmost powerful refutation of their claim. It clears that they are unable to restore one soul from one place to another even if the entire men and Jinn come together to do it. The verse is declaring the Lordship of Allah Almighty and His oneness and power to deal with His slaves and put them under His rule and judgments.

Religion is two types:

i.   Religion based on orders and Shari'ah, and
ii. the religion of judgement and recompense.

Both are exclusively for Allah alone. As a matter of fact the entire religion with all its commands and recompense is property of Allah, and the love is the basis of both religions. What Almighty has decreed and commanded, He loves it and is pleased with it, and what He prohibited, He hates and dislikes because it does not match with His pleasure. The conclusion is that His religion based on command returns to His love and agreement.

The devotion of the slave to Allah will be acceptable if it emanates from love and agreement. The Prophet, Allah's blessing and peace be upon him, said:

"He has found the taste of faith, who has accepted Allah as Lord, Islam as religion and Muhammad as Messenger."[302]

This religion is based on love and for it, it was enacted and regulated and it was founded on it. His system of recompense as well includes rewarding the righteous for his right deeds and recompensing the wrongdoer for his wrongdoing. Both matters are agreeable to the Lord because they represent His justice and His favour. Each one of them is among the Attributes of His perfection. He, glory be to Him, loves His Names and His Attributes and loves those who love them.

Both systems of reward and recompense are His straight path on which Almighty is established. He is on the straight path in His command, prohibition and reward and punishment. Almighty told us about Hud, peace be upon him, that he said to his people:

---

[302]. Muslim (34)

"I call Allah to witness, and you, too, are my witnesses, that I disown those you set up as partners with Allah. So plot against me, all if you, and give me no respite. I put my trust in Allah, my Lord and your Lord. There is no moving creature which He does not control. My Lord's way is straight." (11:54-56)

The Prophet of Allah Hud, peace be upon him, knew that his Lord was on the straight path in His creation, His order and prohibition, His reward and punishment, His decrees and decisions, His withholding and giving, bestowing safety and afflicting people, and supporting or deserting. He knew that the Lord Almighty is never out of His pure perfectness, which is the result of His Names and Attributes such as justice, wisdom, mercy, favour and bounty and putting the reward and punishment in their proper places, and placing the support and desertion, giving and withholding and guidance and misguidance – placing them all in their proper situations, which makes Him deserve the full praise and glory. This knowledge gave Hud strength to announce to the people what has been cited with full confidence and without fear. He also told his people that how he would fear those who are controlled by other and they are under his power. This will be the most serious ignorance and worst injustice!

He also said to his people that Allah, the Exalted, was on the straight path in all that He decrees and decides, therefore, the salve should not be afraid of His wrongdoing and injustice. Almighty's decree is operative in His salves, His decision is just; to Him belongs the sovereignty and praise. Nothing is out of His justice and favour, if He grants, honours, guides and supports someone, it is by His favour and mercy; if He withholds, disgraces, misguides, deserts and causes misfortune, it is because of His justice and wisdom. He is on the straight path in all these acts.

In an authentic Hadith the Prophet, Allah's blessing and peace be upon him, said:

"No one has ever suffered from grief or worry and says: 'O Allah, I am Your slave and the son of Your slave and the son of Your maiden, my forelock is in Your hand, Your judgements about me is effective, Your decree about me is just. I ask You, O Allah, by every name You have, You have named Yourself with it, or revealed it in Your Book, or taught one of Your creature, or have kept secret in hidden knowledge with You: to make the Great Qur'an the spring of my heart, light of my breast, removal of my grief and eradication of my worry and sorrow', (No one says it) but Allah will take away his worry and grief and replace them with happiness."

They said: 'Should we not learn it, Messenger of Allah?'
He replied:

"Yes, indeed. It is appropriate for anyone who hears it to learn it."[303]

This includes all kinds of judgement of Allah concerning the slaves, optional or destined. Every decree concerning the salve is just and effective. This Hadith is reflecting what has been cited from the Qur'an.

7.15 The Immediate and later evils effects of the passionate love of images

Now we conclude the answer to the question related with the passionate love of images and its immediate and later bad consequence. They are several times more than anyone can say. This love targets the heart and spoils it , and when the heart is spoiled intentions, speeches and deeds, all are corrupted, and the front of Tawhid is damaged as we will explain, if Allah will.
Allah described this disease about women and sodomites. He related the passionate love of the wife of Aziz for Joseph when she seduced him and was about to trap him. Almighty told us the situation of Joseph in his patience, chastity and consciousness despite the fact that what he was tried was a matter against which only those can control whom Allah provided with the strength of endurance. The illicit act depends on the power of the motive and absence of the barrier. The motive here was extremely strong from various ways:

First, Allah, the Glorious, has set in the nature of a man to be inclined towards women as he is inclined to food and drink. He is unable to control himself from women; it is not censured if there is a solution, but rather is praised. The Prophet, Allah's blessing and peace be upon him, said:

"Women and perfume have been made dear to me from your world; I can endure from the food and drink, but cannot endure from women." [304]

---

[303] Ahmad (1: 391, 452), Ibn hibban (972) Tabarani I Kabir (10352) Hakim (1: 509)
[304] The last part of it is not authentic, the rest is genuine and reported by Ahmad (3: 128, 199, 285), Nisa'i (3939), Abu Ya'la (3482), Hakim (2: 160)

Secondly, Joseph was young, and the sexual desire of a young man is very strong.

Thirdly, He was unmarried without a wife or concubine to reduce the outburst of desire.

Fourthly, he was in a foreign land. A stranger finds ways of satisfying his sexual urge in a remote land more than in his country between his family and friends.

Fifthly, the woman was of a high rank and charming, which were enough to seduce him.

Sixthly, she was not resistant or refusing, as the resistance and refusal of a woman make many men lose their desire; he finds humbleness and asking as a deterrent. There are others whose love and passion increase with the resistance and refusal of the woman, as a poet has said:
'My fondness increased when I was stopped; the dearest thing to a human is the one from which he is stopped.'

The natures of the people are different, the love of some of them increases when the woman consents and agrees and goes down when she resists and refuses.
Some judges told me that his sexual desire and intention fade away when his wife or slave girl refuse and resist, and he is unable to return to her. Others' love and desire double when he is stopped; his desire becomes stronger when he is refused. He gains similar joy which he gets by succeeding an opposite after its refusal.

Seventhly, it was the wife of Aziz who wanted and tried to seduce and did her best to trap him. She did not let him feel the humility of seeking and getting her. She was the one who had interest and been humble, and he was the honourable and target of her desire.

Eighthly, He was in her house and under her rule and authority, and he has the fear that if he does not agree with her, she might punish him. So, both the motives of desire and fear were together.

Ninthly, He was not scared that she will tell about him neither anyone else from her side. She was the one who sought to seduce him and closed the doors and there was no one to watch.

Tenthly, he was apparently a servant in the house, coming and going without any trouble. Before demand there was intimacy which is the strongest motive. It was said to a noble woman from the noble Arabs: 'What prompted you to adultery?'
She replied: 'Closeness of the bed and the length of the night.'

Eleventh, she sought help from the experts of deception and tricks and showed him to them and complained to them about her feeling to get their support; he sought the help of Allah against them and said:

"If You do not protect me from their treachery, I shall yield to them and do wrong." (12:33)

Twelfth, she threatened him of imprisonment and humiliation, which is a kind of forcing him. Here the motive of desire and the motive of safety from prison and humiliation are combined.

Thirteenth, the husband did not show sense of honour and jealousy to cause separation between the two and make each one to be away from the other. The utmost he said to Joseph was:

"Joseph, turn away from this." (12:29)

And said to the woman:

"Seek forgiveness for your sin; you have indeed done wrong." (12:29)

The strong sense of honour of a man is a powerful barrier, but here the man did not show that sense.

With all these motives Joseph chose the pleasure and fear of Allah, and Allah's love made him choose prison on the adultery and said:

"My Lord, the prison is dearer to me than what they are inviting me to do." (12:33)

He knew that he by himself is unable to turn it away from him, and if his Lord did not protect him and foil their treachery, he would yield to them by his nature and do wrong. It was his perfect knowledge of his Lord and himself.

In this story there are lessons, useful points and wisdom exceeding one thousand. If Allah gives us support, we will describe them in a separate book.

7.16 The other group about which Allah spoke

The second group Allah described their passionate love, are the sodomites. Allah said:

"The people of the town came along, revelling, and he told them: 'These are my guests, do not disgrace me. Fear Allah, and do not shame me.' They answered: 'Have we not told you not to interfere (between us and) anyone else? He said: 'My daughters are here, if you must.' By your life, they wandered on in their wild intoxication." (15:67-72)

This community was passionately in love and Allah described both groups, each one of them loved what was forbidden to them, but they did not care about the harm of the love of images.

This is a disease which rendered the physicians incapable of treatment and bring cure to them. It is, by Allah, the most serious disease and destructive poison, which once affects a heart the whole world is unable to release the person from its effect, when its fire rages in the soul of the person, it is difficult for the creature to extinguish it.

It has various types:
Sometimes it is disbelief like the person who takes his beloved as rival, loves him as he loves Allah. How will it be if his love is greater in his heart than the love of Allah? It is a passion which will not be forgiven; it is more serious than association of partner with Allah, and Allah does not forgive association with him; He forgives less than that with eradicating repentance.

The sign of this blasphemous passionate love is that the lover puts the pleasure of his beloved over the pleasure of his Lord. When there is a clash between the right of his lover and the right and dues of his Lord, he gives preference to the right of his beloved, and chooses his delight over the pleasure of the Lord. He offers for his lover the best of what he can, while chooses for his Lord, if he at all does, the worst of what he has. He does his best to please his lover, and to bring him closer, and if he shows obedience to his Lord, he spends the time which remains after his lover.

Consider the condition of most of the lovers of images, you will find exactly as said. Put their condition in one side of scale and their faith and devotion to Allah in the other and see the result. Sometimes a lover declares that union with his lover is dearer to him than the devotion to his Lord. A wicked poet has said:

'They suck from my mouth sips which are sweeter than the exclusive devotion to Allah.'

Another wicked poet said:
'The union with his lover is more desirable to him than the mercy of his Lord'. We seek refuge in You, O Allah, from this setback!
He said:
'Union with you is more desirable to my heart than the mercy of the Great Creator.'

Undoubtedly this passionate love is among the greatest shirk. Many lovers say that there is no space in their hearts for anyone besides their beloved. Some of them further claim that his beloved had completely possessed his heart and he had become his slave from every side. This person has chosen the slavery of a created over the devotion of the Creator. Devotion means full love and submission and this person directed all the power of his love and submission to his beloved and thus become the real slave of him. There is no relation between the corruption of this serious offence and the corruption of the immoral act. The immoral act is a grave sin for which there is a ruling but the evil of this love is same as associating partners to Allah.
Some pious people used to say:
'It is better for me to be afflicted by illicit relation with that image than being in passionate love with it, which keeps my heart devoted to it and turns away from Allah.'

7.17 The cure of this lethal disease: passionate love

The cure of this lethal disease for a person is to realise that the disease he is afflicted is opposite of devotion to Allah alone, and he was tested for the ignorance and carelessness of his heart concerning Allah. He is required to know the Tawhid of his Lord and His ways and signs first, and then carry out the outer and interior worships in order to keep his heart busy from thinking about his love. He should beseech and plead to Allah to turn it away from him. He should devote his heart to Him because there is no medicine more useful than to be sincere to Allah. This is the treatment He mentioned in His Book saying:

"We did this in order to keep evil and indecency away from him, for he was truly one of our chosen servants." (12:24)

Allah, the Exalted, informed that He kept the evil of love and indecent act away from Joseph because of his sincerity. When the heart is sincere and makes his deeds purely for Allah, the love of images will not get an opportunity to set in; it targets only the empty heart. A poet has said:
'Her love approached me before I knew the love, it found an empty heart and settled in it.'

A sensible person should know that the reason and the Shari'ah require him to acquire the beneficial matters and complete them, and to destroy the corrupt ones and reduce them. When a sensible person is faced with a matter which has both the benefit and harm, he has to follow two ways: one based on knowledge and the second related to action. The matter of knowledge requires him to find out which of the ways is superior, the one of benefit or the one of harm. When it becomes clear to him, he must choose what is more suitable for him. It is well known that there is no religious or worldly benefit in the love of images; its religious and worldly evils are far more than estimated benefit for the following reasons:

One: To engage in the love and remembrance of the created being on the expense of the love and remembrance of Allah cannot come together in the heart; one of them will dominate and overpower the other.
Two: His heart will suffer because of his lover; anyone who loves something other than Allah is necessarily afflicted by the torment of it.
It is said in the following lines of a poem:

'There is no one more wretched than a lover though he finds love sweet in taste.
You will see him crying every time in the fear of separation or longing.
He cries if they are far in yearning to them, and cries if they are close for the fear of departure.
His eye is hot at the time of departure, as it is hot at the time of meeting.'

Love though is one of the greatest suffering yet the lover finds it sweet.
Three: The heart of the lover is in the control of his beloved who subjects him to humiliation, but because of the intoxication of love he does not realise his misfortune. His heart is:
'like a small bird in the hand of a child who subjects it to destruction, and the child plays and is amused.'

The life of a lover is the life of an enchained prisoner while the life of a free person is unstrained and at liberty. It is also said:

'He is seen to be free while he is sick roaming on the pole of perish,
He is dead but appears in the form of living and walking while he has no
power to rise until the Day of Resurrection.
He is a man of emotional exuberances in which his heart is lost and he
will not come to sense until death.'

Four: It keeps the person busy from his affairs of the world and the religion. There is nothing more devastating to the affairs of the religion and the world than the passion for the images. As for the interests of the religion are concerned they are attached with putting in order the heart and making it to focus on Allah while the passionate love of the images is the greatest cause of shattering and disturbing the heart. As regard the interests of the world they are actually subject to the interests of the religion. Anyone whose interests of the religion were destroyed and broken up, the interests of his world would be more vulnerable.

Five: The calamities of the world and the Hereafter are destroying the lovers of the images quicker than the fire is for the dry wood.

This is because whenever the heart approaches the love and its link with it becomes stronger, it becomes far from Allah. The farthest hearts from Allah are the hearts of the lovers of images. When the heart is removed from Allah, it becomes the target of calamities, and Satan surrounds it from every side. A person who is surrounded and controlled by the enemy, he will afflict him with trouble and will not spare him from any possible harm but will make him suffer from it. If this is the situation, then what do you think about a heart which is dominated by its enemy who is very much interested in misguiding and damaging it? This person is removed away from his supporter and the one without whose support and help he cannot achieve happiness, success or delight.

Six: When this love takes hold of the heart, becomes deep-seated and its power becomes strong, it spoils the mind and creates confusion sometimes leading the person to the circle of insane people whose reasons have been corrupted and become useless for them.

The stories of the lovers in this respect are cited in their places; rather some of them are witnessed. The noblest part of the human is his reason which makes him distinguished from other animals. If that faculty is lost, he joins the dumb animals; the animal may be in better condition than him. Did anything else take the reasoning power of Majnun of Lyala and people like him except passionate love? His craze may have gone beyond the craze of others. It is said:

'They said: 'you have been crazy', I said to them: love is much more serious than what the crazy people have.
The man affected by love never recovers while the crazy suffers from time to time.'

Seven: It may spoil the senses either mentally or physically. The mental spoiling is subject to the spoiling of the heart, because when the heart is corrupted the eye, the ear and tongue also get corrupt, and an ugly image appears beautiful to them, as the Prophet, Allah's blessing and peace be upon him, said:

"Your love of a thing makes you blind and deaf."[305]

It renders the eye of the heart unable to see the evils and defects of the loved, so the eye does not see them, and it makes the ear deaf from listening to the blame. The desires cover the faults. A man interested in a thing does not see its defects till his desire disappears, he becomes able to notice the defects. The intensity of the desire is a veil on the eye, which prevents from seeing the object as it is, as it is said:
'I loved you when there was a veil on my eye, but when the veil was removed, I started blaming my soul.'
A man inside an object is unable to see its faults, and so is the one who is outside and did not go in; the only person who can see its faults is the one who went inside it then came out of it. This shows that the Companions who embraced Islam after disbelief were superior to those who were born in Islam.

'Umar ibn al-Khattab said:
'The hand-holds of Islam will disintegrate bit by bit when the people are born in Islam and did not know the period of ignorance.'

As for the corruption of the senses physically it is noticed in the weakness and illness of the body, which may result in its ending as it is known from the news of those who were killed by extreme love.
A man was brought to Ibn Abbas at 'Arafah, who was young but greatly emaciated till he became skin on the bones. He asked: 'What happened to him'?
They replied: 'He is affected by passionate love.'
Ibn Abbas continued seeking refuge from love throughout that day.

---

[305] Ahmad (5: 194; 6: 650), Abu Dawud (4967)

Eight: Passionate love, as indicated earlier, means extreme love in such a manner that the loved takes control of the heart of the lover so much that he is always busy in thinking about him and remembering him, and he does not go away from his mind and thought. In this situation the soul becomes unable to use the physical and mental powers, which become inactive. This condition produces such calamities for the body and the soul that the treatment of which is difficult. As a result his actions, qualities and objectives change and are disturbed and no one can put them in order. It is said:

'The love starts with insistence brought by fate;
When the young man plunges into the depth of it, unbearable matters appear.'

The beginning of the love is easy and sweet; its middle is worry, illness and disquiet of the heart; and its end is ruin and perish if the help of Allah does not come. It is said:

'Live free because the love starts with trouble and its middle is illness and the end is perishing.'

Another person said:

'He was drawn to love till he fell in it. When it took hold of him, he was unable.
He saw abyss and thought it was wave, when he went in it he was drowned.'

The mistake lies with the person, and he is responsible for his destruction.

7.18 Three stages of the lover

A lover has three stages: the beginning, the middle and the end.

In the first stage he is required to resist it with all his powers if reaching his loved is difficult by fate or religion. If he fails in it and his heart refuses but to travel to his loved one and this is the middle and final stage, he should try to hide it and not to disclose it to the people and mention him and disgrace him among the people. If he does so, he combines the association and injustice together, and injustice in this regard is the most serious one. It may be more harmful for the loved and his family than any harm in his property. This is because by revealing his love he exposes the loved person to the criticism of the people and making them divided between the believer and the denier. Most people tend to believe the story with little suspicion. If it is said that so and so did it with so and so, one person will reject it and nine hundred and ninety nine will believe it.

The information about a dishonourable lover is taken as certain. Not only that but if the object tells lies and fabricates the story about him, they will believe him beyond any doubt. If they happen to be seen together in one place, the people will believe that it was agreed between them. Their certainty is based on suspicions, doubts, imagination, and false news, but they believe as though they have seen it. That is how the people of accusation were trapped about the pure and decent, the beloved of the Messenger of Allah, Allah's blessing and peace be upon him, 'A'ishah who was cleared from above the seven skies. Their doubt was based on coming of Safawan ibn al-Mu'attal alone behind the army. Those who took part in accusation were condemned; and had it not been that Allah undertook to clear her and remove the lie from her and deny those who accused her, it would have been something very serious.[306]

The aim is to highlight that the disclosure of a person affected by love of the one with whom his link is not permitted, is injustice and aggression against him and his family. It is an exposure of suspicion of many people about him. If the lover seeks help of someone who can make the loved inclined to him by desire of fear, the injustice becomes more grievous and spreads, and that middle man is an unjust pimp. The Prophet, Allah's blessing and peace be upon him, has cursed the person who acts as the middle man between the one who gives the bribe and the one who takes it. If it is so then what will be case of the person who plays the role of middle man between a lover and loved in an illegal union? In this way the lover and the pimp cooperate against the loved and do wrong to him and to others who will be subject of injustice concerning his self or his property or honour. It may lead to killing of a person whose existence poses a barrier to reach his goal. How many close relative including husbands have been victims of it!

Many women were persuaded against their husbands and the slave girl and slave against their masters. The Prophet, Allah's blessing a peace be upon him, has cursed those who are involved in doing it.[307] It is one of the gravest sins.

The Prophet, Allah's blessing and peace be upon him, has forbidden a man to seek engagement over the engagement of his brother,[308] or enter in bargain on the bargaining of his brother.[309] How serious will be the act of a person who is trying to separate a woman and her husband or a slave girl and her master in order to establish relation with them!

---

[306] See the full account of the story of accusation in Bukhari (2661), Muslim (2770)
[307] Ahmad (2: 397), Abu Dawud (5170), Ibn Hibban (568), Hakim (2: 196)
[308] Muslim (1408)
[309] Muslim (1515)

The lovers of the images and their helpers do not consider it wrong while seeking of the lover to have link with his loved and share the husband and the master is as a serious sin as is the harming a person if not greater. The right of another does not go away by repentance from the immoral act. Allah's right may be removed but the right of the servant will remain and he will have to account for that on the Day of Judgement. To do wrong to the husband by spoiling his wife and commit crime on his bed is greater injustice than taking all his money. It is more painful to him than taking his money and to him there is no retribution but to kill the perpetrator.

What a serious injustice which is greater than committing immorality! If it is concerning a man who is on expedition in the cause of Allah, the criminal will be held on the Day of Resurrection and the victim will be told to take from his good deeds as much as he wished as the Prophet, Allah's blessing and peace be upon him, has said, and he asked: "What do you think?"[310]

Meaning what do you think will remain from his righteous deeds? And if the victim happens to be his neighbour or close relative the crime becomes multi fold including breaking the ties of relationship and causing harm to the neighbour. The Prophet, Allah's blessing and peace be upon him, said:

"A person who severs the ties of relationship will not go to Paradise."[311]

"A man from whose misdeeds his neighbour is not safe will not enter Paradise."[312]

If the lover seeks help from the Devils from Jinn by magic or other methods, the crime of magic will be added to the association and injustice. If he himself did not do it but approved it, he will be regarded as approving the disbelief and accepting it to achieve his goal, which is not far from disbelief. The point is that cooperation in this regard is cooperation in sin and aggression.

As for the common injustice the extended harm, which is connected with achieving the objective of the lover, its gravity is not hidden. When the lover achieves his goal regarding the loved, the latter may have some other aims and want the lover to help him to achieve them. Now the lover cannot refuse and the situation will be that each of them will be helping

---

[310] Muslim (1897)
[311] Bukhari (5984), Muslim (2556)
[312] Bukhari (5670), Muslim (46)

the other in injustice and aggression. The loved helps the lover against those who are related to him from among his family, relatives, master and husband; while the lover will help the loved to cause harm to those the loved is interested in his harm. So, each one of them will be helping the other on matters which are harmful to the people, and the people will suffer from their joint effort in causing corruption among them. It is usual that a lover helps his loved in matters, which are unfair, unjust and aggression. The lover may try to get a position for the loved, which he is unable to manage and it does not suit him. He may seek his help in acquiring money from unlawful sources or harm someone unnecessarily. When there is a competition between the loved and another person, he will side with his loved, regardless of him being right or wrong. And that the lover's attempt to trick the people to take their money unlawfully by stealing, betraying or false swearing or robbery or any other abominable ways and use it to approach the loved. It may lead to killing the soul which Allah has made sacred in order to gain money to please his loved.

All these calamities and many times as much are the result of infatuation of images, which sometimes drag to the open disbelief. Many people who were brought up in Islam converted to Christianity because of love. It happened to a person who used to call for prayer. He saw a beautiful woman on the roof and was infatuated by her, went to her house and negotiated with her. She said that she was Christian and said to him: 'If you embrace my religion, I will marry you.' He did, and he climbed a stair in their house, and fell from it and died.

When the Christians intended to convert a prisoner to their religion, they showed him a beautiful woman and told her to seduce him till her love takes hold of his heart; she becomes ready to consent to him if he enters her religion. In this situation:

"Allah gives firmness to those who believe in the firmly rooted word, both in this world and the Hereafter, but the evildoers He leaves to stray. Allah does whatever He will." (14:27)

In love each of the lover and the loved do wrong by helping and cooperating on immoral act. Each one is unjust for himself and his partner, and their wrong extends to others, and the greatest wrong committed by them is association. In this way the love includes all kinds of wrongdoings. If the loved is not conscious of Allah, he will cause the lover to perish. He will create in him interest for him, decorates him and induce him by every means to take out his money, but will give him opportunity to have contact with him to satisfy himself. He causes him great trouble, and the lover may kill his loved to vent his anger on him especially if he has union with others. How many are killed by love from both sides! How much favour was taken away, wealthy man rendered to poverty, lost his status and his affairs scattered!

A sensible person is required not to let his soul fall in the love of images so that he is safe from theses damages. If he does not take care, he is responsible for his harm and deluded by it. If he perished, he is the cause. If his repeated looking at the face of his loved were no there and he had not been interested in union with him, his love would have not taken root in his heart. The first cause of the love is to regard the object as good whether it was the result of looking or hearing. If it is not accompanied with desire of union and there is no hope of it, the love will not take possession of his heart. When he has desire, but turned his mind away from thinking about him and did not occupy his heart by him, he will be safe. If he prolong thinking in the beauty of the loved and it is accompanied with the fear of what is more serious than the joy of the union, either a religious fear like going to Hell and being subject of the Powerful Lord and carrying the burdens of the sin, and this fear dominates the desire and thought of the loved, he will be saved from the love. If he does not have religious fear but a worldly fear of damage like the fear of destroying himself or his wealth or his status or losing his honour to the people and this fear overwhelms the motive of the love, he will repel it. When he is scared of losing something which is more beloved and useful to him than having the loved, and he puts that fear over the love of the loved, the fervour of the love will go away. If all these matters are absent and the love of the loved one dominates, the heart will be dragged to him totally and the soul will move to him fully.

If it is said that you mentioned the bad features of the love and its harms and damages, why did you not say something about its positive sides and useful effects like mild nature, amusement of the soul and its amiability and disappearance of the rudeness, and its inducing for the noble characters like courage, kindness, manliness and kindness of the nature?

Yahya ibn Mu'adh al-Razi was informed that his son had fallen in love with a particular girl and he said:
'Praise is to Allah Who instilled in him the nature of human being.'

Some people said:
'Love is the cure of the hearts of the noble people.'
Another said:

'Love is not suitable but for a man of clear chivalry, pure character or for a person of excellent tongue and perfect kindness or for a man of outstanding etiquette and shining family background.

Another man said:

'Love strengthens the heart of a cowardly person, purifies the mind of stupid, moves the stingy to generosity, humbles the arrogance of the kings, and pacifies the antipathetic characters. It is the close friend of the one who has no friend and the companion of who has no companion.

Someone else said:

'Love removes burdens, refines the soul, purifies the dirt of the heart and produces appreciation of the deeds of the noble people.'

A Poet said:

'An affectionate person in the world will perish concerning you if he is faced by a destructive matter of love.
A noble person who hides the secret to the extent that when they ask him about you as though he does not know.
He wishes to be ill with hope that when she knows about his pain she may write to him.
He is energetic in search of high ranks so that one day his noble characters are praised to Layla.'

So, it is love that induces people to noble characters.

Some wise man said:

'Love tames the soul, rectifies the characters; its exposure is natural and its hiding is pretension.'

Another man said:

'The one whose soul does not get excited by touching voice and bright face, his nature is spoiled and he needs treatment. He recited the following line:

'If you did not love and did not know what passion is, you have got no share in pleasant life.'

Another poet said:

'If you did not love and do not know what the passion was you and a donkey in desert are equal.'

Another said;

'If you have not experienced the love and do not know what passion is, be a solid stone in a rock.'

Another said:

'If you have not experienced the love and do not know what passion is, rise and eat grass because you are a donkey.'

Some lovers said:
'The lovers are the people of chastity and preservation. Be chaste, you will be noble, and get in love, you will be smart.'
One of the lovers was asked:
'What would you do if you succeed with your beloved?
He replied:
'I would make my eye to enjoy sight of his face, will comfort my heart with his mention and his talk, would hide what he does not like to be exposed and I would not approach any evil act which may lead to break our relations. Then he recited the following lines:
'When I am alone with him, I abstain from him because of respect and fear of the religion not because of his lovers;
Like water in the hand of a fasting person who likes it for being thirsty, but exercises patience from its joyful taste.'

Ishaq ibn Ibrahim said:
'The spirits of the lovers are fine and aromatic; their bodies are thin and light. Their pleasure trip is friendliness and their talk gives life to dead hearts and increases understanding. Had there been no love and passion, the pleasure of the world would have gone.'
Another person said:
'Love for the souls is like nourishment for the bodies; if you abandon it, it will harm you; and if you take too much of it, it will kill you.'
It is said about it:
'My two colleagues, love and joy, and it has lasting trouble and misfortunes.
Without it the life is not pleasant; no life is enjoyable without the beloved. There is no good in the world without ardent love and there is no pleasure in it without a beloved.'

Abu Bakr al-Siddiq passed by a girl who was singing:
'I loved him before my amulets were detached, he was moving like a soft twig.'
He asked her: 'Are you free or owned?'
She replied: 'owned.'
He asked: 'who is your beloved?'
She paused and he entreated her to speak. She said:
'I am the one the love has played with her heart; I am afflicted by the love of Muhammad ibn al-Qasim.'

He bought her from her master and sent her to Muhammad ibn al-Qasim ibn Ja'far ibn Abi Talib. He said: 'These are the trials of the men. How many noble men have died because of them and how many healthy ones perished!'

A girl went to 'Uthman ibn 'Affan complaining against a man from the Helpers. He asked her about her story and she said:
'I fell in love, the commander of the faithful, with his nephew and I remain attached to him.'
'Uthman sent for the man and said to him: 'Either you gift her to your nephew or I give her price from my money.'
He said: 'I make you witness, the commander of the faithful that she is for him.'

We do not deny the corruption of the love related with the immoral act with the beloved, we are talking about chaste love of an elegant person whose religion and chastity insist on keeping away from forbidden act what is between him and Allah and his beloved. This is like the love of the pious ancestors and well known Muslim scholars. This is 'Ubadullah ibn Abdullah ibn 'Utbah ibn Mas'ud, one of the leading seven learned people in fiqh, his story of love spread among the people and it was not denied and anyone who blamed him was considered unjust. Among his poetry are the following lines:

'You tried to keep your love secret till this attempt caused you harm, and some people blamed you, which was wrong from them.
The secret enemies revealed your affair, and before that the love itself had betrayed if hiding could work.
You became like the lover of Hind who died out of sorrow after her or like a person who suffered from poison.
Do you consider meeting with the beloved as sin, the desertion of the beloved is the real sin.
Now taste separation from her and you were claiming that it was good. Your claim turned out to be false.'

This is 'Umar ibn Abd al-Aziz whose love for a slave-girl of his wife Fatimah bint Abd al-Malik is famous. She was a girl of outstanding beauty. He fancied her and asked his wife to gift her to him. But she refused, and the girl remained in the mind of 'Umar. When he was appointed as the Caliph, Fatimah ordered the girl to be prepared. She was exemplary in beauty and charm, went to 'Umar and said to him:

'Commander of the faithful, you were fascinated by my slave girl so and so and you asked me to give her to you, but I refused. Now I am pleased to give her to you.'

When she said this, happiness appeared on his face and said:

'Bring her quickly to me.'

When she brought her to him, his admiration for her increased. He told her to undress, she did then he said to her:

'Wait, tell me to whom did you belong? How did you come in the possession of Fatimah?'

She replied:

'Hajjaj fined one of his governors in Kufah huge amount of money. I happened to be owned by that governor. He took me and sent me to Abd al-Malik who gave me as gift to Fatimah.'

He asked: 'what happened to that governor?'

She said that he had died.

He asked: 'Did he leave any children?'

She said: 'Yes.'

'What is their condition? He asked.

She replied: 'Very bad.'

He said to her:

'Put on your dress and go to your place.'

He wrote to his governor of Iraq to send immediately so and so to him. When he arrived he said to him:

'Tell me about all that Hajjaj fined your father.'

Then he ordered the girl to be handed to him and said to him: 'Be careful because your father may have contacted her.'

The boy said: 'She is for you, Commander of the faithful.'

He said:

'I have no need of her.'

He said: 'Purchase her from me.'

He said:

'In that case I will not be among the people who prevented their souls from desire.'

When the young man decided to leave with her she said:

'Where is your passion, Commander of the faithful?'

He replied: 'The same but rather has increased.'

The girl remained in the mind of 'Umar until he died.

This is Abu Bakr Muhammad ibn Dawud al-Zahiri, the well known scholar of many subjects like fiqh, Hadith, Tafsir and literature, and he had opinions in law. He is among the great scholars, and his love is famous.

Niftawayh said:

'I went to him in the illness in which he passed away and ask him:
'How do you feel?'
He replied:
'The love of the one you know has caused me what you see.'
I said:
'What stops you from enjoying his company when you are able to do it?'
He said:
'Enjoyment is in two ways: permissible looking and forbidden enjoyment. It was the permissible looking that caused me what you see. As for the forbidden enjoyment I could not go to it for what my father has reported from Ibn Abbas that the Prophet, Allah's blessing and peace be upon him, said:

"Whoever was afflicted with passionate love, and kept it secret, remained chaste and patient, Allah will forgive him and admit him into Paradise."

Then he recited the following lines:
'Look at the charm running in his eyes and look at the deep black in his tranquil eye.
Look at the hairs on his cheek as though they are ants moving on an ivory.'
Then he recited:
'What is wrong with the people reject blackness in his cheeks and they do not reject the rose of the branches?
If the defect in his cheeks is due to hair, then the defect of the eyes should be regarded because of the hair of eyelids.'
I said to him:
'You denied analogy in fiqh and established it in poetry?'
He replied:
'The domination of strong emotion and talent of the soul called for it.'
He died that very night.
For his loved he wrote the book "al-Zuhrah."
He said in it:
'Whoever experienced despair from the one he loves and did not die instantly, he will find comfort. This is because the first alarm of desperation comes to the heart while it is not prepared for it. The second one comes to the heart while it is prepared by the first one.'

He (i.e. al-Zahiri) and Abu al-Abbas ibn Surayj met in the gathering room of the Minister Abu al-Hasan Ali ibn 'Isa, and debated the issue of 'ILA' (i.e. swearing of not approaching one's wife). Ibn Surayj said to him:

'Your statement that anyone who constantly gazes will have much distress is more accurate than your talk about legal matters.'
He replied;
If it is so then I also said:

'I let my eye wander around the meadows of the beauty, but control myself from committing the prohibited matter.
I carry such heavy burden of love that if it is put on a solid rock, it will crush.
My eye speaks on behalf of my thought, if it were not my glancing furtively, it would have spoken.
I found the claim of love by all the people, but I do not see any right and pure love.'

Abu al-Abbas Surayj said:

'For what you are priding upon me? If I wanted, I would have said:
'A companion tasting like honey in his melodies I passed the night preventing him from the joy of his sleep by love and by his beauty and talk. I let my eye wander around his cheeks.
Until when the sign of the morning appeared, he left with the ring and freedom of his Lord.
Abu Bakr said:

'The minister should take notice of what he has confessed and set two witnesses on that he left with the ring and freedom of his Lord.
Ibn Surayj responded saying:
'I bear the charge of it as you are required to do in your saying:
'I let my eye wander around the meadow of beauty and control myself from committing the forbidden matter.'
The Minister laughed at this and said:
'You both combined elegance and gracefulness.'[313]

Zahiri received a question which said:
'Son of Dawud, the jurist of Iraq, give us fatwa about the killers by looks, do they bear responsibility of what they are doing or the blood of lovers is allowed for them?'

He wrote the answer on the same paper by his hand:

---

[313] See the story in Tarikh Baghdad (5: 260-263), Siyar A'lam al-Nubala' (13: 111)

'I have answer for the questions of the lovers, listen to it from a man who is lover and restless inside his heart.

When you asked about love, you stirred me up, and shed tears which were not to be shed.

If a loved causes distress to a lover, the distressed person is the most pleasant lover.'

Shihab al-Din Mahmud ibn Fahd, the author of 'Manazil al-ahbab' said that he had composed answer to the question in following lines:

'Say to one who came asking about gazes which play with the blood of the lovers.

There is no harm on a sword if it blunts from shedding blood.

The swords of gaze deserve more to be ignored of what they do to the lovers.

All those whom they kill are martyr, but the victim of this remains alive though he is weak.'

A similar question was sent to Shaykh Abu al-Khattab Mahfuz ibn Ahmad al-Kaluzani, the leader of the Hanbali people in his time.

'Tell Imam Abu al-Khattab that there was a question for you which only you can answer.

What about a man who intended to perform prayer and the thought of a beautiful person came to his mind and he was distracted?'

He answered below the question:

'Tell the writer who approached me with a question which pleased my heart when I listened to it.

The one who captivated him from his worship is a beautiful virgin and he turned to her and became unmindful.

If he repents and makes up for his duty, Allah's mercy covers anyone who commits a mistake and becomes distracted.'

Abdullah ibn Ma'mar al-Qaysi gave the following account:

'Once I went for pilgrimage, and at night I entered the mosque of the Prophet, Allah's blessing and peace be upon him. While I was sitting between the grave and pulpit, I heard moaning and I listened. Someone was saying:

'Is it the wailing the pigeons of lotus tree roused in your breast the worries?

Or your sleep was disturbed by the memory of a girl who despatched to you the whispering of thought.

Oh the night which became long for a weak man who complains sleeplessness and lack of patience!

You surrendered the one you love to the heat of ardent love burning like the flame.

The moon is witness that I am enchanted by the love of the one who is like the full moon.

I never thought I will be love of her till I was trapped without noticing.'

Then the voice cut off and I did not know from where it had come. Then he resumed crying and moaning and recited:

'The visiting thought of Rayya saddened you while the night is dark and black.

The love came to you with force and the visiting thought agitated your eye.

I called Rayya when the dark was as the sea in which roaring waves were moving.

The full moon moves in the sky as though it is a king who is walking and the stars are his soldiers.

You see Gemini dancing in the dark like dancing of the lover who was affected by intoxication.

O night you became long on a lover for whom there is no helper or assistant but the morning.

It replied to me: Die a natural death and remember that the love is the available disgrace.'

I sneaked to him when he had started singing, so he did not notice me until he saw me. I saw a youth in the prime age; tears had drawn two lines in his cheeks. I greeted him; he said: 'Sit down. Who are you?'

I said: 'Abdullah ibn Ma'mar al-Qaysi.'

He asked: 'Do you need anything?'

I replied: 'Yes, I was sitting in the meadow and was alarmed by your voice. I ransom you with my soul! What is your trouble?'

He said:

'I am 'Utbah ibn al-Hubab ibn al-Mundhir ibn al-Jamuh al-Ansari. I went one day to the mosque of al-Ahzab and performed prayer, then sat in a corner not very far. I saw some women coming swaying to and fro like sand grouse; in their middle was a beautiful young girl. She was extraordinary charming and nice. She stood before me and said:

'Utbah, what would you say about the union of the one who is interested in being with you?'

She left me and went; I did not have any news about her neither did I find any trace of her. I was puzzled moving from one place to another. At this point he screamed and fell unconscious. When he came back, his cheeks were as though they have been coloured with saffron. He said:

'I see you by my heart from far away countries, I wonder whether you see me by the heart despite the distance?
My heart and my eye lament over you; with you is my soul and with me is your memory.
I will not find life joyful till I see you even if I were in Firdaus or Paradise of Eternity.'

I said: 'The son of my brother, turn in repentance to your Lord and ask Him for forgiveness for your sin; there is before you the horrible time.'
He said: 'I will have no comfort forever.'
I remained with him till morning, and then said to him:
'Rise up, and let's go to the mosque of al-Ahzab. May be Allah removes your suffering.'
He said: 'I hope so because of the blessed appearance.'
We walked and came to the mosque of al-Ahzab, and I heard him saying:

'Oh people! It was Wednesday, and is there any delight coming to me after understanding?
A gazelle continues killing me; it comes to the mosque of al-Ahzab covered in veil.
He tells people that he will get his reward because he did not come seeking reward for any good deed.
If he were seeking reward, he would have not come perfumed with musk and having his hair coloured.'

We sat there till we performed noon prayer, then the women appeared but the girl was not with them. They stood on him and said:
''Utbah, what do you think about the one who was interested in union with you, who had made your heart gloomy?'
He asked: 'What happened to her?'
They said:
'Her father took her and left for the land of Samawah.'
I asked them about the girl and they told me that she was Rayya daughter of al-Ghitrif al-Sulami. 'Utbah raised his head to them and said:

'My two friends, Rayya left early in the morning and her camel went to the land of Samawah.
My friends, I have become dim-sighted; has anyone an eye which I could borrow?'

I said:
'I came with huge amount of money to spend on the people of blameless record. By Allah, I will spend it for you so that you gain your goal and more than you seek. Let us go to the mosque of the Helpers. We marched

till we approached a prominent group of them. I greeted them and they nicely returned my greeting.

I said to them: 'What is your opinion about 'Utbah and his father?' They replied: 'He is one of the nobles of the Arab.'

I said: 'He has been afflicted with disaster of love; I need your help to reach to Samawah.'

They said: 'Very well.'

We rode and they accompanied us till we approached the lodgings of Banu Sulaym. Al-Ghitrif was informed about us and came out in hurry and received us saying: 'Welcome noble people!'

We said: 'And you may Allah bless you! We are your guests.

He said:

'You have come to the noblest place.'

Then he called: 'Assembly of servants, honour the people.'

The cushions were put and table clothes were spread, and animals were slaughtered.

We said:

'We are not going to eat your food until you fulfil our need.'

He asked; 'What is your need?'

We said:

'We came to ask the hand of your daughter for 'Utbah ibn al-Hubab ibn al-Mundhir.'

He said:

'The one you are asking her hands has free will. I am going to tell her about it.'

He went to his daughter in anger; she asked:

'Father, why I see anger on your face?'

He replied: 'The Helpers have come asking for your marriage.'

She said:

'They are noble and honourable people. The Prophet, Allah's blessing and peace be upon him, asked Allah to forgive them. For whom they are proposing?'

He said: For 'Utbah ibn al-Hubab.'

She said:

'By Allah, I have heard about this 'Utbah that he fulfils what he promises and is available when approached.'

He said:

'I have sworn that I will never give you in marriage to him. Some of your talk has been conveyed to me.'

She said: 'It is not true. But since you have sworn, the Helpers should not be refused in an unacceptable manner. Refuse their request in a best way.. He asked: 'How?'

She replied:

'Ask for an exorbitant dower; they will go and will not come back.'
He said:
'You said the best thing.'
He came out and said:
'The young woman has accepted but I require a dower for her similar to the amount given to a girl like her. Who is going to pay?'
Abdullah ibn Ma'mar said: 'I will, say what you wish.'
He said:
'One thousand *mithqal* of gold, one hundred garments and five bags of amber.'
Abdullah said: 'You will have all that. Do you agree?'
He replied: 'Yes.'
Abdullah said:
'I despatched some people to Madinah, and they returned with all that was demanded. Wedding party was arranged, and we stayed for few days. Then he said:
'Take your bride and return with her.'

He put her in a howdah and provided her with thirty camels loaded with materials and gifts. We bid farewell to him and left. When there remained only a short distance from Madinah, a troop attacked us, I assume they were from Sulaym. 'Utbah attacked them and killed many and injured many. He returned with a wound gushing blood with force; he fell down on his cheek and died. The attackers were repelled but 'Utbah lost his life. We cried: 'Oh 'Utbah!
When the girl heard us, she dropped herself from the camel and cried in pain and said:

'I struggled to have patience but I did not succeed. I indulged in hope he is going to meet us.
If my soul had been just, it would have been ahead of you to death.
No one after me and you is going to do justice to his friend and no souls will be in agreement with another.'

She broke out in loud weeping and lost her life. We dug a grave for both of them and buried them in it. After that I returned to Madinah and stayed for seven years, then travelled to the Hejaz and went to Madinah. I said: 'I must visit the grave of 'Utbah.' I went to the grave and found on it a tree with yellow and red wraps. I asked the people: 'What this tree is called?' They replied: 'The tree of newly-wed couple.'

If there were no concession for love against the stern opposition other than the Hadith reported with good chains, it would have been enough. It is what is reported from Ibn Abbas from the Prophet, Allah's blessing and peace be upon him, that he said:

"Whoever loved, and remained chaste, hid it and died, he is a martyr."

It is the master of the earliest and latest generations, the Messenger of the Lord of the World who looked at Zaynab and said:

"Glory is for the turner of the hearts!"[314]
She was married to Zayd ibn Harithah, and when he decided to divorce her, the Prophet to him:

"Fear Allah and keep your wife with you." (33:37)

When Zayd divorced her Allah, the Glorious, married her to His Messenger, Allah's blessing and peace be upon him, by ordering from above the seven skies. Allah acted as the guardian for her and for His Messenger. Her contract was completed above Almighty's Throne and Allah revealed the following verse:

"When you said to the man who had been favoured by Allah and by you: 'Keep your wife and be mindful of Allah.' You had in your heart what Allah would later reveal, and you were afraid of people, while it is Allah whom you should fear. (33:37)

Take David, the Prophet of Allah, peace be upon him; he had ninety nine wives, then he loved that woman and married her and completed hundred.

Al-Zuhri said:
'The first love in Islam was the love of the Prophet, Allah's blessing and peace be upon him, for 'A'ishah.'[315]
Masruq used to call her 'the beloved of the Messenger of Allah, Blessing and peace be upon him.
Abu Qays the freed slave of Abdullah ibn 'Amr said:
'Abdullah ibn 'Amr sent me to Umm Salmah to ask her whether the Prophet, Allah's blessing and peace be upon him, used to kiss his wives while he was fasting?
She said: 'No.'

---

[314] Ibn Sa'd in Tabaqat (8: 101), Hakim (4: 23) The story has been rejected by the author himself in Zad al-Ma'ad (4: 266-267). See also Ahkam al-Quran of Ibn al-Arabi (3: 1530) and Fath al-Bari (8: 404)

[315] It is a false report. See al-Mawdu'at (2:267)

He said:

''A'ishah said that the Prophet, Allah's blessing and peace be upon him, used to kiss her while he was fasting.'

Umm Salmah said:

The Prophet, Allah's blessing and peace be upon him, was unable to control himself whenever he saw 'A'ishah.'[316]

'Amir ibn Sa'd reported from his father who said:

'Abraham, the friend of Allah, peace be upon him, used to travel every day from Syria on Alborak to see Hagar because of his passionate love for her and inability to control himself from her'

Al-Khara'ti mentioned that Abdullah ibn 'Umar bought a slave girl and loved her extremely. She fell one day from her mule, Abdullah started wiping the dust from her face and kissed her. She very often said: 'O Batroon, you are Qalun,' Which means that my master you are very nice. Then she ran away and he felt very sad and said:

'I considered myself Qalun, then she left, and today I realise that I am not Qalun.'

Ibn Hazm said:

'Many people among the rightly guided Caliphs and leading Imams had love affairs.

A man said to the Commander of the Faithful, 'Umar ibn al-Khattab:

'Commander of the Faithful, I saw a woman and fell in love with her.'

He said:

'This is something you cannot control.'

Now the answer for the question is as follows, and help comes from Allah:

To discuss this issue requires distinguishing between unlawful and lawful, and useful and harmful matter. It is not possible to pass a rule in general for rejecting and condemning or accepting and endorsing it. Its condition and ruling can be decided with the matter connected with it. Otherwise the passionate love as such cannot be praised or condemned. We are going to mention the useful and harmful, and lawful and unlawful love.

Know that the most useful love without exception, and the highest and noblest one is the love of the one for whose love the hearts are created.

---

[316] Ahmad (6: 296, 317), al-Tahawi (1: 346). This report has been criticised.

He is the one the entire creation is created to worship Him, and with it the heavens and the earth are standing and all things created for it. It is the secret of the witnessing that there is no god except Allah. It is God to Whom the hearts are devoted with love, glorification, exaltation, submission and surrender. Worship is appropriate only to Him. Worship or devotion is the complete love with full submission and humbleness. Any association in this worship is the gravest crime which Allah will not forgive. Allah is loved for Himself from every way while others are loved as the result of His love.

The obligation of His love is attested by all the Books He revealed and by the call of all His Messengers. It is also substantiated by the natural disposition on which He has created His servants, and instilled it in their minds and by the favours He showered on them. The hearts are created on the love of the one who shows favour and bounty to them. Then what about the being who has shown all the kindness? There is no favour to any creature but it is from Him alone without there being any partner with Him.

"Whatever favour you receive comes from Allah, and when hardship afflicts you, it is to Him alone you cry out for help." (16:53)

He made Himself known to His slaves by His beautiful Names and magnificent Attributes and through His works which indicate His perfection, Majesty and Sublimity.

There are two motives for love: beauty and honour. The Lord Almighty has the both of them in absolute form. He is beautiful, loves beauty, and all honour emerge from Him. There is no one who deserves to be loved by himself except Him.
He said:

"Say, if you love Allah, follow me, Allah will love you." (3:31)

"You who believe, if any of you go back on his faith, Allah will soon replace you with people He loves and who love Him, people who are humble towards the believers, hard on the disbelievers, and who strive in Allah's way without fearing anyone's reproach. Such is Allah's favour; He grants it to whoever He will. Your true allies are Allah, His Messenger, and the believers, those who keep up the prayer, pay the prescribed alms, and bow down (to Allah). Those

who turn for protection to Allah, His Messenger and the believers (are Allah's party); Allah's party is sure to triumph." (5:54-56)

The basis of friendship is love, there is no friendship but with love; as the basis of the enmity is hatred. Allah is the friend and ally of the believers and they are His allies. They are His friends for their love for Him, and He supports them because of His love for them. Allah supports His slave according to his love for Him. For this reason He criticised those who took allies besides Him, unlike those who befriend His allies; there friendship with them is a part of His friendship for them. Almighty also has rejected those who love Him and others in the same way and said that anyone who does it has assigned rivals to Him and loves them like Allah. He said:

"There are some who choose to worship others besides Allah as rivals to Him, loving them with the love due to Allah, but the believers have greater love for Allah." (2:165)

Almighty informed us about those who put Him and the rivals on the same footing in love. He said that they will say in the Fire to their deities:

"By Allah, we were clearly misguided when we made you equal with the Lord of the Worlds." (26:97-98)

With this unity in love Allah sent all His messengers and revealed all His Books. The Messengers, the first to the last called to it. For this He created the heavens and earth and Paradise and Hell. He made Paradise for His obedient servants and the Hellfire for those who associated with Him.
The Prophet, Allah's blessing and peace be upon him, asserted that by saying:

"No one will be perfect believer until I am dearer to him than his children, his parents and all the people."[317]

He said to 'Umar ibn al-Khattab:

"No, until I become dearer to you than yourself."[318]

---

[317] Bukhari (14, 15), Musllim (44)
[318] Bukhari (6632)

When the Prophet, Allah's blessing and peace be upon him, is above ourselves in love and its requirements is not the Lord, Bestower of the honour, whose Names are holy and are exalted, His power is high and there is no god besides Him – is He not more deserving for the love of the servants for themselves?

Everything which pleases the believer or displeases him has come from Him and calls him to love Him. His giving and withholding, His granting safety and affliction, His expansion of the provision and restraining, His justice, favour, His giving life and causing death, His kindness and benevolence, His mercy and sympathy, His covering and forgiving, His forbearance and being patient with His slave, answering his supplication, removing his anxiety and distress and driving away his grief without having any interest in it but being fully free from it – all these are appealing the hearts to worship Him alone and love Him. He gives His servant an opportunity to disobey Him, helps him then covers him till he satisfies himself in committing the sin all these are the strongest motive of His love. If a person does the least of this favour to someone, he cannot help loving him. How then the servant will not love by his heart and the parts of the body the one who shows His kindness to him permanently despite the misdeed of him. Allah's good is coming down to him, and his evils ascending to Him. He comes close to His servant with His favour and He is not in need of him in any way while the servant himself commits deeds hateful to Him while he is in need of Him. His kindness, favour and benefaction do not prevent the slave from doing evil deeds, neither his disobedience nor wickedness cut off the favour of the Lord to him. The worst ignominy of the hearts is to keep away from the love of the one who does all this and turn to others beside Him.

Anyone from the creatures you love and he loves you, his love is for himself and for some purpose, but Allah, the Exalted, wants you for yourself, as it is said in a Divine report:
"My servant, everyone wants you for himself but I want you for yourself."
How the servant does not feel ashamed that his Lord treats him in this way and he turns away from Him and is busy with the love of others, his heart is drowned in the love of someone else?

Also anyone you deal with from among the people if he does not get profit from you, he will not keep his relation with you. He is looking for some benefit from you while the Lord Almighty deals with you to profit you; one dirham for ten to seven hundred to much more, and the evil for one and it may be wiped out.

Allah, the Exalted, created you for Himself and created everything for you in the world and the Hereafter. Who then deserves more to be sought for love and do best in acquiring his love?

All that you need but all that the entire creature needs is with Him. He is the most generous of all the generous ones and the kindest of all kind people. He gives His servant before he asks him and more than he expects, appreciates small deed and develops it, forgives big mistakes and erases them. Everyone in the heaven and the earth begs Him; every day He attends to some task. One hearing does not keep Him away from the other. He is not irritated by the multitude of issues and is not fed up by the insistence of the people on committing misdeeds. He loves those who insist in supplication, and loves to be asked, gets angry if He is not asked. He feels ashamed of His servant whereas he does not have shame from Him; He covers him where he is unable to cover himself and shows mercy to him where he cannot have mercy on himself. He called the man by His favours, generosity and benefits to His honour and pleasure but he refused. He sent His messenger to look for him and despatched with His covenant. He comes down Himself to call:

"Who is there to ask Me, so that I give him? Who is there to ask Me for forgiveness so that I forgive him?"

As it is said:
'I invite you for meeting but you refuse, I send My messenger to look for you and descend Myself to you; I meet you in dream.'

How the hearts do not love the One who alone brings good things and removes evils? No one answers the supplications, erases the shortcomings, forgives evils, covers faults, removes the worries, helps the distressed and grants the requests besides Him.

Allah is more entitled to be remembered, to be thanked, to be worshipped and to be praised. He is more aware of what is sought for. He is more beneficent than a king, the most generous to be asked, the most magnanimous to grant, the most merciful to the one who seeks mercy, the most noble among those who are intended, the most sufficient of those whose protection is sought. He is the most sufficient for the servant to put his trust in Him, and more compassionate to His servant than the mother is to her child. He is more pleased with the repentance of a person than a man who lost his camel which had his food and drink in a dangerous desert and lost his hope for life, then he found it.

Allah is the King, has no partner, Unique without rival, everything will perish except His Face. He cannot be obeyed without His permission, and will not be disobeyed without His knowledge. He is obeyed and appreciates it, and by His help and grace He was obeyed; He is disobeyed and He forgives and pardons while His right was abandoned. He is the closest Witness and the noblest Guard. He honours His pledge and upholds justice in the perfect way. He controls the souls and He rules every one. He has written the decisions and fixed the time of the death. The hearts are inclined to Him, and the secrets are open to Him and the hidden is exposed to Him. Everyone is eager towards Him; the faces are humbled before Him and the reasons fail to grasp His true nature. The natural dispositions and all evidences indicate there is no one like or similar to Him. Darkness is deleted by the light of His Face, and the heavens and the earth are illuminated for Him and the entire creations are set right by Him.

A Hadith further explains:

"He does not sleep and it is not appropriate for Him to sleep, He lowers the justice and raises it; the deeds of the night are taken to Him before the deeds of the day and the acts of the day are ascended to Him before the acts of the night. His veil is light; if He removes it, the august splendours of His Face will burn all that comes under His vision of His creation."[319]

The perfect happiness and joy are based on two things and this is an important matter to which an intelligent man must pay attention. The perfect joy, delight, happiness, the comfort of the heart and rejoicing of the soul are subject to two matters:

1. One is the excellence of the beloved in himself and his beauty, and the certainty that he is more entitled for love than anything else.
2. Second is the full exertion to his love and doing all that is possible to achieve his love and preferring his closeness over everything else and struggling to reach him by any means.

Every sensible person is aware that the joy of gaining the beloved depends on the strength of his love. The more the love is stronger; the joy will be more perfect. It could be compared with joy of a person who is extremely thirsty when he gets sweet water, and the joy of a hungry man

---

[319] Muslim (179)

who finds delicious food and similar things where the joy depends on his desire and force of his love.

If this is known, then the joy, happiness and delight are matters which are desired by their self, but rather they are the objectives of every living sensible person. If the joy is sought for by itself, it is not appreciated if it results a greater trouble and prevents a bigger joy. What will be the case if it produces the greatest sorrow and causes the loss of the most important joy and delight? It is to be praised if it helps to achieve great and permanent joy with no trouble or problem of any sort; this is the joy of the Hereafter, its delight and comfortable life in it.

Allah, the Glorious, said:

"Yet you prefer the life of the world, while the Hereafter is better and more lasting." (87:16-17)

The magicians said to Pharaoh:

"So decide whatever you will: you can only decide matters of this present life, we believe in our Lord, so that He may forgive us our sins and sorcery that you forced us to practice. Allah is better and more lasting." (20:72-73)

Allah, the Exalted, created people to grant them this lasting joy in the Home of Eternity. This present home is going to end and its joys are not pure and lasting unlike the Hereafter, the joys of which are permanent and its pleasure is pure from any trouble and pain. There will be all that the souls desire and the eyes find comfort forever. No soul knows what joy Allah had kept hidden in store in it for His worshippers; it has things which no eye has ever seen, no ear has ever heard of and it has passed in the mind of any human.

This is the message which the sincere advisor tried to pass to his people when he said:

"My people, follow me! I will guide you to the right path. My people, the life of this world is only a brief enjoyment; it is the Hereafter that is the lasting home." (40:38-39)

He told them that the world is a commodity to be passed to others while the Hereafter is the real settlement.

When it is known that the joys and pleasure of the world is temporary and a means of achieving the pleasure of the Hereafter, and the world and its joys are created for this purpose, it should be clear that any joy that helps to achieve the joy of the Hereafter and takes the slave to it is not condemned, it is rather praised because it is the source of acquiring the joy of the Hereafter.

When this is clear then it should be known that the greatest joy and pleasure of the Hereafter is to look at the Face of the Lord, the Most Glorious, and to hear His words and be close to Him. It is confirmed in the following statement of the Prophet, Allah's blessing and peace be upon him:

"By Allah, He did not grant them anything more pleasant than looking at Him."[320]

In another Hadith he said:

"When He appeared to them and they saw Him, they forgot all the pleasure they had."[321]

Ammar ibn Yasir reported in the prayer of the Prophet, Allah's blessing and peace be upon him, that he prayed:

"I ask You to have the joy of looking at Your Noble Face, and desire of meeting with You."[322]

Abdullah ibn Ahmad reported in his book 'al-Sunnah' that the Prophet, Allah's blessing and peace be upon him, said:

"When the people listen to the Qur'an from the Most Beneficent on the Day of Resurrection, they will feel as though they had never heard it before."

When this is known, then learn that the most significant means that brings this joy is the absolute desirable joy of the world, which is the joy of

---

[320] Muslim (181)

[321] Ibn Majah (184) al-Bazzar (2253). It is declared as weak.

[322] Ahmad (18351), Nisa'i (3: 54) Ibn Hibban (1971)

being aware of Allah and His love. It is the Paradise of the world and its greatest pleasure. Other vanishing pleasures compared to it are like a drop in the sea. The soul, the heart and the body have been created for it. The most pleasant of what is in the world is to know Him and to love Him. What will be the enjoyable pleasure in the Garden while looking at Him and watching Him. His love and looking at Him are the comfort of the eyes, the pleasure of the soul, and the delight of the hearts. All felicities and happiness of the world, and entire joys of the world will end up in torment and pains, and their people will be in depressed life. There is no pleasant life except with Allah.

Some of the devotees experienced ecstatic condition and said:

'If the people of Paradise are in similar condition, then they are having pleasant life.'
Another person said:
'If the kings and their children know the pleasure we have, they would fight us about it with swords.'

If the people of the false love, which is a torment on the heart of the lover can say:
'People are no more than lovers and of affectionate; there is no good in a person who does not love and is not affected by passion.'
And
'Shame for the world if the man in it is not lover or loved.'
Another said:
'There is no good in the world and its pleasure when you arw alone and not involved in love.'
Another said:
'The lovers complain the ardent love, oh I wish I had alone all that they suffer from;
My heart had the delight of all the love, which no one had experienced before or after me!'

If this is what the lovers of the worldly desire say, then what will be the case with the love which is the life of the hearts and nourishment of the soul? There is no pleasure, delight or success and life for the heart without it. When this love is missed the heart feels more severe pain than the pain of losing the sight of the eye, and ability of hearing by the ear, and the power of smelling by nose and the speaking power of the tongue. The corruption of the heart when it is empty from the love of its Creator, Designer and true Deity is greater than the corruption of the body when it is empty from the spirit. This cannot be understood but by the one who has life. A dead person does not feel the pain of the wound.

The gist of all that has been said is that the greatest joy of the world is the one which is the surest mean of achieving the greatest joy of the Hereafter.

The joys of the world are of three types:

1. The most important and perfect of them is the one which can take to the pleasure of the Hereafter. A man is rewarded fully on this joy. A believer gets reward on any act by which he means the pleasure of Allah even his eating, drinking, dressing and having intercourse and taking out his anger by overpowering his enemy and the enemy of Allah. He deserves to be given full credit for having faith and knowledge of Allah, and acquiring His love and being desirous of meeting with Him and in looking at His Noble Face in the Gardens of bliss.

2. It is the joy that keeps away the pleasure of the Hereafter and results in severe pains like the joy of those who take idols besides Allah as a bond of affection among them in the life of the world. They love them as it is due to Allah, and benefit from one another. They will say in the Hereafter when they meet with Allah:

"Lord, we have profited from one another, but now we have reached the appointed time You decreed for us.' He will say: 'Your home is the Fire, and there you shall remain, unless Allah wills otherwise. Your Lord is All-Wise, All-Knowing. In this way, We make some evildoers have power over others through their misdeeds." (6:128-129)

The same will be the fate of those who were engrossed in evil deeds, wrongdoing, aggression in the earth and unfair haughtiness.
The pleasures are in reality respite from Allah to make them taste the greatest pains and deprive them of the enormous pleasures. It is like someone who offers to a person delicious poisoned food to lure him to his death.

Allah, the Exalted, said:

"We will lead them step by step without them realising it, and I will give respite, My plan is firm." (7:182-183)

Some early scholars explained it by saying:
'Whenever they got involved in a sin, we provided them with a source of joy.'

"When they had forgotten the warning they had received, We opened the gates to everything for them. Then as they revelled in what they had been given, We struck them suddenly and they were dumbfounded. The evildoers were wiped out. Praise be to Allah, the Lord of the Worlds." (6:44-45)

Allah Almighty also said about such people:

"Do they reckon that, by giving them wealth and sons, We race to give them good things? They really have no idea." (23:55-56)

Almighty said to His Prophet about them:

"Do not let their possessions or their children impress you. Through these Allah intends to torment them in this world and for their souls to depart while they disbelieve." (9:55)

This pleasure will at the end turn pains of the severe torment as it is said:

'Desire which were torments for their people became punishment in the Hereafter.'

3. The third type is that which does not result in joy or pain in the lasting home, and does not bar the basic joy of the lasting home though it prevents its full advantage. This is the permissible joy which does not help on the joy of the Hereafter. Its period is short and for the enjoyment of the soul in it there is no scope, and it necessarily will be engaged from what is more beneficial and useful for it.

This is the type which the Prophet, Allah's blessing and peace be upon him, meant in his saying:
"Every enjoyment which a person gets engaged in is useless except his engagement in shooting the arrow, training his horse and playing with his wife: These are right."[323]

---

[323] Abudawud (2513), Tirmidhi (1637), Nisa'i (3580), Ibn Majah (2811), Ahmad (4: 444), Hakim (2467)

Anything that helps to achieve the desired joy is right and actions, which does not lead to such achievements are useless.

This type of love is not rejected or condemned but it is the best of the types of love, and it is the same with the love of the Messenger of Allah, blessing and peace be upon him. We mean the special love which keeps the heart of the lover and his memory and thought busy with his beloved, otherwise every Muslim has the love of Allah and His Messenger in his heart; he cannot be considered Muslim without it. People are on different scales in this love known only to Allah. Between the love of the two friends and the love of others there is a great distance. The love of the Messenger is the one which makes the burdens of duties light and bearable, encourages a stingy man to be generous, and a cowardly to be courageous, purifies the mind and trains the soul. It is the one which makes life pleasant in reality not the love of the forbidden images. When the secrets are disclosed on the Day of Meeting, the character of the person of this love will be the best one. It is said:
'There will remain in the hidden part of the heart a secret of love on the Day when secrets are laid bare.'

This is the love which brightens the face, opens the breast and gives life to the heart. The same is true about the love of the speech of Allah; it is the sign of the love of Allah. If you want to know how much do you and others love Allah, see the love of the Qur'an in your heart, and how much do you enjoy listening to it; do you enjoy it more than the people of amusements and singing to the singer. It is clear that anyone who loves a person his talk and speech is the sweetest thing to him, as it is said:
'If you claim my love then why did you neglect my book? Why did you not look in it my beautiful address?'

'Uthman ibn 'Affan said:
'If our hearts were pure, they would have been satisfied from the speech of Allah.'

How can a lover be satisfied from the talk of his beloved? It is what he desires most.

Once the Prophet, Allah's blessing and peace be upon him, said to Abdullah ibn Mas'ud:
"Read to me."
He said: 'I read to you while it is revealed on you?'
The Prophet said:
"I love to listen from another person."

Abdullah started reading chapter of women (ch.4) and when he reached the verse:

"What will they do when We bring a witness from each community, and We will bring as a witness against them?" (4:41)

He said:
"Enough."

Abdullah said that he raised his head and saw the eyes of the Messenger, Allah's blessing and peace be upon him, shedding tears.[324]

When the Companions were together and Abu Musa was among them, they would say to him:
'Abu Musa, make us remember our Lord. He would read and they would listen.'

Those who are attached to the Qur'an have the ecstasy, taste, sweetness and delight much more than those who love to listen to Satan's singing. If you see a man whose taste, delight, ecstasy and longing to listening to the poetry are more appealing than listening to the verses of the Qur'an, he is as said:
'The whole Qur'an is read to you and you are stiff like a stone, and a line of poetry is recited and you start moving like a drunkard.'

It is the strongest proof of his heart being empty from the love of Allah and His speech, and devoted to the love of listening to the singing of Satan. This deluded person still thinks that he has achieved something. In the love of Allah, His speech and His Messenger, Allah's blessing and peace be upon him, many more benefits are than the person who asked the question mentioned about the benefits and profits of the Love. In fact there is no love more profitable than it and every love beside it is useless unless it takes the lover to the love of Allah and His speech.

7.19 Love of the wives

There is nothing wrong in showing affection to one's wives; it is as a matter of fact the completion of it. Allah, the Exalted, has mentioned it as a gracious favour to His servants saying:

---

[324] Bukhari (5055), Muslim (800)

"Among His signs is that He created spouses from among yourselves for to live with in tranquillity, and ordained love and kindness between you. There truly are signs in this for those who reflect." (30:21)

Almighty tells that He made the woman a source of tranquillity for the man; his heart finds peace in her. He put pure love between them which is affection joined with kindness. Allah, the Exalted, said after citing the women whom He made lawful or unlawful for men:

"Allah wishes to make His laws clear to you and guide you to the righteous ways of those who went before you. He wishes to turn towards you in mercy. He is All-Knowing, All-Wise. Allah wishes to turn towards you, but those who follow their lusts want you to go far astray. Allah wishes to lighten your burden; man was created weak." (4:26-28)

The Prophet loved the women. Jabir reported that the Prophet, Allah's blessing and peace be upon him, saw a woman and went to Zaynab and satisfied himself with her and said:

"A woman comes forward in the shape of Satan and turns back in the shape of Satan. When one of you looks at a woman and is fascinated by her, he should go to his wife. It will take away what he feels."[325]

This Hadith includes many guidelines:

One is to advise men to satisfy their desire by having sexual act with their wives as any food is good substitute for another food and only clothes are substitute for another set of clothes.

Second to order men to treat the fascination by a woman which causes the desire with the most useful treatment that is to fulfil his need from his wife; it will suppress his desire of that particular woman.
The Prophet, Allah's blessing and peace be upon him, advised two lovers to get married and said:

"There is nothing more useful to two lovers than marriage."[326]

---

[325] Muslim (1403)
[326] Ibn Majah (1847), Hakim (2: 160) Bayhaqi (7: 78)

The marriage with the loved one is the cure of the passion, which Allah has made a cure religiously and naturally. This was the treatment use by David; he did not commit any illicit act, but married the woman and added her to his wives because he loved her. His repentance was according to his status and high ranking with Allah. Nothing more is appropriate to be said in this respect.

The story of Zaynab bint Jahsh is as follows:
Zayd had decided to divorce her but she did not agree. He consulted the Prophet, Allah's blessing and peace be upon him, concerning separation from her, and the Prophet asked him to keep her. He spoke to the Messenger of Allah, blessing and peace be upon him, that he is definitely going to get rid of her. The Prophet had in his mind that if Zayd divorced her, he would marry her. However, he was scared of the gossip of the people that the Messenger of Allah, Allah's blessing and peace be upon him, married his son's wife. He had adopted Zayd before Islam. Allah, the Exalted, willed to ordain a general rule which had benefits for His slaves. When Zayd divorced her and her waiting period passed, the Prophet sent the message to her seeking marriage with her. Zayd came from behind the door; she became magnificent in his heart when the Messenger, Allah's blessing and peace be upon him, mentioned her. So he called her from behind the door and said: 'Zaynab, the Messenger of Allah, Allah's blessing and peace be upon him, is proposing to marry you.
She replied: 'I am not going to do anything till I seek the guidance from my Lord.'
She stood in her place of prayer and prayed. Allah, the Glorious, undertook her marriage with His Messenger, Allah's blessing and peace be upon him, and concluded her marriage above His Throne. The following revelation came saying:

"When Zayd had no longer need of her, We married her to you."
(33:37)

The Messenger, Allah's blessing and peace be upon him, immediately went to her and marriage was contracted. She used to boast to the wives of the Prophet, Allah's blessing and peace upon him, for that and say:
'Your marriage was conducted by your families, but Allah conducted my marriage above the seven skies.'[327]
This is the story of Zaynab with the Messenger of Allah.

---

[327] Bukhari (7420) , Muslim (1428)

Certainly the Prophet, Allah's blessing and peace be upon him, loved women as he said:

"From your world women and perfume have been made lovable to me; but my comfort of eyes has been put in prayer."[328]

Imam Ahmad added in his al-Zuhd:

"I have patience from food and drink but cannot have patience from them."[329]

The Jews, the enemies of Allah envied him and said: 'His mind was only in Marriage.'
Allah, the Most High, defended His Messenger, Allah's blessing and peace be upon him, and said:

"Do they envy people for the bounty Allah has granted them? We gave the descendants of Abraham the Scripture and wisdom, and We gave them a great kingdom." (4:54)

This is Abraham, the friend of Allah, who has Sarah the most beautiful woman of the world, yet he loved Hagar and took her as concubine.
Here is David who had ninety nine women as wives, yet he loved that woman and married her, and thus he completed hundred.
His son Sulyman used to have intercourse with ninety women in one night.[330]

The Messenger, Allah's blessing and peace be upon him, was asked about the most beloved person to him, and he said that it was 'A'ishah.[331]

He said about Khadijah:

"I have been gifted her love."[332]

The love of women is part of the perfection of the human. Ibn Abbas said:
'The best of this community had more women than others.'[333]

---

[328] Ahmad (3:128, 199, 285), Nisa'i (3939), Abu Ya'la (3482), Hakim (2:160), Bayhaqi (7:78)
[329] This addition is not accepted by the scholars.
[330] Muslim (6654) See Bukhari (5242) where the figure is given as hundred.
[331] Bukhari (3462), Muslim (2384)
[332] Muslim (2435)
[333] Bukhari (5069)

Imam Ahmad wrote that Abdullah ibn 'Umar was given after the battle of Jalawla a girl whose neck was like the pitcher of silver. Abdullah said: 'I couldn't control myself and kissed her while the people were looking.'

The Prophet, Allah's blessing and peace be upon him, interceded for a lover to his beloved asking her to marry him, but she refused. It is the case of Mughith and Barirah. The Prophet saw him walking behind her after she left him crying and tears flowing on his cheeks. The Messenger, Allah's blessing and peace be upon him, said to her:

"If only you could go back!"

She asked:
'Is it an order from you, Messenger of Allah?'
He replied:
"No, I am only interceding."
She said: 'I have no need for him.'
The Prophet said to his uncle Abbas:

"Abbas, are you surprised by the love of Mughith for Barirah and her hate for him?"[334]

The Prophet did not object to his love for her though she was separated from him because it was something which he had no control on it.
The Prophet, Allah's blessing and peace be upon him, divided the days equally between his wives and said:

"O Allah, this is my division in what I have power, so do not censure me about what I have no power over it."[335]

Allah, the Exalted, has said:

"You will never be able to treat your wives with equal fairness, however much you desire to do so." (4:129)

That is in love and intercourse.
The rightly guided Caliphs and kind people used to intercede in favour of the lovers to their beloved with whom their relation was alright, as we have seen from Abu Bakr and 'Uthman.

---

[334] Bukhari (5280)
[335] Abu Dawud (2134), Tirmidhi (1140), Nisa'i (3943), Ibn Majah (1971), Ahmad (6: 144)

It was done by Ali, the Commander of the Faithful. He was presented an Arab young man who was found in the house of some people in night. He asked him about his case.

He said: 'I am not a thief, but I tell you the truth:

'I became affected by a beautiful girl in the house of Riyahi, so beautiful that even the full moon will surrender to her because of her fascinating look.
She has among the Romans beauty and good appearance. If she boasted about her beauty, the boasting is scared.
When I knocked at the door out of my heat of the soul and tried to pass the night where the house was brightened because of her brightness,
The people of the house shouted at me and said he was thief who is to be killed or put in prison.'

When Ali ibn Abi Talib heard his lines of poem, he had mercy on him and said to al-Muhallab ibn Ribah: 'Grant her to him.'
He said: 'Commander of the Faithful, ask him who he was?'
He replied: 'al-Nahhas ibn 'Uyaynah.'
He said: 'Take her, she is for you.'

Mu'awiyah purchased a slave girl and was immensely fascinated by her. He heard her one day singing some lines among them was:

'I departed him; he was like a twig moving on the earth, fresh and beautiful after his moustache came out.'
He asked her and she told him that she loved her previous master. He returned her to him; still his heart was busy with her.

It is said that Zubaydah read on the way to Makkah following lines written on a wall:

'Isn't there among the servants or maidens of Allah a noble person who can remove the worry of a person who has lost his reason?
The corners of his eyes are injured and inside him is fire burning.'

She vowed that if she finds the person who said it, she will bring him together with his beloved. While she was in Muzdalifah she heard someone reciting those lines; she sent for him and asked him. He said that he wrote those lines of poetry about a cousin of him whose family have vowed not to give her in marriage to him. She sent the envoys to the people and continued spending money till they married her to him. She discovered that the woman was more enchanted with him than he was in her.

Zubaydah counted it among her greatest good deeds. She said:

'I am not happier with anything than bringing that young man to his beloved.'

Sulayman ibn Abd al-Malik had a boy and a girl who were in love with each other. The boy wrote one day to the girl:

'I saw you in dream as though you supplied me with the saliva of your cold mouth,
And as though your hand was in my hand and we passed the night in one bed.
I kept sleeping throughout the day so that I can see you while I was not sleeping.'

The girl responded by saying:

'You saw good thing and all that you saw you will get it despite the envy of envious.
I hope that you hug me and pass the night above a swelling breast. And I see you between my anklets and bangles and I see you on my chest in a bed.'

Sulayman got the news of it and married the boy to the girl, and helped them to live peaceful life despite his sense of shame.

Jami' ibn Murhibah said:

'I asked Sa'id ibn al-Musayyinb, the outstanding scholar of Madinah: 'Is there anything wrong in a love which takes us unawares?'

He replied:

'You are blamed on matters which are under your power. By Allah, no one asked me about it before you; and if he asked me I would have given the same answer.'

The love of women is three types:

One which a good deed and doing the duty, that is the love of a person to his wife and his slave girl. This love is beneficial because it helps to achieve the objectives for which Allah has ordained the marriage. It promotes patience and prevents from longing for others beside his family. This lover is praised by Allah and by the people.

The **second** is the love that causes the anger of Allah and drives far from His mercy. It is the most harmful for a man in his world and his religion.

It is the love of young boys. No one was afflicted with it but he was dropped from the sight of Allah. He is thrown away from His door and his heart is banished from Him. It is the greatest barrier from Allah. Some early people have said:

'When the servant is dropped from the sight of Allah, He afflicts him with the love of young beardless boys.'

This is the love which caused the people of Lot suffering; they were punished because of this love. Allah Almighty said:

"By your life, they wandered on in their wild intoxication." (15:72)

The treatment of this disease is to seek the help of the Turner of the hearts, to sincerely return to Him, keep busy in His remembrance and struggle to love Him and be close to Him. It is also useful to think about the pain which will come as the result of it, and the joy which will be missed. It will cause missing of the greatest desirable matter and receiving the most severe hateful torment. If his soul still goes ahead and prefers it, he should perform funeral prayer for it and be sure that the trouble has surrounded him.

The **third** type is the permissible love which is out of the power of a man like someone to whom a beautiful was described or he saw her suddenly without intention and his heart became attached to her and he fell in love. As long as this love did not lead to an evil act, he is safe; it is out of his power and he will not be punished for it. The best thing for him is to repel it and get busy in what is more useful for him. He is also required to hide, exercise chastity and patience on this trial. Allah will reward him for that and grant him substitute for his patience and keeping away from sin for the sake of Allah. He deserves it because he desisted from the obedience of his desire and preferred the pleasure of Allah.

7.20 Categories of the lovers

Lovers are of three categories:
   a) those who have affection for general beauty
   b) those who are attached to particular beauty whether he wishes meeting with him or not
   c) those who love only the one with whom he expects meeting

All these categories are different as regards strength and weakness. The heart of the lover of the general beauty wanders in every valley and he is fascinated by every beautiful image.

'One day he is in Hazwa, and one day in 'Aqiq, another day in 'Udhayb and then in al-Khulaysa'. Sometimes he heads to Nejd, and sometimes to valley of 'Aqiaq and sometimes the palace of Tayma'.

This person's love is wide but not stable and moving constantly.
'He is in love with this one then is affected by another, and in the morning he feels satisfied.'

The lover of the particular beauty remains steady with his beloved and is firm in his love; his love is more powerful that that of the first person. They differ in the desire of union. The lover who is interested in union is the most intelligent and practical person, and his love is sturdy because the desire supplies it with strength and power.

The Hadith 'Whoever loved and remained modest'

This Hadith is reported by Suwayd ibn Sa'id, but the scholars have rejected it. It has been rejected by Ibn Adi and al-Bayhaqi and Ibn Tahir. Ibn al-Jawzi included it among the fabricated ones. Even Hakim despite his leniency rejected it and I am amazed from him.
I say:
'This statement is from Abdullah ibn Abbas and Suwayd made mistake in attributing it to The Prophet, Allah's blessing and peace be upon him. It does not resemble the words of the Prophet.
Al-Khatib narrated it from Hisham ibn 'Urwah from his father from 'A'ishah, which is clearly wrong. This type of Hadith can never come from 'A'ishah. We assert that she never reported it from the Messenger, Allah's blessing and peace be upon him, neither did Hisham and his father narrate it.

Other chains of this Hadith are all fabricated. The statements of the scholars of Hadith in rejection of it are the criterion. To them reference should be made, and no one of them has authenticated or passed it. Even those who are known for their leniency in judging the reports have denied it.
Yes, it could have been said by Ibn Abbas.
Ibn Hazm mentioned that he was asked about a man who was killed by love and he replied:
'There is no retaliation or blood money for a person killed by love.'

A young man who had become like a chick was brought to him in Arafat, and he asked: 'What is wrong with him?'
They replied: 'Love.'

He sought refuge from love the whole day.
How can he say: 'Whoever fell in love, preserved his chastity, kept his love secret and died, he is martyr'?

The falsehood of this report becomes clear from the fact that the Prophet, Allah's blessing and peace be upon him, counted the categories of martyrs and did not include among them the one who was killed by love. The people mentioned are: Those who are killed in jihad, those who died in the disease of stomach, by fire, the woman in child birth, the drowned and those who died in pleurisy.

It is enough for the person killed by love to hold to the statement of Ibn Abbas, but he will not be included in it until he shows patience for the sake of Allah, preserves his chastity and hides his feeling for the sake of Allah. He does it after getting access to his beloved and preferring the love of Allah and having fear of Him and seeking His pleasure.
Such a person deserves to be under the following words of Allah:

"For anyone who fears meeting with his Lord and restrained himself from base desires, Paradise will be home." (79:40-41)

"For those who fear standing before their Lord there are two gardens." (55:46)

We beg Allah, the Majestic, the Lord of the Magnificent Throne, to include us among those who prefer His love over their desires, and seek through it His pleasure and closeness.

The blessed book has been completed and praise is to Allah in the beginning and the end, openly and secretly, a praise which conforms with His favours and measures up to His additional graces.
The noble fatwa was completed by the help and praise of Allah.

INDEX

W